The Submerged Reality:

Sophiology and the Turn to a Poetic Metaphysics

The
Submerged Reality

Sophiology and the Turn to a Poetic Metaphysics

⊕

Michael Martin

Foreword by
Adrian Pabst

Angelico Press

First published in the USA
© Michael Martin 2015
Foreword © Adrian Pabst 2015
Angelico Press, 2015

For information, address:
Angelico Press
4709 Briar Knoll Dr.
Kettering, OH 45429
angelicopress.com

978-1-62138-113-6 pb
978-1-62138-114-3 ebook
978-1-62138-115-0 cloth

Cover image: *Saint John the Evangelist on Patmos* (detail)
Pedro Orrente (1588–1645)
Cover design: Michael Schrauzer

CONTENTS

For Fr. Cyril Attak

"Confitemini Domino quoniam bonus:
quoniam in sæculum misericordia eius."
Psalmus CXVII, i

Acknowledgements

PUTTING THIS BOOK together has been nothing short of miraculous. From the time John Riess, publisher of Angelico Press (to whom I owe much gratitude), invited me to submit a proposal in summer of 2013 to the act of writing these acknowledgements, the process has, at every turn, revealed previously unknown connections, initiated beautiful new friendships, and fostered the growing awareness that this was a book I was meant to write. I have many people to thank.

Some portions of this book first appeared in other forms in the journals *Logos: A Journal of Eastern Christian Studies* and *Second Spring* and I extend my gratitude to their editors, Adam DeVille of *Logos,* Léonie and Stratford Caldecott of *Second Spring,* for their permission to include them here. Stratford and I had corresponded for a number of years about various topics—Vladimir Solovyov, Valentin Tomberg, and education, to name a few—and I always came away from our encounters with the feeling of almost uncanny familiarity: an experience, I think, many of his friends and colleagues would affirm. With his unfortunate passing, the world of Christian letters has experienced a great loss. *Grant him, O Lord, eternal memory.*

I am also indebted to a number of scholars, friends, and colleagues whose ideas and encouragement have been extraordinarily rewarding and nourishing as I moved through the project: Brandon Gallaher, Francesca Aran Murphy, David Parry, Yaakov Mascetti, James Morgante, James Wetmore, George Alcser, Donald Levin, Kari Riess, Douglas Gabriel, and Robert Powell. And I am more than grateful to Adrian Pabst for his Foreword.

I also offer my thanks to Marygrove College for the reception of a grant that helped me successfully complete this project.

But my deepest appreciation goes to my wife, Bonnie, and my children—Brendan, Dylan, Thomas, Mae, Aidan, Zelie, Isabel, Gabriel, and Daniel—through whom I daily see beauty shine into the world.

Feast of the Encounter /Presentation
2 February 2015

Foreword

by Adrian Pabst

M ichael Martin's *The Submerged Reality* is a narrative about fall and redemption. It links the crisis of contemporary culture to the nominalist divide—between immanent nature and the transcendent supernatural—upon which modernity rests. It also charts an alternative modernity stretching from late medieval realism—via the Renaissance, Protestant mysticism, and Romanticism—to the sophiology of the nineteenth and early twentieth centuries. Linking these strands is the notion that nature is dynamic and that our human embeddedness in a creative cosmos discloses the presence of God in the world, this presence being revealed most of all in God's kenotic self-giving. The one triune God gives Himself absolutely and without reserve, and the radical simplicity of divine essence is paradoxically reflected in the diversity of creation. God's essence is both incommunicable and self-sharing—a paradox that finds its supreme expression in the mystery of divine Wisdom. As Martin's book shows perhaps more clearly than other contemporary works on sophiology, wisdom is at once creative and created, divine and human. It is the "relational *between*" (or *metaxu*) of Creator and creation that draws fallen humanity into union with God. Thus the shape of God's unreserved gift of participation in the divine is sophianic.

This narrative shows in novel ways why the modern shift toward the individual knowing subject and the primacy of epistemology (exemplified by the work of Descartes and Kant) was neither necessary nor normative, and how the underlying theology of nominalism and voluntarism has ended up de-naturalizing humanity and de-humanizing culture. By sundering reason from faith, nominalist theologians such as Roscelin and Occam separated philosophy from theology, and knowledge from wisdom. In turn, these divisions go back to the double denial that universals are in real things and that intellect is more primary than the will in ordering human desire in the direction of the supernatural Good in God. Without universals that bind all beings together and intellectively directed desire, the self turns inward and fideistically views its own isolated individuality as an unmediated mirror of divine simplicity. In the words of Martin, "thus, at least at a conceptual level, the microcosm of the mind (or the soul) had been cut off from an integral, cosmological, and spiritual reality, at least as far as medieval epistemology was concerned" (p. 14). Over time, nominalist and voluntarist theology operated a rupture with cosmic, sacramental, and corporeal mediation that fostered a growing pessimism underpinning Cartesian rationalism, Baconian empiricism, and Hobbesian realism about God's remoteness or even absence from the world. With deep roots in the perverted theology of Jansenist Augustinians who were convinced of man's near or total depravity, this pessimistic outlook led to a new exaltation of human self-determination that left humans disconnected from the cosmos and reduced culture to the artifice of human will.

Crucially, Martin's work shows how the alternative modernity of poetic metaphysics can renew both cosmos and culture, and also begin to redeem our fallen nature in this life. Wisdom governs the metaxological realm between Creation and creation that not only binds reason to faith but also connects both with intuition, feeling, habit, and *poesis*. Accordingly, all human faculties are more fully integrated with one another and the universe we inhabit. In this manner, theology retains its status as queen of sciences precisely because it is not limited to some logicized ontology or epistemology (as in much of modern thought) but rather combines metaphysical speculation with cosmic contemplation—including mystical experience and artistic activity. Building on *nouvelle théologie* and Radical Orthodoxy, this account rejects the mind-world dualism that characterizes Cartesian and Kantian philosophy in favor of the analogical participation of the human soul in the divine intellect that defines the participatory metaphysics of both realism and intellectualism in the Christian Neo-Platonist tradition.

The significance of Martin's contribution is to outline more precisely than hitherto the centrality of Sophia in seemingly disparate strands of modern Christian theology, thereby developing the idea of an alternative modernity that outflanks the shared pessimism of the rationalist and empiricist Enlightenment. At the heart of this re-reading of the Western tradition lies the notion that God's wisdom is at the same time the creative source of nature and all souls therein and also the created nature or world-soul. As such, Sophia discloses the irreducible relationality of natural immanence to supernatural transcendence—not a separate pole in space, but instead the "mediate immediacy" of God's presence in the world. And in the giving, receiving, and returning of the gift of divine wisdom, God's ecstatic self-donation deifies creation and unites us ever-more closely to the Creator.

More specifically, Martin traces this alternative modernity to the work of the Silesian Lutheran mystic Jacob Boehme, whose writings exalt intuition and feeling beyond the limitations of blind faith and formal reason. Reinforced by his religious experience, Boehme's philosophical speculation led him to describe divine wisdom as a cosmological force and as a sense of being that is open to the reception of grace. In and through His infinite wisdom God creates man according to his image and likeness. For this reason, "the human soul's desire for Sophia is correlative to Sophia's desire for the human soul. Nowhere is this reciprocity more evident than in Boehme's considerations of the Incarnation of Christ" (p. 49). The coincidence of divinity and humanity in Jesus Christ is reciprocated by Mary's union with Sophia, and thereby creates the condition of possibility for *theosis*. With extraordinary concision and clarity, Martin also shows how Boehme's metaphysical mysticism connects late medieval realism to the Romantics, including German and English Romanticism. What emerges from his synthetic reading of this tradition is the sense that divine wisdom is the supreme cosmic power—a personal agent that mediates grace and helps each creature fulfill its being. Instead of lapsing into pantheism or panentheism, Romantic sophiology articulates the analogical co-inherence of Creator and creation whereby the invisible, mysteriously appearing through the visible, discloses God's presence in the world.

By contrast with this enchanted and sacramental theology, modern materialism—whether in Descartes' rationalist or Bacon's

empiricist philosophy—coincided with a growing disenchantment of the world, as Charles Taylor has argued in his seminal
book *A Secular Age*. Martin links this process of theological secularization to a fundamental change in outlook—treating the Fall
as absolute, inevitable, and therefore more real than God's creative
activity. Connected with this is human self-assertion over against
the receiving and returning of the gift of wisdom. What underpins
both is the nominalist negation of God's mediated self-revelation
in the world. Here the notion of "reverence" in the writings of
Goethe is key, as it describes the paradoxical coincidence of passive reception and active agency involved in cosmic contemplation, and an openness to divine beauty that shines forth through
the harmonious ordering of the universe. In this manner, reverence is more empiricist than what Goethe described as Newtonian
science's "gloomy empirical-mechanical-dogmatic torture chamber" (p.109) because the latter locks theology into an iron cage of
abstract, general categories.

Far from focusing on a vague, irrational feeling of the whole,
sophiological Romanticism shifts the emphasis away from formal
laws and impersonal forces toward the embodied and the particular in an attempt to perceive the imperceptible and feel the impalpable. By contrast with the Gnostic claim of pre-existing matter,
Martin seeks to recover the theological *poesis* articulated by the
early German Romantics, above all Novalis:

> Novalis's perception is sophianic; that is, he sees the world of the
> senses in participation with the divine reality undergirding it, a
> reality he attempts to disclose in his poetry. This participation rises
> to awareness only in the act of imagination, but it is not, therefore,
> only an imaginative act, an act of phantasy. Imagination, rather, is
> an interactive perception in Novalis, what he called "romanticiz-
> ing," a commerce, a congress at the highest level with the things of
> this world. "The world must be romanticized," he writes. "Then
> one will again find the original sense. Romanticizing is nothing
> more than a qualitative involution" (p.119).[1]

1 The quote from Novalis can be found in Frederick C. Beiser (ed.), *The
Early Political Writings of the German Romantics* (Cambridge: Cambridge University Press, 1996), p.85.

The theme that runs through Martin's meditations on Romanticism is the mutually augmenting role of faith and art in articulating a vision that captures Sophia's living dynamic between nature and the supernatural.

Most importantly of all, wisdom is neither a *tertium quid* nor a fourth divine person, but rather the very middle between divine transcendence and created immanence—as the Russian tradition of sophiology teaches. For nothing can subsist outside God, whether between humanity and God, or between God who was made man and mankind that is destined to be deified. Likewise, Sophia is no third term between the three divine persons or between the essence of the Godhead and the persons of the Trinity—for otherwise persons, relations, and essences would be specific instances of something more general and fundamental than God.

At the same time, there is a middle or *metaxu* (the term used by Sergei Bulgakov), because without mediation the relations within the Trinitarian Godhead would dissolve either into independent univocal substances or into a self-founded equivocal monism. Moreover, mediation cannot be an endless dialectical oscillation, either between such substances or within a monistic ground of being, for dialectics would then be reducible to the opposing poles or an ontological extra that too remains unexplained. Therefore, sophianic mediation is best understood as something that is coextensive with the divine essence, the persons and their substantive relations—an ineffable communication between them that exceeds the grasp of human cognition and is accessed experientially.

According to Vladimir Solovyov, Sophia describes the "pan-unity" that envelops the whole of creation and reunites it to God—the process of deification through which humanity can perfect its God-given form. Unlike the formal identification of God with nature that would warrant the charge of pantheism, Russian sophiology—like Boehme's mysticism and early German Romanticism—draws our attention to divine self-revelation through the natural world. For wisdom is both the energy that enables the internal and intentional act of perception, and the essence of that which is perceived. Similarly, Bulgakov's work overcomes modern dualism and monism, as well as post-modern pluralism, in the direction of "integralism"—the idea that there is an underlying unity that binds creation to its Creator. This unity neither stands apart from God nor is identical with God, but rather springs forth from God as the shaping power of wisdom, or the manifesting power of the divine super-abundant light of glory. To receive and return the gift of divine wisdom is to realize our God-given being and uplift creation to an ever-closer union with the Creator, so that "we evermore dwell in him and he in us" (1 John 4:12–13).

Martin's masterly book makes a vital contribution to sophiology as the fusion of metaphysics with mysticism that avoids the separation of nature from the supernatural, such has characterized modern philosophy, politics, and culture. Metaphysical speculation combined with cosmic contemplation can help to reimagine theology and renew humanity's quest for its transcendent *telos*.

London, 1 February 2015

Introduction:
The Call of Beauty

The LORD begot me, the beginning of his works, the forerunner of his deeds of long ago; From of old I was formed, at the first, before the earth.
⁓Proverbs 8:22–3

The Report and Fame that Solomon gave of Wisdom, did much excite me to see her Favour and Friendship demurring in my self from whence she was descended, still questioning whether she was a distinct Being from the Deity or no? Which while in this debate within my Mind, there came upon me an overshadowing bright Cloud, and in the midst of it the Figure of a Woman, most richly adorned with transparent Gold, her Hair hanging down, and her Face as the terrible Crystal for brightness, but her Countenance was sweet and mild. At which sight I was somewhat amazed, but immediately this Voice came saying, Behold I am God's Eternal Virgin-Wisdom, whom thou hast been enquiring after; I am to unseal the Treasures of God's deep Wisdom unto thee, and will be as Rebecca was unto Jacob, a true Natural Mother.
⁓Jane Lead[1]

Now, Wisdom is said to build herself a house wherein she sets out solid food, cups, and a mixing bowl, so that it will be clear to anyone properly pondering godly things how for all things she is the perfect Originator of their being and welfare, goes forth to all, unfolds to all, and encloses all things.[2]
⁓St. Teresia Benedicta of the Cross (Edith Stein)

L ET US START A WAR.
The subject of Sophia, God's Wisdom, has a long and contentious theological history that has covered much of the last two millennia. The irony, of course, is that Sophia as described in the Old Testament, in mysticism, in poetry, and even in the most militant strains of feminist theology, is the divine

---

1 Jane Lead, *A Fountain of Gardens*, vol. 1 (London, 1696), 1:18.
2 Edith Stein (Sister Teresa Benedicta of the Cross, Discalced Carmelite), *Knowledge and Faith*, trans. Walter Redmond (Washington, DC: ICS Publications, 2000), 92.

repository of harmony, grace, and life—that is, of the Good, the True, and the Beautiful. On the one hand, Sophia seems to bring out the best in those who have claimed immediate experience of this divine reality. This was the case with Jacob Boehme, Jane Lead, Robert Fludd, and Sergius Bulgakov, for example, who were all noted for their kindness, magnanimity, and, even, saintliness. On the other hand, their respective sophiologies have often brought out the worst in their critics and continue to do so. I expect no less from this book.

This book is not a cultural history of Sophia. Even though, as a poet, I find the Gnostic mythos of Sophia and her metaphysical kidnapping a fascinating story, to be honest, the theologians and critics who tend to view anything remotely sophiological as flirting with the "Gnostic heresy" bore me. Nor am I at all interested in the conspiratorial projections of the vast number of unstable individuals and groups who hold out Sophia as "the goddess who was erased" from Judeo-Christian consciousness, a neurotic sensibility that internalizes the Gnostic mythos to an almost surreal degree. There is something inherently ugly about the hermeneutics of suspicion and the scholarship of heresy hunting. Likewise, myth-making steeped in paranoia proves an especially sterile enterprise, self-destructive as well as self-deconstructive. Other ways, I think, are more useful. So, I say again: Let us start a war.

Confusions of Semantics, Power, Politics

The most confusing aspect of Sophia, in the first place, is the name. The feminine figure of the Old Testament depicted in Proverbs, Wisdom, Sirach, and elsewhere is very different from her later, Gnostic counterpart. The Old Testament Sophia (הכמה— *Hokmah* in Hebrew) is God's handmaid at the Creation of the world and likewise attends his abiding presence in it. The Sophia (Σοφία—Sophia in Greek) of Gnosticism is quite different. On the one hand, she is considered a syzygy (or divine emanation) of Jesus, as well as part of the human soul, the Church, and so forth—all themes (re)discovered by later sophiologists. On the other hand, the Gnostic Sophia is rather an archetypal screwup who contributes to the fall and captivity of man in matter, the ultimate evil in the teachings of Valentinian Gnosticism. Some sophiologists—Vladimir Solovyov, for example—were obviously knowledgeable of the limited Gnostic literature available to them when they lived (the treasure trove of Gnostic literature revealed by the discovery of the Nag Hammadi archive would not be available until the mid-20th century). Other sophiologists and religious writers, such as the cobbler Jacob Boehme and the poet and engraver William Blake, were not, and it is amazing, indeed, how closely some of their intuitions regarding Sophia resonate with those of the Gnostics who wrote as much as a millennium and a half before them. The Gnostics, however, were not too fond of the Creation, of matter, and it is in this regard that sophiology most explicitly distinguishes itself from their mythos and aligns itself with the Sophia of the Bible. For sophiology, especially as articulated from the 17th century onward, asks us to attend to the grace of God, his presence, *in* Creation: a presence which, despite the world's fallenness, can only be described (in the words of Genesis) as "good."

Unfortunately, a good number of feminist theologians have appropriated Sophia for their own political projects, typically ignoring all sophiologies prior to 1968 in a case of scholarly amnesia and a very consciously undertaken, deliberately executed *violence du texte*. No doubt they follow Simone de Beauvoir in rejecting any sophiology they associate with men as grounded in "a false Infinite, an ideal without truth,"[3] but they create their own false infinite in the process. In their enthusiasm, they subject Sophia to their own creative genius, turning an organic biblical notion and metaphysical reality into what amounts to a team logo. As philosopher Jean-Luc Marion has noted such an image "acts as a mirror, not as a portrait: a mirror that reflects the gaze's image, or more exactly, the image of its aim and the scope of that aim."[4] The beholder in this case closes herself from the divine

---

3 Simone de Beauvoir, *The Second Sex*, trans. H.M. Parshley (New York: Vintage Books, 1989), 187.

4 Jean-Luc Marion, *God Without Being: Hors-Texte*, Religion and Postmodernism, trans. Thomas A. Carlson (Chicago: University of Chicago Press, 1991), 12.

horizon, as the idol captures the gaze and returns to the viewer her own desires "consign[ing] the divine to the measure of a human gaze."[5] One tendency of this theology is to dwell on "interconnectedness"—certainly an important traditional sophiological theme—but a theme that is often compromised by a wishy-washy, "I'm okay, you're okay" postmodern ecumenism similar in many respects to the theology of the former Dominican Matthew Fox: a religious self-fashioning that may have been considered *au courante* in its heyday, but now comes off as more the theological equivalent of bell bottoms.[6]

Some of these scholars and theologians have turned to historiography as an attempt to legitimize their convictions, arguing that Sophia is the Hebrew appropriation of a Near Eastern goddess whose teachings have been "pirated" into the Bible and abused by "Roman ecclesiology and Mariology."[7] For them, the "christology of Jesus Sophia shatters the male dominance carried in exclusive language about Jesus as the eternal male Logos or Son of the Father"[8] in much the same way, one assumes, *The Da Vinci Code* shattered the Catholic Church; which is to say, not at all. Other misguided souls go so far in this direction as to replace God the Father with Sophia, praying, "Our maker, Sophia, we are women in your image, with the hot blood of our wombs we give form to new life . . . with nectar between our thighs we invite a lover . . . with our warm body fluids we remind the world of its pleasures and sensations."[9] The unintended comedy of such a "prayer" inflicts a kind of pain.

---

5 Marion, *God Without Being*, 14.

6 See, for example, Alice A. Keefe, "Visions of Interconnectedness in Engaged Buddhism and Feminist Theology," *Buddhist-Christian Studies* 17 (1997): 61–76. For Matthew Fox's "creation spirituality," see his *The Coming of the Cosmic Christ* (San Francisco: HarperOne, 1988).

7 Susan Cady, Marian Ronan, and Hal Taussig, *Sophia: The Future of Feminist Spirituality* (San Francisco: Harper and Row, 1986), 77.

8 Elizabeth Johnson, "The Maleness of Christ," in *The Special Nature of Women?* ed. Anne Carr and Elisabeth Schüssler Fiorenza (Philadelphia, PA: Trinity, 1991), 108–16, at 113.

9 Susan Cyre, "Fallout Escalates Over 'Goddess' Sophia Worship," *Christianity Today* (4 April 1994): 74.

This is also the method of Elisabeth Schüssler Fiorenza, whose entire theology seems to be an elaboration on her optative misreading of Luke 7:35, "Wisdom is vindicated by her children."[10] In her many discussions of Sophia, Schüssler Fiorenza fails to mention the representatives of the sophiological tradition at all, even the 17th century English religious leader Jane Lead. Carrying this political agenda to its (il)logical conclusion, Schüssler Fiorenza's colleague Jane Schaberg offers the altogether unconvincing thesis in her work that the Virgin Mary did not receive her child through the Holy Spirit, but that she became pregnant through seduction or rape. In an audacious manner, Schaberg describes her theory as derived from the "illegitimacy tradition,"[11] though this is rather an abuse of the definition of "tradition." But, as we shall see, nominalism such as Schaberg's is intrinsic to the kind of thinking that destroyed an integral view of Christian metaphysics and its accompanying promise of human flourishing that are central to sophiology and central to the argument of this book. The problem here is that Christianity is a revealed religion: what these theologians propose with their innovations, however, is not the fruit of revelation, but self-fulfilling prophecy masked as scholarly excavation; psychological drive married to rationalization. Such a religious epistemology can rightfully be described as "anti-sophiology," even, perhaps especially, when it invokes the name of Sophia.

Feminist theology is hardly alone in the endeavor to create a politically motivated, metaphysically impoverished way of thinking about God. Some of these theologians clearly take as their unspoken first principle the Marxist notion of "taking control of the means of production," as they saturate theology departments, turning them into deserts of intellectual monoculture. Theology, indeed, has been allowed to be overwhelmed by materialistic, political, or agnostic hermeneutics to the point where one need not be a believer to be considered a "leading theologian." Contem-

10 See Elisabeth Schüssler Fiorenza, *Jesus: Miriam's Child, Sophia's Prophet: Critical Issues in Feminist Christology* (New York: Continuum, 1994).

11 Jane Schaberg, *The Illegitimacy of Jesus: A Feminist Theological Interpretation of the Infancy Narratives* (San Francisco: Harper and Row, 1987), 74.

plation, as the point of theological departure, is no longer assumed. "Does it not make one suspicious," wrote Hans Urs von Balthasar in the 1960s, "when Biblical philology's first move in its search for an 'understanding' of its texts is to dissect their form into sources, psychological motivations, and the sociological effects of the milieu, even before the form has been really contemplated and read for its meaning *as form*?"[12] Much has changed since then, for the worse, even in ostensibly Catholic colleges and universities. There is something clearly disordered about the way a good deal of contemporary theology approaches questions of God.

In contrast to these materialistic and premediated hermeneutical projects, sophiology resonates with the ethical commitments of phenomenology in the ways that both return "to the things themselves" in order to enter into the tastes and colors of the real and honor the qualities and character of that which one beholds. Sophiology, like phenomenology, that is, abides in a contemplative engagement with the world, a method rooted in the "suspension of the inessential modalities in the presence of the transcendental truth."[13] The Catholic phenomenologist St. Teresia Benedicta of the Cross (Edith Stein), through her own phenomenological reduction, finds in Sophia a reality absolutely congruent with what the Bible says about her:

> She (Wisdom), abiding therein (or in herself), accomplishes the entire, perfect work of Providence, at once going forth to all yet abiding in herself, at once ever standing and moved yet not standing nor moved. Rather, so to speak, does she possess, at once in nature and above nature, the effect of her Providence in abiding and her abiding in her Providence.[14]

Sophiology attends to this abiding and finds it in religion, science, and art; that is, in Goodness, Truth, and Beauty.

---

12 Hans Urs von Balthasar, *The Glory of the Lord: A Theological Aesthetics, Volume I: Seeing the Form*, ed. Joseph Fessio, SJ and John Riches, trans. Erasmo Leiva-Merikakis (San Francisco: Ignatius, 1982), 31. Von Balthasar's emphasis.

13 Paul Evdokimov, *Woman and the Salvation of the World: A Christian Anthropology on the Charisms of Women*, trans. Anthony P. Gythiel (Crestwood, NY: St. Vladimir's Seminary Press, 1994), 9.

14 Edith Stein, *Knowledge and Faith*, 92.

The Call of Beauty

Sophiology is actualized in the contemplation of the beauty of Creation (the nexus of art and science) married to the contemplation of Holy Scripture (the nexus of art and religion), which discloses what von Balthasar has called a "theological aesthetics." Sophiology is art as much as it is theology, as much mysticism as it is natural science. And it is all these things. Sophiology, furthermore, is concerned with *theosis* (or *deification*), the spiritualization of matter, of the flesh, through the disclosure of the unfallen aspects of natural bodies. Sophiology is concerned, that is, with regeneration—of the human person (religion), of nature (science), of culture (art)—and attests to the sacramental nature of All that is.

The diminished status of beauty in both theology and science diminishes both. As von Balthasar has written, beauty is "a word from which religion, and theology in particular, have taken their leave and distanced themselves in modern times by a vigorous drawing of boundaries."[15] In that, theology has erred in interiorizing the hard sciences' suspicion of beauty. Science can tell us a lot about the world. It can offer us insights into why starlings gather in murmurations in the autumn, why worker bees form a cluster around their queen in winter, how Mozart's *Requiem* affects the brain—but it cannot tell us why these things are beautiful. And the scattered attempts wherein science attempts to do so—for example, in suggesting that men who created the most beautiful music as a "fitness display" in the Stone Age were the most successful in securing mates[16]—are categorically less than convincing. Science, in this way, has sacrificed an important part of its vocation. Theology, in its appropriation of scientific modalities, has done the same.

Some 16th and 17th century natural scientists—such as the Catholic apologist Sir Kenelm Digby (1603–1665), for instance—

---

15 Hans Urs von Balthasar, *The Glory of the Lord: A Theological Aesthetics, Volume I*, 17.

16 Geoffrey Miller, *The Mating Mind: How Sexual Choice Shaped the Evolution of Human Nature* (New York: Anchor Books, 2001), 282.

intuited a kind of sophiological science, for one example, in their experiments in palingenesis, the attempt to raise the perfected form of a plant or animal phoenix-like from its own ashes.[17] Taking the Resurrection as proof, they concluded that there must be a logic (a *logos*) of the glorified body. And if glorification is logical, they assumed, it must be discoverable. They were, it seems, unable to discover it, though the Russian Cosmists, particularly Nikolai Fedorov, were engaged in a similar project nearly 300 years later.[18]

The glorified body can, indeed, be described as the nexus at which art, science, and religion are/will be irrevocably united, which may help to explain why so many sophiologists concerned themselves with eschatology. "But when that which is perfect is come, that which is in part shall be done away" (1 Cor 13:10). The perfect is synonymous with the Beautiful. In visionary accounts of her, for example, the Virgin is invariably described as a young woman, beautiful in both purity and form, and in every sense glorified.[19] This manifestation of the Beautiful, more than admiration, invites us to participation, as St. Bernadette Soubirous explains:

> There came from the interior of the grotto a golden-colored cloud, and soon after a Lady, young and beautiful, exceedingly beautiful, the like of whom I had never seen, came and placed herself at the entrance of the opening above the bush. She looked at me immediately, smiled at me, and signed to me to advance, as if she had been my mother.[20]

---

17 See chapter three, "Love's Alchemist: Palingenesis and the Unconscious Metalepsis of Sir Kenelm Digby," in my *Literature and the Encounter with God in Post-Reformation England* (Farnham, UK: Ashgate Publishing, 2014).

18 George M. Young, *The Russian Cosmists: The Esoteric Futurism of Nikolai Federov and His Followers* (Oxford: Oxford University Press, 2012).

19 Particularly in the apparitions beheld by St. Bernadette Soubirous in 1858, by Eugene and Joseph Barbadette in 1871, in Fatima in 1917, but the phenomenon is nearly universal.

20 J. B. Estrade, *My Witness, Bernadette: The Authentic Source-Book of the Apparitions at Lourdes by an Eyewitness*, trans. J. H. le Breton Girdlestone (1946; reprt., Springfield, IL: Templegate, 1951), 26.

Authentic visionaries do not behold a ghost or "spiritual form," but the Virgin glorified. As was the case with Jesus after the Resurrection,[21] she no longer seems exactly as the person people knew prior to her Dormition and appears differently depending on time and circumstance. Her beauty signifies the sophianization of the flesh, the apotheosis of matter. Tellingly, Bernadette's almost instinctive response to the encounter was to reach for her rosary. An encounter with beauty—through a vision of the Virgin, through one's deep attention to a great work of art, or when standing before the sea at a fiery sunrise—often compels the beholder into a state of profound reverence. Indeed, as Stratford Caldecott has said, the Virgin is nothing if not "God's work of art."[22] Beauty is inherent (though often hidden) in the world, even down to the chemical level.

Solovyov, in an essay entitled "The Universal Meaning of Art," gives three requirements for the manifestation of the fullness of beauty. He designates the first two of these as the "direct materialization of spiritual essence" and "complete animation of material phenomena, as the proper and inalienable form of ideal content."[23] The third is still more profound. Here he designates the manifestation of ideal beauty (supposedly in art) as proceeding from the first two in which

> During the direct and inseparable unification in beauty of spiritual content with sensual expression, in their full mutual penetration, a material phenomenon actually having become beautiful, that is, really having embodied in itself Idea, it should become in the very same way as abiding and immortal as Idea itself.[24]

21 Even St. Mary Magdalene, who knew Jesus very well during his earthly life, was not able to recognize him after the Resurrection (John 20), as was also the case with the disciples on the road to Emmaus (Luke 24). In Mark 16:12, the Evangelist writes that Jesus "appeared in a different form" (ἐν ἑτέρᾳ μορφῇ) to two of his disciples.

22 Stratford Caldecott, *The Radiance of Being: Dimensions of Cosmic Christianity* (Tacoma, WA: Angelico Press, 2013), 217.

23 Vladimir Soloviev, *The Heart of Reality: Essays on Beauty, Love, and Ethics*, ed. and trans. Vladimir Wozniuk (Notre Dame, IN: University of Notre Dame Press, 2003), 73.

24 Vladimir Soloviev, *The Heart of Reality*, 73–74.

Surely, Solovyov's schematic here illustrates more than the ideal potential of art. It points as well, I think, toward a theology of the glorification of matter.

The incorruptible bodies of saints quite literally embody what Solovyov treats here. St. Bernadette, in particular, died from a debilitating illness, tuberculosis, yet her body remains intact in the convent chapel of St. Gildard in Nevers nearly one hundred and forty years after her death. She appears to be peacefully asleep, beautiful, truly a work of art. While not the realization of the glorified body, in which body and soul will be reunited in the true chemical wedding, the uncorrupted corpse of St. Bernadette gives us at least a foreshadowing of that glory. As Pavel Florensky writes, "In a saint the beautiful original creature is revealed to us for contemplation."[25] The beauty of the Virgin described by visionaries, on the other hand, *is* an image of the body glorified.

Beauty, then, is the indicator of God's presence, his Wisdom, Sophia, as it shines through, reveals itself in, matter. Metaphysical poet Henry Vaughan describes this phenomenon in his poem, "Cock-crowing":

> O thou immortal light and heat!
> Whose hand so shines through all this frame,
> That by the beauty of the seat,
> We plainly see, who made the same.
> Seeing thy seed abides in me,
> Dwell thou in it, and I in thee.[26]

Sophiology acknowledges a participatory metaphysics, a metaphysics of reciprocity. For the Beautiful to exist without a being to perceive it is absurd. The categories "subject" and "object," in sophiology, cease to maintain their alleged distinctness, for that

25 Pavel Florensky, *The Pillar and Ground of Truth: An Essay in Orthodox Theodicy in Twelve Letters,* trans. Boris Jakim (Princeton: Princeton University Press, 1997), 234.

26 Henry Vaughan, "Cock-crowing," *The Complete Poetry of Henry Vaughan,* ed. French Fogle (New York: New York University Press, 1965), lines 19–24.

which lies between the two (the *metaxu* in the terminology of William Desmond) is that through which Sophia appears. And so it is with the spaces between art, science, and religion. For this reason, it comes as no real surprise that many of the figures discussed in this book simultaneously followed the vocations of scientist, poet (or artist), and theologian. Categories tend to vanish in the face of the real.

The category, however, since Aristotle's *Organon* first made an impact on medieval learning and culture, has been the overriding paradigm in Western history and, as a result, continues to impact every modern and postmodern culture. But what was once regarded simply as a tool or instrument (*organon*) has become a kind of cage. The subject of this book is a response to the hegemony of this paradigm, though it is far from an out and out rejection of it. Categories are useful things, but I am not convinced they are all that useful for understanding God and his presence in Creation. As the 17th century poet and Anglican priest Thomas Traherne writes, "Infinite is the first thing which is naturally known. Bounds and limits are discerned only in a secondary manner."[27] Sophiology attempts to transcend the "secondary manner" of bounds and limits (i.e., categories) and restore the faculty of beholding what is, the infinite, phenomenon as well as noumenon, nature and its dance with supernature. For the one never exists without the other.

27 Thomas Traherne, *Centuries* (Wilton, CT: Morehouse-Barlow, 1985), 94.

Chapter One

The Repercussions
of a Left-Brain Theology

I find you, Lord, in all Things and in all
my fellow creatures, pulsing with your life;
as a tiny seed you sleep in what is small
and in the vast you vastly yield yourself.

The wondrous game that power plays with Things
is to move in such submission through the world;
groping in roots and growing think in trunks
and in treetops like a rising from the dead.
~Rainer Maria Rilke.[1]

For he fashioned all things that they might have being,
and the creatures of the world are wholesome.
~Wisdom 1:14

S CHOLARS often name the seventeenth as the century in which secularization, aided by the scientific revolution and its attendant fetishization of reason, began its ascent toward cultural supremacy. What transpired in the intellectual and spiritual life of the West during that century clearly changed the previously accepted understanding of the world from one of holistic integrity and sacramental relationality to one of fragmentation and ever-increasing, ever more sophisticated specialization. But, in truth, the seeds of secularization had been sewn long before the age of Descartes, Hobbes, and Bacon. In one of her notebooks, Simone Weil offers an insightful observation into the historicity

---

1 Rainer Maria Rilke, *The Selected Poetry*, ed. and trans. by Stephen Mitchell (New York: Random House, 1982).

of the problem: "Resemblance between modern science and scholasticism: manipulation of signs."[2] Those setting the terms of an argument control the discussion.

I am not saying that reason is a bad thing. Rather, the story I want to tell in this chapter is one of the imbalance consequent to relying too heavily upon one aspect of being, rationality in this case, and the cultural and spiritual fallout that can (and did) ensue. The theologians of the Latin Middle Ages played with syllogisms, categories, and quiddities with all the enthusiasm of children playing with new toys. Yet their enthusiasm inclined toward one-sidedness, and by the seventeenth century this propensity had been institutionalized and internalized by Latin Christendom. No longer an innovation or academic passion, rationality had become a characteristic of high culture. To be sure, various figures of the period bucked this trend—the Beguine mystics and St. Francis of Assisi, for example—but they were not generally professional theologians or teachers and did not have much impact on the intellectual life of the Church, though, especially in the case of St. Francis, they might exert tremendous popular influence. During the medieval period as well as our own, the intellectual class, for the most part, sets the cultural trajectory, though it usually unfolds slowly and according to its own evolution. And while the Church has taught and continues to teach that Revelation has a role to "assist reason in its effort to understand the mystery" of divine truth,[3] the cultural history traced in reason's ascent through Scholasticism, to scientific rationality, and eventually to the dominance of postmodern secularism demands that we consider deeply the assumptions and entailments accompanying such a commitment. Reason, that is, may incline one toward faith, but it does not compel.

A Rage for Rationality

An important component of secularization, the elevation of reason had been prevalent from the beginnings of Scholasticism and came

2 Simone Weil, *First and Last Notebooks*, trans. Richard Rees (London: Oxford University Press, 1970), 6.

3 John Paul II, *Fides et Ratio* (www.catholic-pages.com) pdf, 14.

to a head in the debates between the philosophical schools of real-ism and nominalism. Indebted to Plato and his Christian Neopla-tonist interpreters, realism affirms the existence of universals: abstract, general concepts possessing objective reality anterior to particulars.[4] For realism, universals, that is, are real *things* (*res*). The ideas of "woman" and "man," for instance, precede and inform the actualities of particular women and men. Medieval nominalism, on the other hand, held that only particular things are real and that what the realists called "universals" are only names (*nomina*), possibly useful for categorization (conceptualism), but devoid of any kind of reality in themselves. In a famous example, Roscelin (1050–1125) held that the idea of the Trinity is, in fact, only a concept and that only the Divine Persons—the Father, the Son, and the Holy Spirit—can claim reality.[5] This, to put it deli-cately, "created a difficult situation in regard to nominalism."[6]

Two centuries after Roscelin, the nominalist William of Occam (c. 1287–1347) divided reality into two categories: 1) that which we can know through intentionality (observation and experi-ence); and 2) that which we can know by faith. Nominalism, that is, separated knowledge from wisdom and effectively divorced philosophy from theology. It placed most of what had been tradi-tional metaphysics under the sphere of faith and claimed logic and analysis as the tools of the philosopher.[7] Thus, at least at a conceptual level, the microcosm of the mind (or the soul) had been cut off from an integral, cosmological, and spiritual reality, at least as far as medieval epistemology was concerned.

---

4 Lothar Schafer, *In Search of Divine Reality: Science as a Source of Inspira-tion* (Fayetteville, AR: University of Arkansas Press, 1997), 212.

5 Simo Knuuttila, "Philosophy and Theology in Twelfth-Century Trinitar-ian Discussions" in *Medieval Analyses in Language and Cognition: Acts of the Symposium, The Copenhagen School of Medieval Philosophy*, ed. Sten Ebbesen and Russell L. Friedman, Historisk-filosofiske Meddelelser 77 (Copenhagen: The Royal Danish Academy of Sciences and Letters, 1999): 237–50, at 239–40.

6 Rudolf Steiner, *The Redemption of Thinking: A Study in the Philosophy of Thomas Aquinas*, trans. and ed. by A.P. Shepherd and Mildred Robertson Nicoll (London: Hodder and Stoughton, 1956), 71.

7 Frederick C. Copleston, *Medieval Philosophy* (New York: Harper Torch-books/The Cathedral Library, 1961), 120.

Such a division was one consequence (and, arguably, the most significant) of the introduction of Aristotle's philosophy into the Christian thought of the West. Aristotle's penchant for division and categorization, rendered into schematic form in the *Organon*, offered medieval intellectuals (all of them clerics) a model and method for arranging received ideas, pursuing new knowledge, and disseminating both through the universities. This desire to categorize and classify has, not too hyperbolically, been called a "rage for order," but this movement in Latin Christendom might just as easily be called a "rage for reformation," as the trajectory set by the Occamist desire to reform philosophy (and, with it, theology) led directly over the arch of the centuries following Occam's to the more culturally disruptive notion of reformation associated with Luther, Calvin, and Zwingli.[8] Indeed, like that of his sixteenth century inheritors, Occam's project was originally intended to *cleanse* Christendom of what he considered to be pagan metaphysics. In that, Occam may, in the long run, have succeeded, but as a result Latin Christendom was also essentially cleansed of Christianity.

Philosopher Charles Taylor has described this rage for order in terms of a desire for a "one-speed religion," which he sets in contrast to "multi-speed religion." For Taylor, a multi-speed religion is one that accommodates a variety of religious ways-of-being. On the side of the laity it allows for popular piety, pilgrimages, and veneration of saints and relics, alongside carnival, the enjoyment of jokes and entertainment, raising a family, the general pursuit of human flourishing, and what has called "the spirituality of work."[9] On the side of the clergy, it likewise encompasses a variety of religious ways-of-being: contemplative life, pastoral care, the life of the mind occupied with theological problems, cenobitic or eremitic monasticism, and so forth. The rage for reformation, however, attempted to collapse these ways-of-being into a homogenized singularity and actualize what Taylor calls "the

8 Charles Taylor, *A Secular Age* (Cambridge: Harvard University Press/ Belknap Press, 2007), 63.

9 Simone Weil, *An Anthology*, ed. Siân Miles (New York: Weidenfeld & Nicolson, 1986), 159.

myth of the single, omnicompetent code."[10] The advent of the Reformation, then, comes as no surprise, as "Protestantism is in the line of continuity with medieval reform, attempting to raise general standards, not satisfied with a world in which only a few integrally fulfill the gospel, but trying to make certain pious practices absolutely general."[11] Nominalism made a significant contribution to this continuity of medieval reform, and it also touched on the theology of the Eucharist.

The Eucharist

In the eleventh century, Berengarius of Tours, though he affirmed the Real Presence of Christ in the Eucharist, expressed doubts that the Body and Blood of Christ partaken in the sacrament are synonymous with those born of the Virgin Mary. His opponents, whom he derided as "sensualists," however, held that the two are identical.[12] Though he was forced to an uncomfortable recantation, Berengarius stirred up no little degree of anxiety in theological circles, and, as it tends to do throughout Church history, anxiety forced *Mater Ecclesia* to come more clearly to grips with the issue and provide an authoritative definition for what the Eucharist *is*, especially in a material sense.

The theology of the Real Presence was clarified somewhat with the promulgation of the doctrine of Transubstantiation at the Fourth Lateran Council in 1215. In terms framed by St. Thomas Aquinas, "transubstantiation had become *the* official means by which radical ontological change demanded by the real presence was expressed and safeguarded."[13] But the issue was far from settled. In fact, it may be that through a rigorous definition of the Real Presence the Church may have won one battle while unintentionally preparing the way for a much more costly and devas-

---

10 Charles Taylor, *Secular Age*, 52.

11 Ibid., 82.

12 Nathan Mitchell, OSB, *Cult and Controversy: The Worship of the Eucharist outside Mass* (New York: Pueblo Publishing Company, 1990), 141.

13 Teresa Whalen, *The Authentic Doctrine of the Eucharist* (Kansas City, MO: Sheed and Ward, 1993), 25. Whalen's emphasis.

tating war. By the sixteenth century, while far from the only issue, the doctrine of Transubstantiation had become a virulently contentious one that reformers such as Luther, Calvin, and Zwingli used to leverage a much more radical Reformation than that dreamt of by Berengarius. Nominalism deeply informed Luther's understanding of the Eucharist,[14] a characteristic also present in Calvin and in the theology of the early Anglican theologian Thomas Cranmer (who has been described as "hamstrung by nominalism").[15] The more radical Reformers understood Christ's presence in the Eucharist to be a purely spiritual phenomenon, as the English Calvinist Anne Askew defiantly articulated while defending herself on charges of heresy: "in sprete I received never the lesse, the bodye and bloude off Christ."[16] In response to radical reform, through the organ of the Council of Trent (1545–1563) the Church reasserted the Eucharistic theology of Lateran IV in the strongest terms:

> We, therefore, confess that the sacrifice of the Mass is one and the same sacrifice as that of the cross: the victim is one and the same, Jesus Christ, who offered himself, once only, a bloody sacrifice on the altar of the cross. The bloody and unbloody victim is still one and the same, and the oblation of the cross is daily renewed in eucharistic sacrifice, in obedience to the command of our Lord: "This do, for a commemoration of me."[17]

Eucharistic realism (though not really thought of in those terms until the medieval period) had been assumed by the Church from the earliest of times, holding, as Eastern Orthodox theology concurs, that "Nominalism can have no part in church life."[18] It

---

14 Madeleine Gray, *The Protestant Reformation: Beliefs and Practices* (Brighton, UK: Sussex Academic Press, 2003), 51–52.

15 Eric Mascall, *Corpus Christi: Essays on the Church and the Eucharist* (London: Longmans Green and Co., 1958), 121.

16 *The Examinations of Anne Askew*, ed. Elaine V. Beilin (Oxford: Oxford University Press, 1996), 22.

17 *The Catechism of the Council of Trent*, trans. Rev. J. Donavan (Baltimore: Fielding Lewis, n.d.), 175.

18 Alexander Schmemann, *The Eucharist: Sacrament of the Kingdom*, trans. Paul Kachur (Crestwood, NY: St. Vladimir's Seminary Press, 1987), 85

is absurd to think that one can be simultaneously a nominalist in philosophy and a realist in theology, yet this was (and is) often the case. The Fathers of Trent, it has been argued, were operating under a generally Aristotelian set of assumptions, however filtered through the Scholastic tradition they might have been,[19] and this (fed, certainly, by an urgency to address the heresies promulgated by Protestant Eucharistic theologies) may account for their insistence on an ontological understanding of the Eucharist instead of an approach to the sacrament as *mysterion*.

The rage for order and the accompanying rage for rationality of the medieval period were tragically transformed into a rage that was ultimately neither ordered nor rational, culminating finally in the Thirty Years War (1618–1648), a conflict that did nothing to decide religious disputes but did much to pave the way for the rise of the sovereign state. In an early theological work, the Anglican poet and divine (and former Catholic) John Donne entertained his age's ecclesiastical preoccupation with definition and the trouble it invites:

> Almost all the ruptures in the Christian Church have been occasioned by such bold disputations *De Modo*. One example is too much. That our Blessed Saviours body is in the Sacrament, all say; The *Roman* Church appoints it to be there by *Transubstantiation*. The needless multiplying of Miracles for that opinion hath moved the *French* and *Helvetick* reformed Churches to find the word Sacramentally; which because it puts the body there, and yet no nearer then Heaven to Earth, seems to riddle the *Saxon* and such Churches; whose modesty (though not clearness) seems greatest in this Point.[20]

There is no adequate way to explain the mystery of the Eucharist, just as there is no adequate way to completely understand God. "What do you think God is?" St. Augustine writes, "What do you think God is like? Whatever you fix upon, that is not it. Whatever

19 E. Schillebeeckx, OP, *The Eucharist*, trans. N.D. Smith (New York: Sheed and Ward, 1968), 53–63.

20 John Donne, *Essayes in Divinity, being Several Disquisitions Interwoven with Meditations and Prayers,* ed. Anthony Raspa (Montreal: McGill-Queen's University Press, 2001), 95.

you can comprehend by thought, that is not it."[21] There are some truths we can apprehend only by releasing our claims to them.

But the biggest problem resulting from Aristotelian/Scholastic attempts to refine the definition of the Eucharist, however, was that—initially in the Latin West (particularly in Protestantism), but eventually also at a global level—God's transcendence became emphasized at the expense of his immanence so much so that the question of God's presence in the created world—let alone the Eucharist—became a matter of privately-held opinion, a mere interpretation or even a political position, but not at all a shared cultural value. The idea of *perichoresis* (the co-inherence of God and the world)[22] bore less and less importance to a culture enamored of its own brilliance. These developments amounted to an "exile of God" and an accompanying de-sacramentalization of creation. This was not the spirit of reform's intention, of course, though, as it has been argued, "the unintended self-marginalization of theology through doctrinal controversy in the Reformation era played an indirect but critically important role" in the triumph of secularization.[23] In the wake of the brutality and futility of the Thirty Years War, Latin Christendom finally imploded and with it the culture it had created.[24] With Europe rendered more spiritually and culturally divided and, as a result, more religiously impotent, a space was opened for secularism. Contemporaneous with the Scholastic rage for definition that wreaked such havoc on the Eucharist, a theology of *natura pura*, or pure nature, further contributed to the exile of God.

Natura Pura

During the sixteenth and early-seventeenth centuries, a number of Catholic (and particularly Dominican and Jesuit) theologians

21 Augustine, "Sermon 21 [on Psalm 53]."

22 Alexei V. Nesteruk, *Light from the East: Theology, Science, and the Eastern Orthodox Tradition* (Minneapolis, MN: Augsburg Fortress, 2003), 116.

23 Brad S. Gregory, *The Unintended Reformation: How a Religious Revolution Secularized Society* (Cambridge: Harvard University Press/Belknap Press, 2012), 28.

24 Ibid., 160.

entertained the possibility that human beings "in their natural state" might not be created with the Beatific Vision as an end. The theologians of *natura pura* (pure nature) argued that human beings could, indeed, be created with a "natural end" to which God might add the *supernatural* end promised in the Beatific Vision. They reasoned that to assume God has already implanted a desire for the Beatific Vision into human hearts would be to subvert the action of his grace. That is, if the gift of grace is guaranteed, it is not really a gift. God could, of course, create human beings in such a state. But would he? While pure nature theologians did not hazard to guess what God *would* do, they had no qualms in asserting that he *could* create a human person in a state of pure nature. Whether he did or not, for the theologians of pure nature, was an entirely different question.

The subject of pure nature does not appear to have been too hotly contested during the early modern period. Nevertheless, as Georges Chantraine has observed, its appearance "bears witness to a 'turning point' in the Western mind."[25] For one thing, philosophy and theology, if not finally and formally divorced, were further estranged from one another as the pure nature debate's almost schizophrenic oscillation between theological and philosophical modes of inquiry developed languages increasingly foreign to one another. Secondly, the notion that a person can be human apart from God is clearly absurd and, indeed, suggests a form of Nestorianism.[26] Thirdly, pure nature reinforced binary thinking: spirit/matter, church/state, grace/nature, transcendence/immanence, and so forth, which seriously impacted civic and intellectual life. And, finally and tragically, the development of pure nature theology increasingly and strictly limited God's immanence. But who can limit God? It was an act of hubris.

25 Georges Chantraine, SJ, "The Supernatural: Discernment of Catholic Thought according to Henri de Lubac" in *Surnaturel: A Controversy at the Heart of Twentieth-Century Thomistic Thought*, ed. Serge-Thomas Bonino, OP, trans. Robert Whalen, rev. Matthew Levering (Naples, FL: Sapientia Press of Ave Maria University, 2009): 21–40, at 37.

26 Philip Sherrard, *The Eclipse of Man and Nature: An Enquiry into the Origins and Consequences of Modern Science* (West Stockbridge, MA: Lindisfarne Press, 1987), 20.

The Repercussions of a Left-Brain Theology

By accepting pure nature, the Church in effect gave the *Imprimatur* to secularism, albeit unwittingly. Nicolas Berdyaev describes the situation with painful accuracy:

> Western Christian thought has tended to neutralise the cosmos. This occurred alike both in Thomas Aquinas and in Luther. God's cosmos, bearing upon itself the imprint of God the Creator and transfused with Divine energies, tended to wither and die in the consciousness of the Christian West. It was replaced by a neutralised nature, the object of scientific nature-knowledge and technology.[27]

Though Berdyaev gets Aquinas wrong here, his comments are nevertheless germane to the topic of pure nature. Indeed, it was not St. Thomas but his early modern commentators who turned the Angelic Doctor into a pure nature theologian. For St. Thomas, God, in addition to his utter transcendence, is equally immanent, not only in the human person but in creation as a whole: "Being is innermost in each thing and most fundamentally present within all things, since it is formal in respect of everything found in a thing. . . . Hence God is in all things, and innermostly."[28] But, with Neo-Scholasticism's hypothesizing the possibility of God's creation without God's "innermostly" presence, a real violence was inflicted not only on Aquinas's text but on God's.

Yet, these early modern developments, while new in expression, were not original in design. On the contrary, they had been a long time in coming. As Louis Dupré explains, pure nature

> was deeply rooted in nominalist theology. It might have remained a theological abstraction if Renaissance naturalism had not given it an acceptable content, and seventeenth-century philosophy a rational justification. Once the idea of a quasi-autonomous order of nature gained a foothold in Catholic theology, it spread to all schools except the Augustinian, including some of Aquinas's com-

---

27 N.A. Berdyaev, "Studies Concerning Jacob Boehme, Etude II: The Teaching about Sophia and the Androgyne. J. Boehme and the Russian Sophiological Current," trans. S. Janos with Michael Knetchen, www.berdyaev.com (2002), section 6, par. 2. Originally published as "Iz etiudov o yak. Beme. Etiud ii. Uchenie o sophii i androgine," *Put'* 21 (Apr 1930): 34–62.

28 *ST* I, Q. 8, a 1.

mentators such as Sylvester and Cajetan. Thus the medieval synthesis came to an end, and a dualism between nature and a supernatural realm solidly entrenched itself in Catholic theology for four centuries.[29]

Informed by the spirit of nominalism, pure nature's implicit dualism combined with its programmatic theoretical application resulted in what might be called an utterly "left-brain theology," a theology that ignores intuitive modes for apprehending God. There are no pure nature mystics. Through the medieval period and into the early modern, mysticism and theology lived in a delicate tension, each checking the other's excesses. Certainly, mysticism and theology are not mutually exclusive: some of the greatest theologians of Latin Christendom—St. Teresa of Avila, St. John of the Cross, St. Bonaventure, and St. Thomas Aquinas himself, to name a few—were likewise mystics. As their examples show, the idea is that theology and mysticism should "support and complete each other."[30] Without this synergy, theology runs the risk of turning into pedantry or legalism and mysticism could all too easily justify the accusations of delusion or quietism leveled against it.

Mysticism and theology represent two ways of knowing God. Theology speaks an exact, scientific language (in terms of *scientia*): an academic language of objectivity, definition, description, and analysis. Mysticism, on the other hand, employs what has been called "the language of the bed-chamber, of love, and hence of hyperbole and exaggeration."[31] It is a language of subjectivity and immersion, a poetic language. (Mystical theology, of course, attempts to bridge the gap between these two ways.) It is no wonder, then, that so many mystics speak as poets (e.g., St. Francis, St. John of the Cross, the Sufi poet Rumi) and so many poets

29 Louis Dupré, *Passage to Modernity: An Essay in the Hermeneutics of Nature and Culture* (New Haven: Yale University Press, 1993), 178

30 Vladimir Lossky, *The Mystical Theology of the Eastern Church*, trans. members of the Fellowship of St Alban and St Sergius (1957; reprt., Crestwood, NY: St Vladimir's Seminary Press, 2002), 8.

31 Thomas Keating, *Open Mind, Open Heart: The Contemplative Dimension of the Gospel* (Lexington, NY: Continuum Publishing, 2002), 79.

wander into the realm of mysticism. Indeed, in our own time theology itself has been described as divided between "theology at the desk" and "theology at prayer,"[32] a tacit acknowledgement of the danger of an academic theology alien to devotion and intuition.

The emphasis on rationality characteristic of nominalism and pure nature theology is symptomatic of an unbalanced system. By the late early modern period, indeed, mysticism was more and more disparaged as "enthusiasm," a kind of mental illness. In England, Meric Casaubon, for one, campaigned against religious enthusiasm in *A Treatise concerning Enthusiasme* (1655); and the Cambridge Platonist Henry More, for another, wrote disparagingly of it in *Enthusiasmus Triumphatus: or A Brief Discourse of the Nature, Causes, Kindes, and Cure of Enthusiasm* (1656), encouraging the faithful toward a more rational Christianity. Tellingly, for More, the Holy Spirit functions only through our reason.[33] And such disparagement of mystical ways of knowing was not particular to Protestantism. St. Teresa of Avila and St. John of the Cross, to name only two, suffered much at the hands of Church authorities—including torture and imprisonment on the part of St. John[34]—because of their mystical experiences. Such a development could not end well for either theology or culture. Nor did it. For a proposition that was essentially a hypothetical one,[35] pure nature, directly or indirectly, inflicted some serious spiritual and cultural collateral damage on its own and the following centuries.

In the mid-twentieth century, the theology of pure nature was again brought to the Church's consciousness through the

---

32 Hans Urs von Balthasar, "Theology and Sanctity" in *Explorations in Theology, Volume I*, trans. A.V. Littledale and Alexander Dru (San Francisco: Ignatius Press, 1989), 208.

33 On More, see Dewey D. Wallace, *Shapers of English Calvinism, 1660–1714: Variety, Persistence, and Transformation*, Oxford Studies in Historical Theology (Oxford: Oxford University Press, 2011), 39.

34 José C. Nieto, *Mystic, Rebel, Saint: A Study of St. John of the Cross*, Travaux d'humanisme et Renaissance, no. 168 (Geneva: Droz, 1979), 31–34.

35 Edward T. Oakes, SJ, "The *Surnaturel* Controversy: A Survey and a Response," *Nova et Vetera*, 9, no. 3 (2011): 625–56, at 627.

publication of what John Milbank has praised as "arguably the key theological text of the twentieth century," Henri de Lubac's *Surnaturel* (1946).[36] De Lubac's book (which has yet to be translated into English) brought his ideas under ecclesial suspicion and he was for a time forbidden to either teach or publish. So great was the controversy initiated by *Surnaturel* that de Lubac was censured publicly (humiliated is not too strong a word) in Pius XII's encyclical *Humani Generis* (1950), if not by name, then certainly by implication. De Lubac proposes that the theologians of pure nature not only asserted a bad theology, what he dismissed as "from the womb of a decadent Scholasticism,"[37] but that they also enlisted St. Thomas Aquinas as an unwitting accomplice in spreading their malformed ideas. In the spirit of *ressourcement*, de Lubac claimed to be returning to the source to see what Thomas himself said and not what his commentators ventriloquized through him. The French Jesuit did not speak in delicate terms:

> In reality, the idea of "pure nature" had neither the antiquity nor the doctrinal importance that many recent theologians suppose it to have had. Its entrance into theology dates from yesterday, and it was far from having the right to claim all views. This did not concern the religious order which had conceived it. Its origin was mainly philosophical.[38]

---

36 John Milbank, *The Suspended Middle: Henri de Lubac and the Debate concerning the Supernatural* (Grand Rapids, MI/Cambridge, UK: William B. Eerdmans Publishing Company, 2005), 3.

37 From a letter to Maurice Blondel, dated 3 April 1932. In Henri de Lubac, *At the Service of the Church: Henri de Lubac Reflects on the Circumstances that Occasioned His Writings*, trans. Anne Elizabeth Englund (San Francisco: Communio Books/Ignatius Press, 1993), 184.

38 "En réalité, l'idée de la «pure nature» n'avait alors ni l'ancienneté ni l'importance doctrinale que lui supposent trop volontiers quelques théologiens récents. Son entrée dans la théologie datait de la veille, et elle était bien loin d'y avoir acquis droit de cite aux yeux tous. Ce n'étaient pas non plus des préoccupations d'ordre religieux qui l'avaient fait concevoir. Son origine était surtout philosophique." Henri de Lubac, *Surnaturel: Études historiques* (1946; reprt., nouvelle edition, ed. Michel Sales, Paris: Desclée de Brouwer, 1991), 105. My translation.

The notion of pure nature sets up an unnecessary binary and, de Lubac asks, "would this not be in large part responsible for the evil of 'separated theology,' an evil from which we still suffer greatly today?"[39] Indeed, one could argue that the pure nature hypothesis inclines toward Calvin's doctrine of double predestination—if God could withhold his grace from certain persons, even hypothetically, he could just as easily predestine them for damnation. But for de Lubac, a human person, by definition, is not simply a "natural creature":

> For there is nature and nature. If, in contrast with the supernatural order, the being of angels and men as resulting simply from their being created must be called natural, we must allow that their situation, in relation to other natures, is "singular and paradoxical"; for it is the situation "of a spirit which is to become subject and agent of an act of knowledge for which it has no natural equipment, and which is thus to be fulfilled by getting beyond itself." If, then, there is a human nature and an angelic nature, we cannot use the terms *wholly* in the sense in which we speak of animal nature, for instance, or cosmic nature. If every created spirit, before being a thinking spirit, is itself "nature," if, before even being thinking, it is "spiritual nature," then it must also be recognized that, in another sense, spirit is in contrast with "nature." Even in the terminology of the scholastics, and of St. Thomas especially, *natura rationalis* or *creatura rationalis* is not a *res naturalis*. Spiritual beings cannot be confounded with beings known simply as "natural beings."[40]

When St. Thomas writes that "*Every* intellect naturally desires a vision of the divine substance,"[41] de Lubac takes him at his word. Tellingly (and accurately), de Lubac notes that the pure nature hypothesis is absolutely foreign to Eastern Christian thought.[42] The recovery of the Eastern Fathers undertaken by de Lubac and

---

39 De Lubac, *At the Service of the Church*, 184.

40 Henri de Lubac, *The Mystery of the Supernatural*, trans. Rosemary Sheed (New York: Herder and Herder, 1967), 133.

41 "*Omnis intellectus naturaliter desiderat divinae substantiae visionem.*" *SCG*, bk 3, c.57. My emphasis.

42 De Lubac, *Mystery of the Supernatural*, 6.

many of his contemporaries in the spirit of *ressourcement*, indeed, has provided a much-needed point of contact and opportunity for dialogue with the Eastern Church.[43]

Despite de Lubac's clear, historically-informed articulation of the problem, his ideas continue to meet with resistance, especially from Neo-Thomist quarters reinvigorated by the boom in Latin Catholic apologetics from the 1990s through to the current moment.[44] At least some of these studies, I think, miss the mark in trying to recapture a past theology that was a distortion in the first place, the work of a theological coterie for which "Returning to the sources" seems to stop at Trent. But there are more serious problems with such a posture. Indeed, the importance of accepting the pure nature hypothesis for at least one scholar seems to reside in the fact that it provides a way for religious thinkers to engage their secular counterparts in a discussion of "natural law."[45] This kind of return is hardly worth the expense involved in losing such an integral vision of God's involvement in the lives of persons. What becomes obvious is that the *supernatural*, not all that paradoxically (yet still mysteriously), is the real *natural* state of the human person. Pure nature, in an incredibly violent act, separates "our supernatural destiny . . . from a putative natural end extending even to the next life" and further divides "nature

---

43 An excellent introduction to the subject is Andrew Louth, "French *Ressourcement* Theology and Orthodoxy: A Living Mutual Relationship?" in *Ressourcement: A Movement for Renewal in Twentieth-Century Catholic Theology*, ed. Gabriel Flynn and Paul D. Murray with Patricia Kelly (Oxford: Oxford University Press, 2012), 495–507.

44 See, for instance, Steven A. Long, *Natura Pura: On the Recovery of Nature in the Doctrine of Grace*, Moral Philosophy and Moral Theology (New York: Fordham University Press, 2010); Lawrence Feingold, *The Natural Desire to See God According to St. Thomas Aquinas and His Interpreters* (Naples, FL: Sapientia Press, 2010); and Ralph McInerny, *Praeambula Fidei: Thomism and the God of the Philosophers* (Washington, DC: The Catholic University of America Press, 2006), as well as the collection edited by Serge-Thomas Bonio, *Surnaturel: A Controversy at the Heart of Twentieth-Century Thomistic Thought*, trans. Robert Williams, rev. Matthew Levering (Naples, FL: Sapientia Press, 2009).

45 This is particularly the thesis of Long in *Natura Pura*.

and grace into a two-tiered system."[46] If pure nature is true, then the possibility of a loving Father withholding grace from some of his children for his own inscrutable reasons is our default situation and Calvin wins. Then there should be nothing to hinder resuscitating the idea of limbo which arrives of its own accord "*pari passu* with the continued theological reflection on the meaning of a nature not endowed with grace."[47] Though some Neo-Thomists might welcome such a movement,[48] the Church prudently teaches that we trust in the mystery of God's mercy in such matters.[49]

We can see, then, how the nominalist desire for reformation beginning in the Scholastic debates of the medieval period and extending to the Reformation proper proved "an engine of disenchantment"[50] which, due to cultural and intellectual ennui and inertia, has yet to lose momentum. The theology of pure nature contributed directly to the scientific revolution of the seventeenth century, and nowhere more clearly illustrated than in the life and work of philosopher René Descartes.

A Secular Gnosticism: René Descartes and the Scientific Revolution

Descartes (1596–1650) received his education from Jesuits, including Francisco Suarez, at La Flèche and the University of Poitiers. Considering his schooling, he would have been well-versed in the theology of pure nature (which, as de Lubac argued, is in reality a *philosophy* of pure nature). Descartes' own system upholds an extreme dualism, a kind of secular gnosticism, which divides body and mind, creation and God into discrete and mutually exclusive categories. His philosophy significantly impacted the

46 William L. Portier, "Twentieth-Century Catholic Theology and the Triumph of Maurice Blondel," *Communio* 38 (Spring 2011): 103–37, 115.

47 Edward T. Oakes, "The *Surnaturel* Controversy," 641.

48 Lawrence Feingold appears to welcome the notion in *Natural Desire*, 428. Cited in Oakes, "*Surnaturel* Controversy," 641.

49 *CCC*, 1261.

50 Charles Taylor, *Secular Age*, 77.

thought—religious as well as secular—of the seventeenth and subsequent centuries. For Descartes, God is completely transcendent and cannot be understood except by faith. As Hans Küng writes, "With Descartes, European consciousness in a critical development reached an epochal turning point. Basic certainty is no longer centered on God, but on man. In other words, the medieval way of reasoning from certainty of God to certainty of the self is replaced by the modern approach: from certainty of the self to certainty of God."[51] Philosopher Jean-Luc Marion suggests that the theology of pure nature influenced Descartes particularly in the way the seventeenth-century thinker understands *capacitas* (capacity) as synonymous with *potentia* (power), especially in terms of the human person's ability to receive God. For Marion, "From the theologians of pure nature onward, the concept of *capacitas/capax* has tended to undergo semantic shifts; it now no longer involves receiving God (*capax Dei*), but rather the exercise of a power (*capax dominii*)."[52] Marion reads Descartes' *Meditations* in precisely these terms, finding evidence in the philosopher's letter (dated March 1642) to the priest and scientist Marin Mersenne as emblematic of this ethos. "The texts themselves fit into the thematic of pure nature," writes Marion,

> distinguished from the supernatural aim of grace by virtue of its perfect and sufficient autonomy. . . . By a rigorous consequence, supernatural blessedness finds itself, if not refuted, at least placed at a distance, for natural capacity (*posse*) does not possess the *power* to attain it: "I say that it is possible to know *by natural reason* that God exists, but I do not say that this natural knowledge by itself, without grace, merits the *supernatural glory* which we hope for in heaven. On the contrary, it is evident that this glory is *supernatural, more than natural* powers are needed to merit it."[53]

Descartes' theological innovations would later come to their "logical conclusion" in Immanuel Kant's *Religion within the Limits of*

51 Hans Küng, *Does God Exist?: An Answer for Today,* trans. Edward Quinn (New York: Doubleday, 1980), 15.

52 Jean-Luc Marion, *Cartesian Questions: Method and Metaphysics* (Chicago: University of Chicago Press, 1999), 91.

53 Ibid., 92. Marion's emphasis.

Reason Alone (1793) which reduces religion (and Christianity in particular) to a set of moral principles, regulatory in nature.[54] Indeed, Kant has also been accused of bringing nominalism to its logical conclusion and his thought has been lamented as "the lowest ebb of Western philosophy, the complete bankruptcy of man in his search for the truth, a despair that man can in any way find truth in external objects."[55] Clearly, Descartes, "the founder of modern philosophy," was deeply indebted to the theology of pure nature, a gift which he bestowed to his inheritors (such as Kant) in materialistic and mechanistic philosophy and what eventually came to be known as the "hard sciences."

Pure nature and, especially, the philosophy of Descartes—to say nothing of Thomas Hobbes's pessimism and the empiricism of Francis Bacon—provided seventeenth-century Europe "the new view of physical reality, the new conception of nature,"[56] and one which radically shattered the shared epistemology of Christendom that had understood God as an active participant in human life as well as in chemical, biological, cosmological, and historical processes. An often unspoken (because so widely accepted) contribution of the ancient Greeks to pre-Enlightenment Christendom was the idea that the created world, nature (φύσις, *natura*), is an organism. During the seventeenth century, however, nature came to be increasingly understood as a machine.[57] As Richard Westfall explains, "During the scientific revolution nature was quantified; it was mechanized; it was perceived to be other; it was secularized."[58] Alister McGrath, drawing on this thesis, adds that what

---

54 See Francesca Aran Murphy, *Christ the Form of Beauty: A Study in Theology and Literature* (Edinburgh: T&T Clark, 1992), particularly the chapter entitled "Learning from Kant's Mistakes," 23–36.

55 Steiner, *Redemption of Thinking*, 99.

56 Richard S. Westfall, "The Scientific Revolution of the Seventeenth Century: The Construction of a New World View" in *The Concept of Nature: The Herbert Spencer Lectures*, ed. John Torrance (Oxford: Clarendon Press, 1992), 63–93, at 64.

57 Michael Foster, "Greek and Christian Ideas of Nature," *Free University Quarterly* 6 (1959): 122–27, at 122.

58 Richard S. Westfall, "Scientific Revolution of the Seventeenth Century," 65.

Westfall calls "secularization" can also be understood in light of the now nearly universal assumption that nature is an "autonomous entity, to be studied on its own terms" with scientific observations "explained by analogy with similar phenomena within nature."[59] Nature, that is, was at last understood as an entirely closed system.

These developments were completely in keeping with the rage for order and reformation inaugurated during the medieval period, but now this rage had become a kind of obsession-compulsion. As Mary Midgley observes, the mechanistic scientists of the seventeenth century "displayed a new purifying zeal, a passion for disinfection, at times a cognitive washing-compulsion, accompanied by a rather touching willingness to accept a minor role in the great cleansing process. And these too came to be seen as essential to science."[60] Their zeal eventually transmogrified into the kind of atheist missionary activity we witness in the popular projects of Richard Dawkins, Sam Harris, and Lawrence Krauss, among others. Postmodern nominalism, that is, having passed through its philosophical stage, is now a religion.

As a result of losing an integral understanding of nature that includes the supernatural, the mechanizing world view, it has been argued, "removed the controls over environmental exploitation that were an inherent part of the organic view that nature was alive, sensitive, and responsive to human action."[61] Celia Deane-Drummond, on the other hand, following Charles Raven, considers the seventeenth century "the only one in which theological ideas and science came together in a grand synthesis."[62] There is much to be said for this idea, though it bears some qualification. For one, while it is true that many natural philosophers of the period—Robert Boyle, Kenelm Digby, and Isaac Newton,

59 Alister McGrath, *A Scientific Theology, Volume I: Nature* (Grand Rapids, MI: William B. Eerdmans Publishing Company, 2001), 100.

60 Mary Midgley, *Science as Salvation: A Modern Myth and Its Meaning* (London: Routledge, 1992), 79.

61 Carolyn Merchant, *The Death of Nature: Women, Ecology, and the Scientific Revolution* (1980; reprt; New York: HarperOne, 1990), 111.

62 Celia E. Deane-Drummond, *Creation through Wisdom: Theology and the New Biology* (Edinburgh: T & T Clark, 2000), 10.

for example—maintained a vigorous hold to their faith and attempted to justify it by reason, something in their efforts suggests desperation, "the effort of men uneasily aware that the ground was shifting under the traditional foundations of Christianity to construct new ones."[63] For another, this paradigm shift left behind some untidy residues of the paradigm it had superseded. This was not a movement from integral whole to integral whole, but from integral whole to brokenness. It is a picture of incompleteness:

> Removing spirit from the Cartesian system makes serious trouble about what is then left. The concept of the natural world was originally tailored to fit the current supernatural one. It does not make sense on its own. In some ways, it is only a shadow of its supernatural partner. Life and vigour have been deliberately drained from it, as well as the rest of the spiritual realm, to be conferred on the omnipotent Creator.[64]

Removal of the Creator followed in relatively short order.

Other natural philosophers, it is true, rejected this model and strove to uphold a more traditional, integral, indeed, sacramental view of nature. They were, however, increasingly in the minority, as the alchemist and Anglican priest Thomas Vaughan in his boisterous manner complained: "*the* School-men *have got the* Day, *not by* Weight *but by* Number."[65] He nevertheless located the problem of pure nature at its core: "the doctrine of the schoolmen, which in a manner makes God and Nature contraries, hath so weakened our confidence towards Heaven that we look upon all Receptions from thence as impossibilities."[66]

---

63 Richard S. Westfall, "Scientific Revolution of the Seventeenth Century," 82.

64 Mary Midgley, *Science as Salvation*, 94.

65 Thomas Vaughan, Preface to *The Fame and Confession of the Fraternity of R.C* (1652) in *The Works of Thomas Vaughan*, ed. A. Rudrum with the assistance of Jennifer Drake-Brockman (Oxford: Clarendon Press, 1984), 483.

66 From *Anthroposophia Theomagica* (1650) in *Works of Thomas Vaughan*, 83.

The Repercussions of a Left-Brain Theology

What I am suggesting here is that the dualistic epistemology we know as secularism is an outgrowth of a string of dualistic episte-mologies that began life as dualistic theologies: the faith v. reason epistemology of the scientific revolution, the pure nature episte-mology of early modern Catholicism, the over-emphasis of God's transcendence at the expense of his immanence in Protestant Ref-ormation theologies, and the materialism implicit in nominalism. This, as Marcel Gauchet has argued, is an ironic outgrowth of Christianity, what he calls "a religion for departing from reli-gion."[67] But, contra Gauchet, secularization (the disenchantment of the world) is not built into the structure of religion as its teleo-logical inevitability. Rather, my claim is that secularization is a pathology, a kind of cancer that metastasized on the Body of the Church Militant. This pathology, however, generated (and con-tinues to generate) other pathologies.

Our current, postmodern moment—materialistic, technologi-cal, technocratic, atheistic—exemplifies a nominalism writ large. Here there are no universals. There are no ideas, no archetypes. Only names. "Marriage," for instance, no longer embeds univer-sal cultural archetypes of "husband" and "wife" and, indeed, post-modern cultural norms have become increasingly and militantly hostile to "the essential significance of Biblical engendered typol-ogy" and "the Biblical and theological significance of sexual dif-ference."[68] Marriage, previously assumed as the union of a man and woman into organic whole, has been relativized beyond the point of recognition. A collateral ontological shift has also occurred in the postmodern understanding of the word "family." Perhaps most emblematic of this shift is the new conceptualiza-tion of the term "gender," which, tellingly, has proved the most

67 Marcel Gauchet, *The Disenchantment of the World: A Political History of Religion*, trans. Oscar Burge, New French Thought (Princeton: Princeton Uni-versity Press, 1997), 101–06.

68 John Milbank, "Sophiology and Theurgy: The New Theological Hori-zon" in *Encounter between Eastern Orthodoxy and Radical Orthodoxy*, ed. Adrian Pabst and Christoph Schneider (Farnham, UK: Ashgate, 2009), 45–85, at 83.

plastic of all. Does not the notion of elective gender-reassignment surgery, like nominalism, assert in the clearest terms that universals do not exist?

Recent developments in the medical field also confirm the ascendency of postmodern nominalism. The implementation of new plastic surgery norms, a variety of hormone therapies, and the application of technologies purposed to manipulate procreation have brought within reach the long anticipated (albeit anxiously) realization of a *post*-humanity, what has also been called "*trans*humanism." Martin Heidegger's wise observation that technology could easily turn the human person into a product, a standing-reserve (*Bestand*) awaiting employment (think "human resource management"),[69] has come to pass in a profound and, tragically, for the most part profoundly invisible manner. Is this not the case with embryonic stem cell research, where the frozen human embryo awaits its birth as a tool to be employed in research? With sex-selective abortion, in which the parents choose (or cancel) their child as one would a magazine subscription? And is this not also the case with "three-parent babies," technologically manipulated human beings upon whom are imposed the "trademark" (DNA) of their corporate (with its dual connotations of "bodily" and "manufacturing") producers? This is without even mentioning the ghastly utopian transhumanist scenarios envisioned by Ray Kurzweil, Nick Bostrom, and others, a cultural imagination eagerly anticipating the day when the biological and the technological are joined in a grotesque parody of the Parousia. Nicolas Berdyaev's words (written in 1934) take on a chilling significance: "Is that being," he wrote, "to whom the future belongs to be called man, or something other?"[70] It is more than apparent that, for many, this question has lost its relevance. And the human person is not the sole victim of this culture of postmodern nominalist degradation.

---

69 Martin Heidegger, "The Question Concerning Technology" in *The Question Concerning Technology and Other Essays*, trans. with an Introduction by William Lovitt (New York: Garland Publishing, 1977), 18.

70 Nicolas Berdyaev, *The Fate of Man in the Modern World*, trans. Donald Lowrie (1935; reprt., Ann Arbor, MI: University of Michigan Press 1961), 25.

Indeed, the proliferation, especially in the United States, of GMO (genetically modified organism) crops and livestock is just as emblematic of the technological rape of nature as is the promulgation of a transhumanism. GMO corn and other field crops, for example, have had their DNA manipulated in such a way that they are either resistant to herbicides or produce their own pesticides, and these virtually untested substances find their way into the food chain. Likewise, scientists have inserted spider DNA into goats in order to harvest substances for use in bullet-proof vests, cow genes into pigs in order to toughen their hides, and human genes into corn in order to create spermicide. The side effects of these innovations are still untold, though it has been suggested that their impact—in terms of food allergies, cancer, autism, and sterilization (to name just a few)—will be significant. Already, the devastating collapse of honey bee populations (known as CCD, Colony Collapse Disorder) has been blamed on the proliferation (88% of US corn, 95% of US soy beans) of GMO agriculture and its unhealthy relationship with the pesticide culture.[71]

Biotech companies—and, alas, a good many farmers—would not be involved in this project to reimagine agriculture were profit not a motive, even though use of GMO crops has not been shown to increase yields. This economy favors the biotech companies, not the consumer. Sadly (and truly), as activist Vadana Shiva has observed, "The dominant model of economic development has in fact become anti-life."[72] Indeed, the ethos we see in biotech agribusiness is not all that different from the ethos we see in government-sanctioned contraception distribution and the abortion industry: theme and variation on what St. John Paul II

71 See, for example, Andrea Tapparo, Daniele Marton, Chiara Giorio, Allesandro Zanella, Lidia Soldà, Matteo Marzaro, Linda Vivan, and Vincenzo Girolami, "Assessment of the Environmental Exposure of Honeybees to Particulate Matter Containing Neonicotinoid Insecticides Coming from Corn Coated Seeds," *Environmental Science and Technology* 46 (2012): 2592–99.

72 Vandan Shiva, "How Economic Growth Has Become Anti-Life," *The Guardian*, theguardian.com (1 Nov 2013).

called "the culture of death." Such an economic model is not in the least interested in the notion of human flourishing, but, more honestly, in "management of resources."

It may be argued, of course, that human beings have been manipulating plants and animals (through breeding, hybridization, grafting, asexual propagation, and other techniques) since the dawn of agriculture, a prime example of which can be found in Genesis 30. However, the patriarch Jacob, Gregor Mendel, and the unknown founders of agriculture never dreamed of combining species unrelated to one another, an idea archetypally rendered in the nightmare fantasies as the monsters of mythology (probably nowhere so powerfully illustrated as in the story of Pasiphaë) and science fiction. Postmodern nominalism and scientific materialism, rejecting the idea of universals, hold that "corn," "goat," and "human," for instance, are merely terms possessing no existential value or metaphysical significance of their own, signifiers (with no signified) meaning only whatever we wish them to mean. As Humpty Dumpty tells Alice in *Through the Looking Glass*, "When *I* use a word . . . it means just what I choose it to mean—neither more nor less." It all depends on which is to be master: that is all.

But which *is* to be master? This is an important question. GMO "corn" is certainly different from its organic counterparts, despite (or perhaps proved by) the reluctance of biotech companies to label it for what it is. Likewise, postmodern conceptions of gender (or family, or marriage) also exert the primacy of the technological (or technocratic) in the realm of being. Gauchet has traced the history of human culture as moving "from immersion in nature to transforming nature,"[73] and this transformation ethos, blind in its willfulness, now also touches *human* nature. The result of a postmodern nominalist civilization augmented by the technological is, indeed, a kind of blindness, a kind of enslavement. As Heidegger writes in "The Question Concerning Technology,"

---

73 Marcel Gauchet, *Disenchantment of the World*, 67–8.

Everywhere we remain unfree and chained to technology, whether we passionately affirm or deny it. But we are delivered over to it in the worst possible way when we regard it as something neutral; for this conception of it, to which today we particularly like to do homage, makes us utterly blind to the essence of technology.[74]

Heidegger published "The Question Concerning Technology" in 1954. The intervening years have done much to confirm his suspicions if not surpass them. Technology is not something neutral.

The story I have told in this chapter is one of a creeping and eventually totalizing estrangement from God in the Christian West which resulted in a culture focused on the nominalist human subject: self-contained, self-absorbed, materialistic and subsequently calcified, impervious to metaphysics, and desensitized to the supernatural. The Christian East did not follow a parallel trajectory, but, following Russia's fascination with Western ideas and culture during the eighteenth and nineteenth centuries, with the rise of Bolshevik-style Communism, the West's preoccupation with rationality and efficiency indirectly came into its own, in a way "out-Judasing Judas." Western and Eastern Christianity had both struggled to achieve a Christian culture, a wish doomed by their alienation from one another. By the modern period, Christendom—both East and West—was reeling from a lack of integral unity and revealed a brokenness emblematic of the human subject's brokenness. But some have argued that larger forces were at work. In 1881, Vladimir Solovyov took this into consideration:

> Thus, mutilated and then rejected by Western humankind, the Christian truth remained imperfect in Eastern humankind. This imperfection, caused by the weakness of the human principle (reason and personality), could be removed only with the full development of the human principle, a task that fell to the West. Thus, this great Western development, though negative in its direct results, indirectly has a positive significance and goal. . . . In the history of Christianity, the fixed divine foundation in humankind is represented by the Eastern Church, while the Western world represents the human principle. And, here, it had to step away

74 Heidegger, "Question Concerning Technology," 4.

from the Church in order that it might develop all its powers in freedom.[75]

While Solovyov's interpretation of events can be debated, the destructive nature of separation he points to here illustrates the drama I have outlined in this chapter. Will the play end in tragedy or comedy? With slaughter or a marriage? Solovyov is optimistic: "Only after the human principle has completely isolated itself and come to know its helplessness in this isolation, can it enter into a free union with the divine foundation of Christianity, preserved in the Eastern Church, and, as a result of that free union, give birth to a spiritual humankind."[76] In the age of postmodern nominalism it is clear that the human principle has completely isolated itself, but it is unclear if we have recognized our weakness. But, perhaps Solovyov relies too heavily on Hegelian dialectic here. Christian eschatology, need I remind anyone, reads the end as both apocalypse *and* marriage.

Biotech agriculture, the redefinition of gender, and everything I have enumerated above which has contributed to the triumph of postmodern nominalism may seem to have proved the thesis of pure nature: that there is a nature unaffected by God's grace, that God is completely transcendent, if not nonexistent. It is clear—indeed, undeniable—that

> Around 1600, the last comprehensive integration of our culture began to break down into the fragmentary syntheses of a mechanistic world picture, a classicist aesthetics, and a theological scholasticism. Soon a flat utilitarianism would be ready to serve as midwife to the birth of what Nietzsche called modern man's small soul.[77]

But that's not the story I want to tell. The postmodern nominalist triumph is the story the world (*seculum*) wishes to tell; but there is another. The story I want to tell is the story of Sophia, the Wisdom of God, which was "there at the first, before the beginning

---

75 Vladimir Solovyov, *Lectures on Divine Humanity*, trans. Peter Zouboff (1948), rev. and ed. Boris Jakim (Hudson, NY: Lindisfarne Press, 1995), 171–2; 174.

76 Ibid., 174.

77 Louis Dupré, *Passage to Modernity*, 248.

of the earth" (Proverbs 8:23) and continues to inhere creation. This is the story of grace and how grace is able to touch the flesh, to redeem it, even to the chemical and biological levels, and of its presence in cosmology as well as in history. This is the story of how the rise of materialism, mechanical philosophy, and a prideful rationality were met by a spiritual countermovement. This movement appeared primarily among the laity, but it was not of the laity. Rather, the laity—less compromised than theologians and philosophers by the nominalist currents of the age (one might say "Aeon")—were receptive to the whisperings, the intuitions of Sophia. This amounted, not to a theological or religious innovation (as many have suggested) but to a true rebirth: a spiritual, religious, philosophical, and cultural renewal. It began in a cobbler's shop in Germany.

Chapter Two

Jacob Boehme's Sophianic Intuitions

Wilt thou see how I love her that thou might joy with me in the love that I have in her and she in me? ⁓Jesus to Julian of Norwich [1]

> *Mirror of justice, pray for us.*
> *Seat of wisdom, pray for us.*
> ⁓Litany of Loreto

EVEN THOUGH Sophia appears in the Bible and a variety of Sophia mythologies were known to some of the gnostic schools current during the classical era, the understanding of Sophia in the context of an explicitly articulated sophiology properly begins with the writing of the Silesian Lutheran mystic Jacob Boehme (c. 1575–1624). Boehme, a cobbler, experienced at least three aleatory mystical awakenings which resulted in an original and creative mysticism that was to reinvigorate mysticism and religious philosophy, and not only in Protestant contexts, from the early modern period onward. The first event occurred in 1610 when "whereby according to the *Divine Drawing* and *Will,* he was in spirit rapt into the *Holy Saboath*; where he remained seven whole days by his own confession in the highest *Joy*."[2] Later that year Boehme found himself fascinated by light reflected from a pewter dish by which "he was brought to the inward ground or

---

1 *The Shewings of Julian of Norwich,* ed. Georgia Ronan Crampton (Kalamazoo, MI: TEAMS-Medieval Institute Publications, 1994), 25. 893–4. My modernization.

2 [Durant Hotham], *The Life of one Jacob Boehmen, Who Although He Were a Very Meane man, yet wrote the most wonderfull deepe knowledge in Natural and Divine things…* (1644), A2ʳ.

Centrum of the hidden *Nature*."[3] Finally, in 1610 Boehme's third mystical experience inspired him to commit his insights to writing, though, as the story goes, "he wrote privately and secretly for himself, by small means, and no books at all but the *Holy Scriptures*."[4] His theosophic undertakings, nevertheless, soon drew the attention of religious and secular authorities. He was denounced from the pulpit by his pastor, Gregor Richter, and even imprisoned for a time, though "as soon as his book, written in quarto, was brought from his house ... he was released from confinement and warned to cease from such matters."[5] He did not cease. Indeed, his literary output was by any standards immense: thirty-one substantial books in fourteen years, most of them written between 1619 and 1623.

Boehme's mysticism includes elements that might be construed as "alchemical"—terminology such as "tincture," for instance—but it is not anything like alchemical writing. He may have adopted the metaphorical language of alchemy, but he was not engaged in experimentation anything remotely close to that in which John Dee, or Thomas Vaughan, or even Sir Isaac Newton participated. As opposed to the alchemical ethos, Boehme's project is concerned less with what the believer (or operator) wills and struggles to effect than with how the believer learns to place his trust in God's will. As he writes in *The Way to Christ,*

> The will of the creature ought to sink wholly into itself with all its reason and desire, accounting itself an unworthy child, that is no whit worthy of so high a grace, nor should it arrogate any knowledge or understanding to itself, or desire and beg of God to have any understanding in its creaturely self: but sincerely and simply sink itself into the grace and love of God in Christ Jesus, and desire to be as it were dead to itself, and its own reason in the

---

3 [Durant Hotham], *The Life of one Jacob Boehmen*, A2^r.

4 Ibid., A2^v.

5 Ariel Hessayon, "Boehme's Life and Times" in *An Introduction to Jacob Boehme: Four Centuries of Thought and Reception*, ed. Ariel Hessayon and Sarah Apetrei (New York and London: Routledge, 2014), 13–37, at 14–15. Quoting Howard Brinton, *Mystic Will. Based upon a Study of the Philosophy of Jacob Boehme* (New York: Macmillan, 1930), 50.

divine life of God in love, that he may do how and what he wishes with it, as with his own instrument.[6]

Though not unknown to Catholic spirituality, Boehme's spiritual resignation is certainly consistent with Lutheran theology as well as with the words of the Lord's Prayer, "Thy kingdom come, Thy will be done." Boehme's mysticism, however, like Heidegger's philosophy in its context, marks a kind of Great Divide in the history of mysticism. Though Boehme's thought bears traces of the mysticism of Meister Eckhart and other Rhineland mystics, which are likewise concerned with the surrender of the will to God, it is nevertheless unlike anything that went before it and bore a tremendous impact on much of what followed.

Perhaps the best way to describe Boehme's mysticism is to call it "poetic." The German Romantic poet Novalis (Friedrich von Hardenberg, 1772–1801), in fact, thought of the mystic as apperceiving the world poetically, speaking an essentially poetic language, and as evidence points to the ways Boehme exalts intuition and emotion and repeatedly condemns the insufficiency of reason to truly grasp ultimate reality.[7] Friedrich Schlegel (1772–1829) went even further in describing Boehme's thought: "Its form is religious, its content philosophical and its spirit poetic."[8] Indeed, Boehme's writing occupies what philosopher William Desmond calls a metaxological space between religion and philosophy, a field of the poetic. Poetry, as Heidegger argued, by its very nature can provide access to being, and this does not mean that the poetic must be rendered in lines of verse. Truly, besides poetry, prose, architecture, the fine and performing arts, liturgy, and the beauties of the natural world can all—and often do—disclose this

6 Jacob Behmen [Jacob Boehme], *The Way to Christ Discovered* [translation attributed to John Sparrow] (1648 [i.e., 1647]), 2.20.

7 Kristine Hannak, "Boehme and German Romanticism" in *An Introduction to Jacob Boehme*, 163–79, at 163.

8 Friedrich Schlegel, *Die Entwicklung der Philosophie in zwölf Büchern* (Cologne, 1804–05): in Friedrich Schlegel, *Erster Teil: Philosophische Vorlesungen (1800–1807)*, ed. Jean-Jacques Anstett, vol. 12 of *Kritische Friedrich Schlegel-Ausgabe*. Ed. Ernst Behler unter Mitiwirkung von Hans Eichner und Jean-Jacques Anstett (Munich: Schöningh Verlag, 1964), 259. Quoted in Hannak, "Boehme and German Romanticism," 166. Hannak's translation.

access to being. In Heidegger's words, "All reflective thinking is poetic, and all poetry in turn is a kind of thinking."[9] Indeed, every context in which the transcendent becomes immanent opens us to the poetic. In that way, God proves the greatest poet of all. If we try to read Boehme focused only on the logical unfoldment of his discourse, we will fail—which is why Boehme's prose is often described as "simply one of the most difficult reads in the history of Christian thought."[10] Boehme sought a new vocabulary in which to frame his religious intuitions, and, as is the case with many who have attempted to do so (William Blake and Rudolf Steiner come immediately to mind), he created his own idiom—full of idiosyncrasies and neologisms—to which it takes the reader a little time to become accustomed. But, if we read Boehme "agapeically" (to borrow Desmond's term) as we might read a poem, in a state of acceptance and expectation, we can discover the truth lurking behind his strange language. Or, rather, it can discover us as it shines through the discourse in our moments of contemplative repose. Reading Boehme agapeically allows us to experience his Sophia figure as reflective, living, adaptive, simultaneously literal and figurative, as both person and principle.

Sophia and the Language of Wisdom

Sophia in Boehme is not a stable concept, but one which changes according to conditions and contexts, much as an opal responds reciprocally to changing environmental conditions. Boehme's sophiology, at least initially, is grounded in his reading of the Bible, though, after having secured his footing in scripture, he is never hesitant to follow where his contemplation leads. First of all, Boehme connects Proverbs 8's description of Sophia as God's "master worker" at the birth of Creation and then complicates it with his theosophical speculation:

9 Martin Heidegger, "The Way to Language" in *On the Way to Language*, trans. Peter D. Hertz (New York: HarperOne, 1982), 136.

10 Cyril O'Regan, *Gnostic Apocalypse: Jacob Boehme's Haunted Narrative* (Albany, NY: State University of New York Press, 2002), 3.

So the matter of this world, as also the Stars and Elements, must not be looked upon, as if God were not therein: his eternal wisdom and virtue [or power][11] hath formed itself with the *Fiat* in all things, and he himself is the Master-Workman; and all things went forth in the *Fiat*, everything in its own essence, virtue and property. For as every star in the Firmament hath a property different from the other; thus it is with the mother also, out of which the fifth essence of the stars went forth. For when the fiery form of the stars was separated from her, she was not presently severed from the first eternal Birth-right, but she kept her eternal virtue. Only the rising power of the fire is severed from her, so that she is become a pleasant Refreshment, and a kind mother to her children.[12]

This notion is complicated, and for several reasons, not the least of which is Boehme's language of gender. The Wisdom figure of Old Testament is clearly feminine. Indeed, in the kabbalah Wisdom is often associated with the Shekinah, the Presence of God, also a feminine image used to describe God's relationship to Israel in keeping with his promise to "not abandon them wherever they are."[13] In much Patristic literature, on the other hand, drawing on Philo of Alexandria's notion of the Logos as the divine instrument of creation by way of the Prologue to St. John's Gospel and St. Paul's pronouncement that Christ "is the wisdom of God" (1 Cor 1:24), Wisdom is associated with Christ.[14] Boehme is a subtle reader. He moves from the Patristic understanding of

---

11 Boehme's translator John Sparrow often provides the reader with alternative interpretations, here rendered in brackets, of some of Boehme's terminology.

12 Jacob Behmen (Jacob Boehme), *The Second Booke concerning The Three Principles of the Divine Essence of the Eternal Dark, Light, and Temporary World...* [translated by John Sparrow] (London, 1648), 8.5. Hereafter as *Three Principles.*

13 *Zohar: Book of Enlightenment*, trans. and introduced by Daniel Chanan Matt with a preface by Arthur Green (New York: Paulist Press, 1983), 156.

14 Peter Frick, *Divine Providence in Philo of Alexandria*, Texts and Studies in Ancient Judaism 77 (Tübingen: Morh Siebeck, 1999), 76. See also Dennis O'Neil, *Passionate Holiness: Marginalized Christian Devotions for Distinctive People* (Victoria, BC: Trafford Publishers, 2009), 5–11. Some Fathers associated Wisdom with a feminine Holy Spirit, but they were in the minority.

Wisdom as Christ and then, almost unobtrusively, inserts feminine language ("mother") into his description. As is often the case
in Boehme, we need to turn to another passage to deepen our
understanding of his words—and, even then, the understanding
remains incomplete, always receding toward the horizon, drawing
the reader in more deeply. Later in *The Three Principles*, he writes,

> I set you a deep consideration: behold, how the Angelical Thrones
> and Principalities were in the beginning beheld [apprehended or
> aspected] by the Wisdom of God, which aspect [manifestation or
> idea] the Fiat took to Create; and in the Angelical Throne the infi-
> nite multiplicity, according to the Eternal Wisdom in the Wonders
> of God. . . . When God saw and took notice of our miserable Fall,
> he did illustrate [or manifest] himself by the holy Eternal Virgin of
> his Wisdom in the Eternal Wonders, in mercy which always
> floweth out of his heart, and did comprehend with his speculation
> [or manifestation] the Throne, and did further illustrate himself in
> the Throne into many millions without number, and established
> his Covenant with his Oath therein, with his precious promise of
> the Woman's Seed.[15]

The plasticity of this passage at a conceptual level is as astounding as it is subtle. First, the angelic orders are beheld/apprehended/
aspected *by* Wisdom, which we can also read as *through* Wisdom,
as an activity. Wisdom, that is, acts as an agent (we should not let
ourselves be fooled by the passive voice.) God, of course, is the Creator, but Wisdom—personified or not—is *that by which he creates*
("then I was beside him, like a master worker" [Proverbs 8:30]).
Following the Fall, God manifests himself *through* Wisdom (Wisdom as avenue of access), a notion implying that Wisdom can be a
metaphysical principle, or a source of insight (as in the case of the
personification of Wisdom found in the Wisdom literature), as
well as the Virgin Mary, the Throne in whom the Second Person of
the Trinity was manifested. But Boehme, no truster of rationality,
does not wish that his reader rest content with an easy conclusion
when touching the secrets of God. In *The Threefold Life of Man
according to the Three Principles*, for instance, he complicates things
further, writing that "the Spirit of God hath discovered the Image

---

15 Jacob Boehme, *Three Principles*, 23.18.

of God in the Virgin of his Wisdom, and the *Verbum Fiat* hath created it. The Form of this world was from Eternity in the Nature of God, but invisible and immaterial."[16] The preponderance of prepositional phrases is not simply a matter of an unpolished style. Rather, Boehme's prose is performative: it mirrors the illusiveness and hiddenness of God's traces in creation. Furthermore, the word that Boehme's translator John Sparrow here renders as "discovered" might better be translated as "discloses" (a term not available during the early modern period) for revelation is of essence here. Boehme's is an incredibly nuanced reading of Wisdom. Indeed, in returning to the Wisdom of scripture as a *thing-in-itself*—and in reading Wisdom's gender *as-it-is* in the biblical texts—Boehme may, with qualifications, be considered as anticipating religious phenomenology by roughly three hundred years. In general, though, Boehme's understanding of Sophia can be broken into two intimately-connected, yet broadly conceived, categories: 1) as a cosmological agent; and 2) as an immanental and transformative sense of being, as both a property and a condition for receiving grace.

An Anthropological Cosmology and a Cosmological Anthropology

In Boehme's cosmology, Sophia does not act on her own, does not truly possess an independent being, but takes on being as an emanation proceeding forth from God (an idea William Blake later explored to good purpose in his prophetic books). "God's word," writes Boehme, "ariseth out of the power or virtue of the *Wisdom*. And the wisdom is that Exhalation which is breathed forth or expressed from the *Trinity*, viz. God's *perception*, wherein the abyss findeth, feeleth, or perceiveth itself in the bysse or Ground."[17] These words, resonating with those of Psalm 104 ("O

16 Jacob Behmen [Jacob Boehme], *The Third Booke of the Author, being the High and Deepe Searching out of The Threefold Life of Man through [or according to] the Three Principles*, trans. John Sparrow (London, 1650), 5.83.

17 Jacob Behme [Jacob Boehme], *Concerning the Election of Grace, or of Gods Will towards Man, commonly called Predestination...* trans. John Sparrow (London, 1655), 8.7–8.

Lord, how manifold are your works! In wisdom you have made them all" [104:24]), beautifully articulate how the Trinity's act of *perception* engenders being. Unlike human perception, which is a receptive capacity, *God's perception is activity.* Wisdom, then, is the first created of all God's works and, in a sense, the scaffolding of all creation. Furthermore, Boehme argues that Wisdom is that agent by which nonbeing (the "abyss") comes into being ("bysse or Ground"). Wisdom, being absolutely receptive, does not act, yet functions as a kind of catalyst for God's activity, not only in creation but also in the divine will. As Boehme writes in *Six Theosophic Principles,* "And yet the Eternal Geniture or Birth of the Word in the Will in the Looking-Glass of the Eternal *Wisdom*, that is, in the Virgin without generating or bringing forth, is continually effected or produced from Eternity to Eternity." This "non-generating" quality is what renders Sophia a "Virgin."[18] But Sophia is nevertheless not sterile:

> IN THIS VIRGIN OF THE WISDOM OF GOD is the Eternal Principle, as a *hidden Fire*, which becometh thus apprehended as in a LOOKING-GLASS, in its Colours, and hath been known from Eternity to Eternity in the *Figure*, and also thus becometh known in all Eternity in the Eternal Original in the Wisdom.[19]

The idea of the looking-glass takes a significant role for Boehme in explaining the workings of Sophia.

Boehme's notion of the looking-glass opens a rich field of contemplation. First of all, Boehme argues that the Holy Spirit utilizes the Wisdom-mirror as vessel or conduit of revelation. This idea is much in keeping with the Book of Wisdom's description: "For [Wisdom] is the refulgence of eternal light, the spotless mirror of the power of God, the image of his goodness" (7:26). Indeed, as we shall see, even in Protestant religious contexts that exclude Wisdom and Sirach (among other books) from the canon

---

18 Jacob Behme [Jacob Boehme], *A Book of the Great Six Points,* 1.34, in *Several Treatises of Jacob Behme not printed in English before...* trans. John Sparrow (London, 1661).

19 Jacob Boehme, *A Book of the Great Six Points,* 1.35. I have tried to render the emphasis in the text by using all caps here.

of scripture, those seeking Wisdom turn to these texts to a remarkable degree. In discussing Sophia's reflection of the light of God, Boehme writes,

> And in the Light now dwelleth the Will of the Father, and of the Son, and the Holy Spirit is the *Life* therein, which openeth now the *power* of the meek Substantiality in the Light, which is, *viz.*, Colours, Wonders and Virtues.
>
> And that is called the *Virgin-like Wisdom*: For it is NO *Genetrix*, also itself openeth nothing; only the Holy Spirit is the opening of its Wonders.
>
> It is his Garment and fair beauteous ORNAMENT, and hath in it the Wonders, Colours, and Virtues of the *divine World*, and is the *house* of the Holy Trinity, and the Ornament of the Divine and Angelical Worlds.
>
> In its colours and virtues, the Holy Spirit hath the Choir of Angels, as also discovereth [i.e., discloses] all Wonders of *Created* Things, which *all* have become discovered from Eternity in the Wisdom, *without substance*, indeed, but yet in the Wisdom as in the Looking-Glass, *according to their* FIGURES, WHICH Figures in the Father's Mobility are passed into Essence and into a *Creature*, all according to the Wonders of Wisdom.[20]

Notice how, again, Boehme's circuitous style figures the vestiges and presences of God in creation and in the life of the believer through the mysterious workings of Wisdom: flirting with full disclosure, receding to the horizon in figures and signs, creating a condition in which, as Jean Wahl says of poetry, "The mysterious is here very near, and the here-very-near is mysterious."[21]

Perhaps a good way to explain Boehme's concept of this aspect of Sophia's working is by analogy. We know that light is invisible, travelling infinitely through space until it meets with an object which simultaneously reveals itself and the light which reveals it. For Boehme, one function of Sophia is in the way the Holy Spirit simultaneously reveals itself and Creation through the presence of Sophia in Creation. But, without the proper mode of perception,

---

20 Jacob Boehme, *A Book of the Great Six Points*, 1.82–85.

21 Jean Wahl, "La Poésie comme Exercice Spirituel" in *Poésie, Pensée, Perception* (Paris: Calmann-Lévy, 1948), 17–19, at 18. My translation.

one easily misses (or takes for granted) the presence of that which reveals, whether light or the Holy Spirit.

The implications of Boehme's notion of Wisdom-as-mirror further unveil the way his system does not confine the workings of God by limiting them through logically deduced "laws." There is a fluidity to Boehme's thought, and especially his thoughts concerning Sophia. For instance, one way the mirror notion unfolds, transforms, comes about through Boehme's description of Sophia's incorporation into nature as a way to facilitate the revelation of God to fallen humanity:

> And that there should go nothing in vain out of the substances of God, therefore God created Beasts, fowls, fishes, worms, trees and herbs out of all Essences, and besides [created] also figured Spirits out of the *Quinta Essentia* in the Elements, that so, after fulfilling of the Time (when the out-Birth [shall] go into the Ether) they should appear before him, and that his eternal Wisdom in his works of wonder might be known.[22]

What Boehme is saying is that God—contra the theology of pure nature—is implicit in creation, all of creation, through his Wisdom. Again, these ideas are anything but extra-biblical: "For Wisdom is mobile beyond all motion, and she penetrates all things by reason of her purity. For she is an aura of the might of God and a pure effusion of the glory of the Almighty" (Wisdom 7:24–25). Indeed, Boehme calls Sophia, "the Power of the glory of God, which hath shed forth itself in the Creation, in all created things, and lieth in *every* thing, according to the property of the thing, hidden in the Centre, as a Tincture in the living or animate Body."[23] This is not only that the faithful may come to understand creation, but also that they may come to know God, as Boehme writes:

> The concreted *Spiritus Majoris Mundi* [or Spirit of the Great World] is the chaste virgin before God, which the Spirit of the great World, in this world giveth to all Creatures, Mind, sense, and understanding (through the influence of the Stars) and so also

22 Jacob Boehme, *Three Principles*, 15.11.
23 Jacob Boehme, *Concerning the Election of Grace*, 3.68.

[doth the chaste virgin] in the Heaven . . . the virgin of wisdom is the great Spirit of the whole heavenly World (in a similitude) and that not only openeth the great Wonders in the heavenly Earth, but also in the whole Deep of the Deity.[24]

Clearly, for Boehme, "The world is charged with the grandeur of God."

But it is not simply that Sophia is embedded in nature. An aspect of Sophia also inhabits a divine/spiritual space in Boehme's intuition, one which triggers a divine longing in the human person, a divine eros. The heavenly Sophia stands in a synergistic relationship to the creaturely Sophia, the latter acting as a kind of enzyme or activating agent that is drawn to God through the heavenly Sophia. The creaturely Sophia, existing in all of nature but most actively in the human person, becomes then a sort of organ of perception. As the eye is an organ for perceiving light, so, in an analogous way, the creaturely Sophia existing in the human person (and all of nature) is an organ for perceiving the heavenly Sophia who is then capable of leading the repentant seeker to God. In Boehme's words,

the virgin standeth in the second Principle, so that the spirit of this world cannot possibly reach to her, and yet that virgin doth continually behold herself [or appear] in the Spirit of this world, to [satisfy] the lust and longing in the fruit and growing of every thing, therefore he is so very longing and seeketh the Virgin continually.[25]

The Spirit of the World in this passage, though it is informed by Satan, is not identical with him. In Boehme's anthropology Adam and his descendants possess a Spirit of this World, which was originally breathed into Adam by God. But what is important to note is that the seeking Boehme describes here is *reciprocal*: the human soul's desire for Sophia is correlative to Sophia's desire for the human soul. Nowhere is this reciprocity more evident than in Boehme's considerations of the Incarnation of Christ.

24 Jacob Boehme, *Three Principles*, 22.61–62.
25 Ibid., 14.34.

Boehme's Christology has much in common with St. Athanasius's proposal that God became man in order that man might become God. For Boehme, however, the Incarnation of Christ is the template for this in ways that go beyond what Athanasius suggested. Indeed, Boehme's theosophical intuition finds Athanasius's proposal worked out within Christ's own being. He outlines this in *Signatura Rerum*:

> Now when as His Love would give itself into Death, and deprive Death of its might, then the two Worlds, that is, the father's Fire-world with the outward visible World, and also the Divine Love-world with the Divine Heavenly essentiality, that is, with heavenly Flesh and Blood, and also with corrupted flesh and blood, were formed into one Person. God became man and made man to God, the Seed of the Woman, that is, of the Heavenly Virginity, which disappeared in *Adam*, and also corrupted man's Seed in the Anger, that is, *Mary's* Seed, were formed into one Person, which was Christ; and the Seed of the Woman, that is, of the Virgin of God, understand the Heavenly Essentiality, should bruise the head of the Serpent, understand, the wrath of God in the Corrupted man; the head is the might of God's Anger; the Divine man, understand the Divine property, should change the earthly into itself & turn the earth to heaven.[26]

Through the Incarnation, Boehme argues, not only is the human person opened to it, but, indeed, all of creation is able to participate in spiritual regeneration. The Incarnation for Boehme, as for Athanasius, renders *theosis* possible and the repentant sinner able to participate in the life of Christ:

> so the New Man, (which is born to us of God) is the Son of the Virgin: not of Earthly flesh and blood, also not of the seed of Man, but conceived by the Holy Ghost, and born of a pure divine chaste virgin: and (in this world) revealed [or manifested] in our flesh and blood: and is entered with his holy body into Death; and hath separated the earthly [body] together with the might of the Anger, from the holy Element and hath restored the soul again, and hath opened the Gate to the Light of God again, so that the averted

26 Jacob Behmen (Jacob Boehme), *Signatura Rerum: Or the Signature of all Things...* trans. J. Ellistone (London, 1651), 11.11.

soul can (with the Essences of the Father in the holy Will) reach the Light of God again.[27]

In *The Way to Christ* (perhaps his most accessible book) Boehme frames this idea in the language of prayer:

> O thou great and most holy Name and power of God JEHOVA, which hast stirrest thyself with thy most sweet power JESUS, in the limit [goal or mark] of the Covenanted promise to our Father Adam, in the woman's seed; in the Virgin Mary in our disappeared heavenly Humanity, and brought the living essentiality of thy holy power in the Virgin-wisdom of God, into our humanity, which was extinguished, as to thee; and hast given it to us, to be our life, victory, and new Regeneration; I entreat thee with all my strength, beget a new holy life in me, by thy sweet power JESUS, that I may be in thee and thou in me, and that thy Kingdom may be made manifest in me, and that the will and conversation of my soul may be in heaven.[28]

Central to Boehme's Christology—and the locus of its intersection with his Sophiology—is the role of the Virgin Mary.

First of all, Mary is for Boehme the vessel of the Incarnation, "a bright Morning-Star, above other Stars."[29] Boehme esteems her above all other creatures, much in resonance with the notion of hyperdulia, and not at all in harmony with much early modern Protestant theology. The reason she is to be esteemed is clear to Boehme:

> For she bare the Saviour of all the world, without any earthly mixture; and she is also a virgin of chastity, highly blessed by her Son Jesus Christ, in the Divine Light and Clarity, more than the Heavens, like the Princely Thrones of the Angels. For out of her went forth the body, which attracts all Members to it; which are the children of God in Christ. And therefore her Glance [Luster or brightness] is above the Glance of Heaven; and the Glance of her soul is in the holy Trinity, where all other children of *Adam* (which

27 Jacob Boehme, *Three Principles*, 22.26.

28 Jacob Behmen [Jacob Boehme], *The Way to Christ Discovered*, 50. For reasons unknown, John Sparrow did not use his usual method of marking paragraphs for only this chapter of the book.

29 Jacob Boehme, *Three Principles*, 18.83.

are born [or begotten] in Christ) are also Members therein, in that One Christ Jesus.[30]

He knows such an idea will draw suspicion from the Lutheran authorities and he anticipates their concerns, asking, "Or dost thou think I make a God of her?"[31] He does not believe she is: "No, the Invocation does not belong to her." Nevertheless, Boehme believes Mary's place in salvation was built into God's plan, drawing on Genesis 3's promise that the woman's seed would trample the serpent's head.[32] Indeed, Boehme reads Mary's divine role as antecedent not only to the Fall, but to the creation itself: "She was known in God in the highly precious Name JESU, before the foundation of the World was laid."[33] In Boehme, Mary's hyperdulia is intimately related to her sophianic nature.

In Boehme, as the Word incarnated in Jesus, so in a similar (though not identical) fashion Sophia is united with Mary. As he writes in *Three Principles of the Divine Essence*, "the same virgin in the Wisdom of God, in the Word of God, hath in the bosom of the virgin *Mary*, given itself into her virgin-Matrix, and united itself, as a property, not to depart in Eternity."[34] He explains further:

> Therefore we set it down here (according to our knowledge) that the pure chaste virgin (in which God was born [or generated]) is the chaste virgin [that is] in the presence of God: and it is an Eternal virgin; before ever Heaven and Earth was created, it was a virgin, and without blemish; and that pure chaste virgin of God put itself into *Mary*, in her Incarnation, and her new Man, was in the holy Element of God; and therefore she was blessed among all Women, and the Lord was with her, as the Angel said.[35]

This aspect of Boehme's system, indeed, may have been the most

---

30 Jacob Boehme, *Three Principles*, 18.93.

31 Ibid., 18.94.

32 Ibid., 17.97–106.

33 Jacob Boehme, *The Fifth Book of the Author, in Three parts. The First; Of the Becoming Man or Incarnation of Jesus Christ the Sonne of God, That is, Concerning the Virgin Mary...* [trans. John Sparrow] (London, 1659), 1.11.65. Hereafter as *Incarnation of Jesus Christ*.

34 Jacob Boehme, *Three Principles*, 18.37.

35 Ibid., 22.31.

radical for his time. Interestingly, the Incarnation of Christ is answered by Mary's union with Sophia by a reciprocal movement. "We cannot say," writes Boehme,

> that the heavenly virgin of the Mercy of God (that is, that which entered into *Mary* out of the Counsel of God) is become Earthly; but we say that the soul of *Mary* hath comprehended the heavenly virgin: and that the heavenly virgin hath put the heavenly new pure Garment of the holy Element, out of the chaste virgin of God (that is, out of the [*Barmhertzigkeit*, Mercifulness] or Mercy of God) on to the soul of *Mary*, as a new Regenerated Man: and in that same she hath conceived the Saviour of all the world, and born him into this world.[36]

The double event—Christ's incarnation tied to Sophia's manifestation—bears with it important cosmological and salvific consequences upon which Boehme elaborates in ways very different from (though not antithetical to) more traditional Christian notions of atonement.

Cyril O'Regan has argued that "Mary is not in any sense the *theotokos*" in Boehme and that the theosopher emphasizes the "humanness of Mary and Jesus . . . and . . . operates in terms of the Alexandrian axiom that what Christ does not assume, he cannot save."[37] I think this is an extreme representation of Boehme, colored by O'Regan's project—framing Boehme in terms of Valentinian Gnosticism, a school of thought with which Boehme could not have been familiar. As B.J. Gibbons has observed, "If Boehme was a Gnostic, he was a Gnostic standing on his head."[38] Boehme is not writing as a professional theologian, but as a theosopher and as a mystic. Boehme writes in a symbolic and multivalent language. Reading him through a heresy-hunting lens does him (and, conversely, the reader) a great injustice. Indeed, the contrary motion Boehme illustrates through the dynamic of Christ's descent to man and Mary's ascent to Sophia needs to be read in its entirety, not one piece at a time.

36 Ibid., 22.37.
37 Cyril O'Regan, *Gnostic Apocalypse*, 46–47.
38 B.J. Gibbons, *Gender in Mystical and Occult Thought* (Cambridge: Cambridge University Press, 1966), 62.

Just as Mary's union with Sophia provided Christ with a very physical means to make his way to man, for Boehme, that same union also makes it possible for each human person to find his or her way to Christ. In describing this process, he uses what is possibly his most intimate language, as we can see in a passage from *The Way to Christ*:

> When Christ the corner-stone, stirreth himself in the extinguished Image of man, in his hearty conversion and repentance, then Virgin Sophia appeareth in the stirring of the Spirit of Christ, in the extinguished Image, in her virgins-attire before the soul: at which the soul is so amazed and astonished in its uncleanness, that all its sins immediately awake in it, and tremble and shake before her. For then the judgment passeth upon the sins of the soul, so that it even goeth back in its unworthiness, and is ashamed in the presence of its fair love, and entereth into itself, denying itself as utterly unworthy to receive such a jewel. This is understood by them who are of our Tribe, who have tasted this jewel, and to none else. But the noble Sophia draweth near in the essence of the soul, and kisseth it friendly, and tinctureth the dark fire of the soul with her Rays of love, and shineth through the soul with her Kiss of Love: then the soul skippeth in its body for great joy, in the strength of this Virgin-love, triumphing, and praying the great God, in the strength of the noble Sophia.[39]

In most of Boehme's writing, Sophia comes off as a divine principle, a quality (note Boehme's usual employment of the neutral pronoun), while here Sophia is quite clearly a being, and quite clearly feminine. How does one interpret such a passage? Is this poetry? Theology? Do we take Sophia as a reality, that is, as a *person*, supernatural, perhaps, but still a person? When reading Boehme anytime, and perhaps especially when reading Boehme on Sophia, adhering too closely to any conceptualization will result in a shallow understanding. Boehme's Sophia—as is the case with most sophiologies—needs to be read holographically.[40] That is, we need to read Boehme's Sophia on several different lev-

---

39 Jacob Boehme, *The Way to Christ*, 57–59.

40 I am interpreting "holographically" in terms of a kind of quantum mechanics of reading.

els at once, holding that which shines through the text in an attitude of active waiting, allowing its many layers and textures to resonate through our own souls while suspending our critical faculties: faculties which so eagerly wish to lay claim to the victory of interpretive conquest.

An important imagination regarding the human soul's encounter with Sophia for Boehme is what he describes as "the kiss." As critics have noticed, Boehme here speaks in the language of *Brautmystik* (bridal mysticism), though transferred from the Virgin Mary to the Virgin Sophia.[41] The mystical marriage with Sophia, for Boehme, is simultaneously a union with Christ, and, as is typical with his writing, the presence of both is woven into a complex tapestry. But the kiss is not the beginning of the marriage:

> Christ was tempted in the wilderness, and, if thou wilt put on him, thou must progress from his Incarnation to his Ascension: and though thou art not able nor needest to do that which he hath done; yet thou must enter wholly into his process and therein die continually from the vanity of the soul, for the virgin Sophia espouseth not herself to the soul except in this property which springeth up in the soul through the death of Christ, as a new plant standing in heaven.[42]

Here as elsewhere in the spirit of reciprocity characteristic of his writing, Boehme reads Christ's Incarnation as the template for all regeneration. The betrothal period is one of trial and struggle, a characteristic quite at odds with Protestantism's emphases on justification by either *sola fide* or *sola scriptura*. Only after the soul's purification is it prepared for union:

> Now if the soul continue constant and getteth the victory over the devil in all his assaults, disesteeming all temporal things for the love of its noble Sophia, then the precious garland will be set upon it for a token of victory.
>
> Here the virgin, (which manifesteth herself from the dear name JESUS with Christ, the treader upon the serpent, God's anointed) cometh to the soul, and kisseth it with her sweetest love in the essence most inwardly and impresseth her love into its desire for a

41 B.J. Gibbons, *Gender in Mystical and Occult Thought*, 94.
42 Jacob Boehme, *The Way to Christ*, 34–5.

token of victory: and here Adam in his heavenly part riseth again from death in Christ.[43]

There is wonderful circularity, a breathing, to Boehme's mysticism: Sophia is revealed out of Christ and she then engages the soul which, by union with her, is brought to Christ. Furthermore, there is a paradoxical interpenetration of Being and being oscillating between Christ and Sophia, as Boehme writes in *Mysterium Magnum*, "Christ and the virgin Sophia are *one person*; understand the true Manly Virgin of God, which *Adam* was *before* his *Eve*, when he was man and woman, and yet neither of them, but a Virgin of God."[44] This passage requires a little unpacking.

Boehme uses the image of the androgyne when speaking of Adam prior to the arrival of Eve as a way to represent integral unity. There is something of Plato's fable of the separation of the sexes found in the *Symposium* here. For Boehme, as for Plato, the idea of an integral unity when Adam "was man and woman, and yet neither of them, but a Virgin of God" helps to explain in symbolic terms a concept that would be far more difficult to communicate with cold reason. He clearly has biblical precedent for the latter, reading in Genesis: "Let us make man in our image.... God created man in his image, in the divine image he created him; male and female he created them" (Genesis 1:26–27). God's creation of Eve out of Adam's body, on the other hand, does not occur until Genesis 2:21–22. The temptation to interpret the androgynous Adam as intersexed, however, would be a mistake. Nicolai Berdyaev, an astute reader of Boehme, argued as much early in the twentieth century:

> The androgynic image of man does not possess an adequate physical image upon the earth, within our natural conditions. Hermaphroditism is a distorted and sick caricature of it. The myth concerning the androgyne belongs to the very profoundly old myths of mankind. This myth finds its justification upon a quite

43 Jacob Boehme, *The Way to Christ*, 36–37.
44 Jacob Behm [Jacob Boehme], *Mysterium Magnum, or An Exposition of the First Book of Moses called Genesis...* [trans. John Ellistone and John Sparrow] (London, 1655), 50.48.

deep and esoteric interpretation of the book of Genesis, though it be not characteristic to any prevailing theological teachings.[45]

For Boehme, the generation of Eve represents a step in the degeneration and eventual fall of man, a move from integral unity, to division, to alienation from God (a theme Blake explores dramatically in *Jerusalem*). Prior to Eve's generation, for Boehme, Sophia resided with(in) Adam, but afterwards she withdrew:

> But when *Adam* was infested, from the lust to eat of the knowledge of good and evil, and that the Spirit of this world pressed [or swayed] *Adam*, where also the subtle Devil (which in the Spirit of this world slipped in) shot mightily at *Adam*, so that *Adam* became weary, and blind to the Kingdom of God; [then] said God, *It is not good for man to be alone*, for he will not now bring forth the Paradisical virgin; because he is infected from the Spirit of this world, so that the chastity of the modesty is quite at an end: we will make a help for him, to be with him, out of whom he may build his Principality, and propagate himself, it cannot be otherwise now; and he let a deep sleep fall upon man, and he slept.
>
> Here it may be very properly and well understood, how the virgin in *Adam* departed into the Father, into her Principle; for the Text sayeth, *God let a deep sleep fall upon Adam*; now where sleep is, there the virtue [or power] of God is hidden in the Centre: for where that [virtue of God] groweth, there is no sleep; for, the Keeper of *Israel* neither slumbereth nor sleepeth.[46]

This interpretation, certainly, takes more than a few liberties with the biblical text, though Boehme's hermeneutic here has much in common with the kabbalistic meditations on scripture, for instance, such as those found in the *Zohar*.

In *Mysterium Magnum*, his contemplation of Genesis, Boehme reads Adam's sleep theosophically in relation to the Crucifixion. Implicit in both is redemption and regeneration:

45 N.A. Berdyaev, "Studies Concerning Jacob Boehme: Etude II. The teaching about Sophia and the Androgyne. J. Boehme and the Russian Sophiological Current," *Journal Put'* (April 1930): 34–62. Translated by S. Janos with Michael Knetchen, www.berdyaev.com 2002. Retrieved 14 November 2013.
46 Jacob Boehme, *Three Principles*, 17.27–28.

His sleep in the Rest of Christ in the *Grave*, where the new regenerate life in Christ's Humanity, must enter into *Adam's* sleep, and awaken it again to the Eternal *life*, and bring it out of time into Eternal being.

But the breaking [or dividing] of *Adam's* Essence, when the woman was taken out of him, is the breaking or bruising of *Christ's body* on the Cross, from the fixed hour to the ninth; for so long was the *Fiat* in *Adam's* Sleep in the Separating of the Man and Woman; for in such a *space* of time the woman was completely finished [or brought forth] out of *Adam* into a female person [or Image.]

And when Christ on the Cross had again accomplished this Redemption of our Virgin-like Image from the *divided sex* of Male, and female, and tinctured it with his *heavenly blood* in the divine Love; He said, *it is finished*: for before, he stood in *Adam's* thirst: As *Adam* did thirst after the vanity; so Christ did now fill or *satiate* this thirst of vanity, with the holy divine Love-thirst, and turned about the will of the Soul, that it might again introduce its thirst into God: and when this was brought to pass, he said, now *it is finished*, and converted; Christ turned back *Adam* in his sleep from the vanity, and from the Man, and woman, again into the Angelical Image. Great and wonderful are these *Mysteries*, which the world cannot apprehend; for it is as blind in them, as a man that is born blind, is, to behold this world; but he that Regardeth and *findeth* them, hath great joy therein.[47]

This is a fine example of Boehme's method of working poly-dimensionally, reading the text not only in terms of the Old Testament anticipating the New (and the New fulfilling the Old) but also interpreting it in terms of human spiritual psychology. In a sense, what Boehme writes concerning the androgynous Adam is poetry. But does Boehme intend for his reader to take this image as metaphor, as metaphysics, or as ontology? As is usual with Boehme, the answer is multidimensional.

Indeed, he speaks directly to reader reception—but even then leaves the matter unresolved. He is highly distrustful of rationality when exploring the mysteries of God. In *Three Principles*, for instance, he writes, "O thou blind Mind . . . dost thou suppose,

---

47 Jacob Boehme, *Mysterium Magnum*, 19.5–7.

that I write of the fall of Man without light and understanding? Or that I do not look and see into the holy Scripture, what that sayeth of it, [when I say] that Man before his fall was Angelical in his mind and body?" Even this defense, however, avoids making a claim for his non-scripturally-based insights. Yet he denies that he is engaged in myth-making:

> Beloved Mind, we write no conceits and tales, it is in earnest, and 'tis as much as our bodies and souls are worth: we must give a strict account of it, as being the Talent that is committed to us: if any will be scandalized at it, let them take heed what they do, truly it is high time to awake from sleep: for the Bridegroom cometh.[48]

It is important to note, though, that he does not address the reader—at least not directly—and speaks directly to the *mind*. Reason, for Boehme, becomes a hindrance when searching into mysteries: "We must wholly reject our own Reason, and not regard the dissembling flattering Art of this world, it is not available to help us, *to that Light*, but it is a mere leading astray and keeping of us back."[49] The kind of Scholastic wrangling that bequeathed nominalism to posterity has no place in Boehme's project and, combined with the Lutheran milieu of early seventeenth-century Gorlitz, certainly jaded his view of the Catholic Church as well as "all the high-Schools or Universities of this World; with their disputations and *Laws*."[50] Rationality, for Boehme, had become a worthless hermeneutic, whereas a theosophic (that is to say, a poetic) apprehension of scripture might yield richer and truer rewards.

Boehme's intuitions are the product of his essentially contemplative engagement with scripture, with which, under the right conditions, our own contemplation may participate. Contemplation, among other things, is an act of focusing the will and, in religious contemplation, uniting it with God's will. "For if there were but one only will," Boehme writes, "then all essences would do

---

48 Jacob Boehme, *Three Principles*, 17.115.

49 Jacob Behmen [Jacob Boehme], *The Third Booke of the Author, being The High and Deepe Searching out of The Threefold Life of Man through [or according to] the Three Principles*, trans. John Sparrow (London, 1650), 5.32.

50 Jacob Boehme, *Incarnation of Jesus Christ*, 2.1.5.

but one thing, but in the *Counter will* each exalteth itself in itself
to its victory and exaltation; and all life and vegetation stands in
this contest, and thereby the divine *wisdom* is made manifest, and
comes into form to Contemplation, and to the kingdom of joy."[51]
As with other aspects of his thought, human contemplation stands
in a reciprocal relationship with God's contemplation. This is
especially evident in the notion of Sophia as a looking-glass. For
what is this looking-glass if not God's, and what does he see if not
himself? As Boehme writes in *Concerning the Election of Grace,*
"the *Spirit of God* . . . hath, through the wisdom of Eternity, introduced itself into such a *Mysterium Magnum,* to the visibility of
itself."[52] The kind of contemplation Boehme considers results in
what I have called a "double intentionality," a meeting of two cen-
ters of consciousness through the contemplation of a text. Philosopher and priest John Panteleimon Manoussakis recognizes a
similar phenomenon in the discomfort one might feel when praying before an icon: a sudden realization that, while one gazes at an
icon, one is also seen from beyond the image.[53]

Boehme's contemplation of the deep mysteries of scripture and
nature results in what is simultaneously an anthropological cosmology and a cosmological anthropology. The reciprocity
implicit in such an ethos welcomes our participation if only we
are patient enough to give it the time and presence necessary to
allow their unfoldment, employing an agapeic method which
"sets all present beings free into their given presence, and brings
what is absent into their absence."[54] This is a question of interiority, which, as Pope St. John Paul II has said, is something sadly
and tragically lacking in postmodern culture. Like Boehme, he
points to the example of the Virgin as remedy:

> Mary, in addition to being our Mother who is close, discreet and
> understanding, is the best Teacher for achieving knowledge of the

51 Jacob Boehme, *Mysterium Magnum,* 40.8.
52 Jacob Boehme, *Concerning the Election of Grace,* 2.71.
53 John P. Manoussakis, "The Phenomenon of God: From Husserl to
Marion," *American Catholic Philosophical Quarterly* 78 no. 1 (2004): 53–68, at
64.
54 Martin Heidegger, "The Way to Language," 126.

truth through contemplation. *The drama of contemporary culture is the lack of interiority,* the absence of contemplation. Without interiority culture has no content; it is like a body that has not yet found its soul. What can humanity do without interiority?

Unfortunately, we know the answer very well. *When the contemplative spirit is missing, life is not protected* and all that is human is denigrated. Without interiority, modern man puts his own integrity at risk.[55]

The abandonment of interiority is not a risk worth taking. With Pope John Paul, Jacob Boehme invites us to experience the depths of God again for the first time in imitation of the Virgin.

55 Apostolic Journey of His Holiness John Paul II to Spain. Meeting with Young People, Air Base of Cuatro Vientos in Madrid, Saturday, 3 May 2003. www.vatican.va. Emphasis in source.

Chapter Three

Dei Gloria Intacta:
The Wisdom of God in Robert Fludd's Mystical Philosophy

Bright Queen of Heaven! Gods Virgin Spouse!
The glad worlds blessed maid!
Whose beauty tyed life to thy house,
And brought us saving ayd.
~ Henry Vaughan[1]

Sapientiae humanae fructus Lignum vitae est.
~ Michael Maier[2]

F OLLOWING his stunning entrance into the milieu of early modern religious thought, Jacob Boehme's mystical insights inspired a wide variety of individuals and groups interested in a more immediate, more profound experience of God than what they found available to them in their own familiar Protestant religious contexts. Most of these individuals and groups, to be sure, were part of growing aspect of Protestantism that was showing signs of having grown weary of *sola scriptura* and of an absolutely transcendent divinity. On the Continent, and especially in Germany, Boehme found a ready readership among those who found conventional Protestantism too limiting yet who were

---

1 Henry Vaughan, "The Knot" from *The Complete Poetry of Henry Vaughan*, ed. French Fogle (New York: New York University Press, 1965), lines 1–4.

2 "The fruit of human wisdom is the Tree of Life." Michael Maier, *Atalanta Fugiens, hoc est Emblemata Nova de Secretis Naturae Chymica...* (Oppenheimii, 1618), 113.

also wary of Catholicism due to a successful print and political campaign that portrayed Catholicism as fallen from the tradition of the apostles, as corrupted, and as nothing but a beautiful shell of ceremonies and superstition void of any actual Christian substance. This resulted in a curious development of "Protestant mysticism": one mystical enough to be thought heretical by the various establishment forms of Protestantism and just Protestant enough to be considered (at least among its practitioners) as decidedly *not* Catholic.

In early modern Germany, Boehme inspired, among others, the early adherents of Radical Pietism, including Gottfried Arnold (1666–1714) and Johann Georg Gichtel (1638–1710), both of whom elaborated on Boehme's sophiology. Boehme's spirituality also influenced to some degree a number of German Catholics, including the Silesian priest, physician, and poet Johann Scheffler (1624–1677), better known by the name he adopted after his conversion to Catholicism, Angelus Silesius. Boehme's popularity in Germany persisted well into the Romantic Era.

In early modern England, Boehme's ideas made a significant impact. Among those inspired by his theosophy were some in the burgeoning Quaker movement, the Cambridge Platonists,[3] and the Philadelphian Society,[4] as well as the Metaphysical poets Henry Vaughan and Thomas Traherne and Vaughan's twin brother, the Anglican priest and natural philosopher Thomas. From these tributaries, Boehme's ideas later surfaced in the thought of the non-juror William Law (1686–1761) and the poet and engraver William Blake (1757–1827), to name only two. His influence was both pervasive and resilient.

Yet Behmenism was not the only movement that countered

3 Henry More in particular.

4 The Philadelphians were a society devoted to ecumenism and mysticism and developed from a circle gathered around the Anglican priest John Pordage. Notable among the group are Thomas Bromley, Francis Lee, Richard Roach, and the leader of the Philadelphian Society, Jane Lead (sometimes spelled "Leade"). Boehme's influence permeates their work. For more on Lead, see the chapter entitled "The Pauline Mission of Jane Lead" in my *Literature and the Encounter with God in Post-Reformation England* (Aldershot, UK: Ashgate Publishing, 2014).

pure nature theology and the establishment of scientific rationality as the primary epistemological method for engaging the
world. Also originating in Germany, Rosicrucianism likewise
made a claim for an integrated, holistic view of the cosmos, but
one in which religion and science as well as mystical and rational
modes of inquiry complemented one another instead of being
engaged in a struggle for superiority. Indeed, the critical narrative
concerning intuitive epistemological approaches (such as that
expressed in Boehme and Rosicrucianism, but also in religion in
general) has been for the most part articulated in a politically secularist framework in which faith's "inability to adapt" is predicted
to end in religion's assured extinction and science's evolutionary
victory guaranteed through an assumed "survival of the fittest."
In this chapter, I will argue that 17th-century Rosicrucianism (not
to be confused with the later, mostly Masonic, movements co-
opting this name) served as a kind of theoretical framework for
proposing a holistic and integral epistemology that responded to
the radically dualistic and materialistic epistemologies then taking
shape in the wake of pure nature and Descartes. Furthermore, I
will argue that, inspired by the early Rosicrucian manifestos, the
English physician and mystical philosopher Robert Fludd in his
voluminous writings attempted to retrieve a traditional, integral,
and thoroughly Christian understanding of the world (both macrocosm and microcosm) that was quickly being colonized by sec-
ularizing forces and, thereby, vanishing, and that he did so by a
bold and radical act of reimagination. The idea of the Wisdom of
God, Sophia, plays a significant role in his thought.

The Rosicrucian Phenomenon

In the second decade of the seventeenth century, the publication
of a series of works in Germany created what can almost be
described as a kind of hysteria among the learned of Europe. What
are now known as the Rosicrucian manifestos promised a more
comprehensive Reformation than that initiated by Martin Luther
and his allies, one that would transform education, learning, and
politics as well as religion. In 1614 the first of these works, *Fama
Fraternitatis*, written in German, laid out the tenets of the move-

ment in the form of a seemingly mythical narrative concerning its "founder," the legendary "C.R.C." Following in 1615, the Latin *Confessio Fraternitatis* articulated the objectives of the brotherhood. In 1616 a third work appeared, the allegorical romance *Chymische Hochzeit Christiani Rosencreutz anno 1459*, known in English as *The Chymical Wedding of Christian Rosenkreutz*.[5] However, after the publication of these three texts, the "Invisible College" of the Rosicrucian Fraternity grew silent, never to speak again, a phenomenon the German alchemical writer and physician Michael Maier lamented as a "*silentium post clamores.*"[6]

When the manifestos were first published many intellectuals, René Descartes for a famous example, tried—and failed—to contact the fraternity.[7] Public appeals begging admittance, such as Julius Sperber's *Echo der von Gott hocherleuchteten Fraternitet des Lobl. Ordens R.C.* and his shorter *Sendbrieff* (both published in 1615), went unanswered. That is not to say that all responses were

5 The *Chymische Hochzeit* has been attributed to the juvenilia of the Lutheran pastor and theologian Johann Valentin Andreae, who is also suspected of having a hand in the other manifestos. There is much scholarly debate on Andreae's alleged Rosicrucianism. John Warwick Montgomery is highly skeptical about the possibility that Andreae was. See his *Cross and Crucible: Johann Valentin Andreae (1586–1654), Phoenix of the Theologians*, 2 vols. (The Hague: Martinus Nijhoff, 1973). Much scholarship, however, argues that Andreae was connected to the movement. See, for instance, Donald R. Dickson, *The Tessera of Antilia: Utopian Brotherhoods and Secret Societies in the Early Seventeenth Century* (Leiden: Brill, 1998), 19–22; Hereward Tilton, *The Quest for the Phoenix: Spiritual Alchemy and Rosicrucianism in the Work of Count Michael Maier (1569–1622)*, Arbeiten zur Kirchengeschichte, Band 88 (Berlin: Walter de Gruyter, 2003), 127–31; Frances A. Yates, *Rosicrucian Enlightenment* (1972; reprt., Boulder, CO: Shambhala, 1978), 50.

6 Michael Maier, *Silentium Post Clamores, hoc est, Tractatus Apologeticus, quo causae non solum clamorum, seu Revelationem Fraternitatis Germanicae de R.C.* (Francofurti, 1624).

7 Christopher McIntosh, *The Rosicrucians: The History, Mythology, and Rituals of an Esoteric Order*, 3rd ed. (York Beach, ME: Samuel Weiser, 1997), 50. Hilton (*Quest for the Phoenix*, 150) counts more than four hundred 'Rosicrucian' apologies and opposing *Kampfschriften* that appeared following publication of the manifestos. See also the chapter entitled "The Mystery of the Rose Cross" in A.C. Grayling's *Descartes: The Life and Times of a Genius* (New York: Weller & Company, 2005), 69–88.

so welcoming of the Rosicrucian entrance into the intellectual life of Europe. Such was the case with Andreas Libavius (1555–1616) who, in *DOMA Exercitatio Paracelsica nova de notandis ex scripto fraternitatis de Rosea Cruce* and *Analysis Confessionis Fraternitatis de Rosea Cruce*, greeted the publication of the manifestos with skepticism if not outright contempt.[8]

Though the manifestos are often maligned as "occult texts" (whatever that means) their teaching is surprisingly straightforward and more or less traditionally Christian, though they are not untainted by the anti-Catholic polemic that so infected northern Germany prior to the Thirty Years War. However, it should be said, the anti-Catholicism of the texts is rather "stagey," a kind of performance. Some scholars (though I am not in agreement with them) have even suggested that the Rosicrucian manifestos were part of a Jesuit plot intent on winning Protestant souls back to Catholicism.[9] Whatever their origins, the fraternity's primary commitment speaks directly to an intellectual *mise en scène* troubled by pure nature and encroaching scientific materialism and is evident particularly in their affirmation of the presence of God in world-historical processes: "God in these later days hath poured out so richly His mercy and goodness to mankind, whereby we do attain more and more to the perfect knowledge of Jesus Christ and of Nature."[10] The key phrase here is "*the perfect knowledge of Jesus Christ and of Nature.*" For this early Rosicrucianism, the theological and the scientific realms are inconceivable apart from one another and, furthermore, it holds that religious devotion and scientific inquiry cannot be properly and fully realized other than in union. Not only are the manifestos straightforward in their traditional Christian ethos, they are also straightforward in their strongly-held religious commitments.

In the *Fama,* the first of the fraternity's clearly articulated prin-

8 Both works are included in Libavius's *Examen philosophiae novae, quae veteri abrogandae opponitur* (Frankfurt, 1615).

9 See, for example, Frances Yates, *Rosicrucian Enlightenment*, 98.

10 All references to the manifestos are taken from Thomas Vaughan's edition, *The Fame and Confession of the Fraternity R.C., commonly of the Rosie Cross* (1652), 1.

ciples is "That none of them should profess any other thing, then to cure the sick, and that *gratis,*"[11] a gesture indicative of both the theological virtue of charity (*caritas*) and a commitment to the medical profession's ethos of using science in the service of healing. Furthermore, the *Fama* describes C.R.C.'s tomb as inscribed with affirmations of Christian piety:

Round about the first Circle or Brim stood,

Jesus mihi omnia.[12]

In the middle were four figures, inclosed in circles, whose circumscription was,

1. *Nequaquam Vacuum.*
2. *Legis Jugum.*
3. *Libertas Evangelii.*
4. *Dei Gloria Intacta.*[13]

The statement, "*Nequaquam Vacuum*" ("by no means a vacuum") proves intriguing in its inference that there is no place in the creation where God is absent, an idea that certainly touches upon theology of pure nature. Likewise, "*Dei Gloria Intacta*" ("the Virgin Glory of God") suggests the notion of Sophia, an idea, as we shall see, more fully developed in the writing of Robert Fludd.

In the *Confessio* the investigation of the secrets of Nature is anchored in the assumption that these secrets must stand in implicit resonance with the secrets of God, being, as they are, "those great Letters and Characters which the Lord God hath written and imprinted in Heaven and the Earths Edifice."[14] In the Rosicrucian understanding, this way of reading nature is an extension of the Rosicrucian way of reading the Bible:

These Characters and Letters, as God hath here and there incorporated them in the holy Scripture the *Bible*, so hath He imprinted them most apparently into the wonderful Creation of heaven and Earth yea in all Beastes. So that like as the *Mathematician* or

11 *Fame and Confession*, 14.
12 "Jesus is all to me."
13 "1. By no means a vacuum. 2. The yoke of the law. 3. The freedom of the Gospel. 4. The Virgin Glory of God." *Fame and Confession*, 21–22.
14 *Fame and Confession*, 44.

Astronomer can long see and know the Eclipses which are to come, so we may verily fore-know and fore-see the darkness of Obscurations of the Church, and how long they shall last.[15]

The Rosicrucian project, then, is really a re-establishment and reimagination of the medieval notion of "the Two Books" through which God's self-revelation can be known. As Alister McGrath has noted, the idea of the Two Books gained a renewed currency during the seventeenth century and was affirmed by Francis Bacon, Thomas Browne, and Robert Boyle, among others.[16] My contention, however, is that the Two Books of the seventeenth century mirrored the bifurcation of the disciplines of science (nature) and theology (scripture), which were less and less studied or savored as a symbiosis effecting what Peter Harrison has called "a comprehensive hermeneutical practice" that included both within its purview.[17] Rosicrucianism found such a division unacceptable. Therefore, in the Rosicrucian way of understanding it, through the study of nature one can only hope to aspire to any sort of comprehensiveness by an even deeper engagement with and knowledge of the Bible, which results in a transformation of the self or, in theological terms, *theosis*. As the *Confessio* phrases it,

> We do admonish every one for to read diligently and continually the holy *Bible*; for he that taketh all his pleasures therein, he shall know that he prepared for himself an excellent way to come in to our *Fraternity*. For as this is the whole sum and content of our Rule, That every Letter or Character which is in the World ought to be learned and regarded very well; so those are like unto us, and are very near allyed unto us, who do make the holy *Bible* a Rule of their life, and an aim and end of all their studies; yea to let it be a *Compendium* and Content of the whole World: And not only to have it continually in the mouth, but to know how to apply and direct the true understanding of it to all times and Ages of the

15 *Fame and Confession*, 48.
16 Alister E. McGrath, *Christian Theology: An Introduction*, 5th ed. (Oxford: Wiley-Blackwell, 2011), 162.
17 Peter Harrison, "The 'Book of Nature' and Early Modern Science" in *The Book of Nature in Early Modern and Modern History*, ed. Klaas van Berkel and Arie Johan Vanderjagt (Leuven: Peeters, 2006), 1–26, at 7.

World. Also, it is not our Custom to prostitute and make so common the holy *Scriptures*; for there are innumerable Expounders of the same; some alledging and wresting it to serve their Opinion, some to scandal it, and most wickedly do liken it to a Nose of Wax, which alike should serve the *Divines, Philosophers, Physicians* and *Mathematicians*, against all the which we do openly witness and acknowledg, That from the beginning of the World there hath not been given unto Men a more worthy, a more excellent, and more wholesom Book then the holy *Bible*; Blessed is he that hath the same, yea more blessed is he who reads it diligently, but most blessed of all is he that truly understandeth the same, for he is most like to God, and doth come most near to him.[18]

Clearly, there is much of *sola scriptura* in such a statement, but that is not the complete picture. Indeed, the complete picture includes the study of nature and, in this way, the Rosicrucian ethos implies a sacramental vision of Creation—a picture of God's simultaneous immanence and transcendence—that is lacking in most Protestant theologies of the period and, in the case of pure nature, seriously compromised in at least one variety of Catholic theology.

Robert Fludd and the Rosy Cross in England

Robert Fludd (1574–1637) was an important English physician, scientist, and religious philosopher of the early seventeenth century who in his voluminous writings not only argued against the encroaching scientific materialism of his age but articulated a mystical-scientific vision of the relationship of the microcosm to the macrocosm in language that was simultaneously grounded in Christian tradition and *avant garde*. Fludd's life and work, however, are virtually unknown today but for the exception of a handful of specialist scholars and a variety of occultist authors. The latter, to some degree, account for Fludd's fall from academic grace, though his absence from the scholarly mainstream should be more accurately attributed to what has been called "the enor-

18 *Fame and Confession*, 49–50.

mous condescension of posterity."[19] Indeed, occult scholarship (and pseudo-scholarship), it could be argued, arose because of the vacuum created by the ultimately unenlightened Enlightenment ethos that pushed figures such as Fludd to the margins—even though he was an important intellectual in his day, engaged in a vigorous public discourse with the scientists Johannes Kepler, Andreas Libavius, Pierre Gassendi, and Marin Mersenne among others. Post-Enlightenment culture tends to prefer that its science and theology be cordoned off from one another, and any discourse (such as Fludd's) disregarding this unwritten rule immediately becomes suspect and eventually dies of neglect. Indeed, prescientific-revolution thinkers like Fludd have been typically ignored over at least the last two centuries as quaint oddities at best if not condemned as "abnormally eccentric"[20] by the intellectual and cultural gatekeepers of the academy, a dismissive attitude that is now increasingly levied against even the simplest expressions of belief in the supernatural, such as in the possibility of miracles, for instance, or the existence of God.[21]

Fludd graduated from St. John's College Oxford and was licensed to practice medicine in May 1605, though his entrance to the Royal College of Physicians was initially blocked when he was, not without cause, suspected of being a Paraclesian. He did, however, subsequently gain admittance in February 1606 and, after some opposition, became a Fellow in 1609.[22] His medical practice was marked by his interest in iatrochemistry (a chemical/alchemical approach to medicaments) and by his use of astrology in treat-

---

19 E. P. Thompson, *The Making of the English Working Class* (1963; reprt. Harmondsworth: Penguin, 1986), 12.

20 Wayne Shumaker, *The Occult Sciences in the Renaissance: A Study in Intellectual Patterns* (Berkeley: University of California Press, 1972), 239.

21 A relatively recent study treating Fludd as an esoteric loser in the face of *scientia triumphans* is Noel L. Brann's *Trithemius and Magical Theology: A Chapter in the Controversy over Occult Studies in Early Modern Europe*, SUNY Series in Western Esoteric Traditions (Albany, NY: State University of New York Press, 1999). See especially 214–27.

22 Ian Maclean, "Fludd, Robert (bap. 1574, d. 1637)," *Oxford Dictionary of National Biography* (Oxford University Press, 2004), online edn., Jan 2008 [http://www.oxforddnb.com/view/aticle/9776/accessed 11 February 2014].

ing his patients, the former provoking much more suspicion than the latter at the time. He seems to have been particularly effective and successful as a healer and successful enough to have employed both an apothecary and an amanuensis.[23]

Fludd's name first became associated with Rosicrucianism when he published a defense of the invisible brotherhood in 1616. In *Apologia Compendaria, Fraternitatem de Rosea Cruce* Fludd takes issue with the German physician and chemist Andreas Libavius's criticisms that in the manifestos the Rosicrucians (whoever they were) made exceedingly presumptuous and wild claims for their own religious authority and posterity, which caused him to suspect the Rosicrucians of sedition and radicalism. Fludd, on the other hand upheld their integrity pointing to evidence in the *Confessio* that "they embrace Christ purely and sincerely and they encourage a Christian life."[24] He then contextualized Libavius's wrangling within the spirit of religious dissension and suspicion that was then tearing Europe apart, effectively accusing him of being uncharitable.[25] Libavius, to be sure, certainly wrote within a cultural environment—religious as well as political—marked by anxiety and uncertainty. Times much like our own.

Fludd followed up the *Apologia Compendaria* with a much more expansive work, *Tractatus Apologeticus Integritatem Societatis de Rosea Cruce defendens* (1617), which includes the *Apologia* as a proem. In the longer work, Fludd begins to explore the theological and scientific as well as the mystical and metaphysical implications of the manifestos. Foremost among these is the notion that the universe is an integral whole, exemplified in the traditional teaching of the Two Books. For Fludd, "we discover the visible books to be two-fold. For in one God mystically writes in the creation of things, and he sculpts true forms and qualities of whatever creature

---

23 J.B. Craven, *Dr. Robert Fludd (Robertus de Fluctibus), The English Rosicrucian: Life and Writings* (Kirkwall, UK: William Peace & Son, 1902), 29.

24 "Alibi etiam in confessione invenimus, quòd Christum pure & sincere amplectantur, vitamque Christianam agant." Robert Fludd, *Apologia Compendaria, Fraternitatem de Rosea Cruce,* 8.

25 Robert Fludd, *Apologia Compendaria,* 10–11.

he pleases; and with these letters and mysterious characters he completed this scripture by his Word and by his most holy Spirit."[26] Scripture and Nature, for Fludd, are one, though revealing different facets of the one eternal Truth. God, that is, inscribes his word in nature just as he inscribed it on the stone tablets— stone tablets that are for Fludd the signature of God's working in the world, not only at the metaphysical, spiritual, and moral levels, but also at the chemical and biological levels. The Johannine sense of the Word is paramount here: "For by the most holy word (FIAT) it will have wondrous interior and exterior effects and have power in all stars, animals, plants, and minerals continuously to the last violence (PEREAT)."[27] Fludd's language here clearly stands in resonance with the proclamation of Psalms: "The heavens declare the glory of God and the vault of heaven proclaims his handiwork" (19:1).

Dei Gloria Intacta: *Sophia* (*Wisdom*) in *Fludd's Published Work*

Even the most casual reader of Fludd cannot help but notice how often the philosopher quotes scripture. Interestingly, he quotes liberally from the biblical Wisdom literature, particularly the books of Wisdom and Sirach (Ecclesiasticus), neither of which is (or was) part of the Protestant canon. Indeed, so often does Fludd mention Wisdom in his work that one of his critics upbraided him for always having the eternal wisdom of Christ in his mouth.[28] It is a fair and accurate critique. Most of Fludd's writings include at least one (and usually many more) instance of "sacred cento" in which he compiles snippets of disparate scrip-

---

26 "Libros etiam visibiles, duplices esse reperimus nam in uno Deus mysticè scripsit in rerum creatione, & insculpsit veras formas & proprietates cujus libet creaturae, hocque literis & characteribus arcanis, atque hanc ejus scripturam Verbo, & Spiritu suo sacrosancto complevit." Fludd, *Tractatus*, 36.

27 "nam sacrosancto verbo (FIAT) admirabiles effectus interiores & exteriores in omni stella, animali, planta, & mineralis usque ad vltimum (PEREAT) vim atque efficaciam habebit." Fludd, *Tractatus*, 40–41.

28 Robert Fludd, *Clavis*, 27. Original found in Petri Gassendi, *Theologi Epistolica Excercitatio...* (Parisiis, 1630), 11.

tural passages or allusions and arranges them in such a way that they accumulate meaning, as he does, for example, in the inaugural section of his *Sophiae cum Moria* (1629), invoking Wisdom as his Muse: "O Sempiterna Sapientia, tu candor lucis aeternae, Speculum sine macula maeiestatis Dei." ("O Eternal Wisdom! thou warmth of the eternal light, unblemished mirror of God's majesty!")[29] Such an effusion would have caused at least a little concern among English Protestants. Among its anxieties, early modern English Protestantism troubled itself over the Wisdom books so much so that one of the architects of Anglicanism, Richard Hooker, felt a need to address the proper use of them in his monumental *Lawes of Ecclesiastical Politie*. "We marvaile the lesse that our reading of books not Canonicall is so much impugned, when so little is attributed to the reading of Canonicall scripture it selfe. . . . The publique reading of the Apocrypha they condemne altogether as a thing effectual unto evill."[30] Hooker was addressing radical Puritans and their concerns with the so-called Apocrypha, which were nevertheless included in both the Geneva Bible and the Authorized Version (the KJV) in the way of appendices. However, Article VI of *Thirty-Nine Articles of Religion* (1562) justifies the inclusion of the books, if not their canonicity: "And the other books (as Hierome saith) the Church doth read for example of life and instruction, but yet doth it not apply them to establish any doctrine."[31] Puritan anxieties with the books, however, continued from the late sixteenth century, through the Revolution, into the Restoration and beyond. Known primarily to us as a poet, John Donne, Dean of St. Paul's (the King's parish), though he was careful never to take his main text from the Apocrypha, was not loathe to quote from them in his sermons,

29 Robert Fludd, *Sophiae cum Moria Certamen...* (Frankfurt, 1629), 4. He glosses "O Sempiterna Sapientia" "*Sap* 7" (Wisdom 7) and the following lines "1 *Ioan* 5" (1 John 5).

30 Richard Hooker, *Of the Lawes of Ecclesiastical Politie. Eyght Bookes.* (London, [1593]), 5.21 (37)

31 Alister E. McGrath, *In the Beginning: The Story of the King James Bible and How It Changed a Nation, a Language, and a Culture* (New York: Doubleday, 2001), 225.

and seems to have been especially fond of Sirach.[32] Yet these anxieties do not seem to have affected Fludd, who some think was more of Puritan than High Churchman on the Anglican continuum.[33] Fludd does not appear to consider the excluded books, at least Wisdom and Sirach, as extra-canonical.

Fludd reads scripture to be in an intimate, synergistic relationship with the natural world, first of all, by asserting (as he does habitually, almost obsessively, throughout his written work), that "God . . . in and by his Eternal Word or Divine Wisdom, hath first made creatures, and sustained the same unto this present."[34] He finds ontological justification for his opinion in scripture itself, and he argues his case in an extended sacred cento taken from a variety of scriptures:

> God operateth all in all. He vivifieth all things. He filleth all things. His incorruptible Spirit is in all things. By the Word all things were made. In the Word was life, and that life was the light of men. He giveth life, and inspiration, and all things. In him we live, move, and have our beeing. He is the Father of all, who is above all, and through all, and in all of us. From him, by him, and in him, are all things. He sent his Spirit and created all things. He giveth breath unto the people, and spirit unto the creatures that tread on the earth. O Lord, how manifold are thy works; in Wisdom thou hast made them all: the earth is full of thy riches, &c. If thou hidest thy face, the creatures are troubled, if thou takest away their breath they die, if thou sendest forth thy Spirit they are re-created or revivied. By him were all things created, which are in heaven, and which are in earth, things visible and invisible; whether they be Thrones, or Dominations, or Principalities, or Powers; all things were created by him, and for him, and he is before all things, and in him all things consist. *Note here, how the Apostle doth lively set forth in these words, the foresaid three worlds.*

32 Evelyn M. Simpson, Introduction, *The Sermons of John Donne*, vol. 6, ed. Evelyn M. Simpson and George R. Potter (Berkeley, CA: University of California Press, 1953), 17.

33 William H. Huffman, *Robert Fludd and the End of the Renaissance* (London: Routledge, 1988), 28.

34 Robert Fludd, *Mosaicall Philosophy, Grounded upon the Essentiall Truth or Eternall Sapience* (London, 1659), [i]. Note: Fludd's foreword in *Mosaicall Philosophy* is not paginated, though the main text is.

Again, Christ is all and in all things. He sustaineth all things by the word of his Virtue. In him, are all the treasures of Wisdom hid. God by his Wisdom giveth or proportioneth a weight unto the aire, and hangeth the waters or clouds in measure, and maketh a decree for the rain, and ordereth a way for the lightnings of the Thunders. He speaketh in Thunder, and answereth *Job* out of a Whirl-wind. He by his Word giveth Snow like wool, and scattereth the hoary Frost like ashes; he casteth forth his Ice like morsels: who can resist his cold? He sendeth out his Word and melteth them; so soon as he sendeth forth his breath, the waters do flow again. By his breath the Frost is engendered, and the breadth of the waters is made narrow.[35]

Then he concludes this superabundance of scriptural proof with an instance of understated hyperbole:

I could produce an infinity of other places out of Scriptures, to manifest the universall acts and virtuous operations which are effected in the Elementary creatures, by that most essentiall and eternall Wisdom, which is the main ground and true Cornerstone, whereon the purest Mosaicall Philosophy doth rely.[36]

Fludd cannot conceive of a "pure nature," that God could ever be completely absent from chemical or biological, cosmological, or historical processes. This is why he so vehemently engaged theologian-scientists Marin Mersenne and Pierre Gassendi (as well as Johannes Kepler) in such volatile polemics. The attacks of Mersenne and Gassendi (one a Minim friar, the other a Jesuit) in no small part clearly, for Fludd, justified his contempt for Scholasticism (and which he extended to Catholicism as a whole) which he regarded as poisoned by the "Ethnick philosophy" of Aristotle, rendering it, he thought, antithetical to Christianity and Christian culture. It is they, Fludd argues, and not he, who were introducing paganism into Christian philosophy, an unforgivable offense;

35 Robert Fludd, *Mosaicall Philosophy*, [iii–iv]. Fludd's sources are 1 Cor 12:11; 1 Tim 6:13; Eph 4:10; Wis 12:1; John 1; Acts 17:25; Eph 4:6; Rom 11:36; Judith 16:17; Isaiah 42:5; Psalm 104:25; Col 1:16; Col 3:11; Heb 1:3; Col 2:3; Job 28:25; Psalm 17:18; Job 38:1; Psalm 147:4; Job 37:10.

36 Robert Fludd, *Mosaicall Philosophy*, [iv].

indeed, to him, their enterprise was tantamount to heresy.[37] He did not hold back in his condemnation:

> This doctrine of theirs hath so infected our Christian Philosophers, which are of their sect, that they distinguish of Gods Beeing, saying, That he is present *vertualiter*, and not *substantialiter*, or *essentialiter*. As who would say, that Gods vertue can be without his essence, or divided from his divinity, which is indivisible; and so they dream of some accidents to be in God, which are distinguished from his essence.[38]

Is it possible for God to be "virtually present"? What does such a term even mean? Fludd, in essence, accuses his Neo-Scholastic contemporaries of heresy if not outright atheism. Moreover, he was right. Fludd betrays a sacramental sensibility sadly lacking, ironically, in his Catholic interlocutors. Fludd, it has been argued, "transgressed the Baconian injunction against the mixing of philosophy and divinity."[39] He might have replied that his opponents were transgressing an even more significant injunction, a move that could be interpreted as occasioning "a second Fall of man." Fludd's thought cannot be understood without considering the holistic, synergistic dynamism he sees at play in divine and cosmic world processes, a dynamism in which God and his Wisdom play the most important role.

"I was with him forming all things": Sophia's Role according to Fludd

In Fludd's system, Wisdom occupies a multifaceted role in both the creation of the world and as presence/principle in Creation. First of all, Wisdom is that agent by which God creates the world. In a section criticizing the Ethnick Philosophers, for example, Fludd recommends they adopt an appropriately Christian methodology,

---

37 Robert Fludd, *Sophiae cum Moria*, 30–35.
38 Robert Fludd, *Mosaicall Philosophy*, 29.
39 Peter Harrison, "The Book of Nature," 17.

the which, if by a riper contemplation they had understood they would have confessed, being instructed and directed by reasons produced from the eternall unity, or essentiall point and beginning of all things, that the divine light, or sacred emanation (which Scriptures entitle by the name of the holy Spirit of wisdom) was the actuall beginning of all things, as neverthelesse before it, there was another property in one and the same sacred essence, which was termed the divine puissance, or *potentia divina*, which did precede this act or emanation, no otherwise than the Father in time, order, and being, is justly said to exist before the Son, or the Creator before the creature: And thereupon the wise man hath it, *Omnium prior creata est sapientia, Wisdom was created before all things.*[40]

Elsewhere he is not so charitable, haranguing those who would divide knowledge of the Creator from knowledge of the Creation: "How stupid, therefore, is that distinction of the Christian philosophers who wish to distinguish and to separate God from his power and virtue."[41]

Contemplation, according to Fludd, not method, opens the truth to Christian philosophers. Furthermore, in God's creative act, the divine processionism, his Wisdom penetrates the darkness of the abyss and gives form to chaos.[42] Fludd is anything but obtuse or esoteric here. His words, indeed, essentially amount to a meditation on Proverbs 8:

> The Lord possessed me in the beginning of his ways, before he made any thing from the beginning.
>
> I was set up from eternity, and of old before the earth was made.
>
> The depths were not as yet, and I was already conceived. neither had the fountains of waters as yet sprung out:
>
> The mountains with their huge bulk had not as yet been established: before the hills I was brought forth:

40 Robert Fludd, *Mosaicall Philosophy*, 41. Citing Sirach 1:4.

41 "Quam stulta ergo est illa Philosophorum Christianorum distinctio, qua DEVM a sua potentia & virtute distuingere & separare voluerunt." Robert Fludd, *Philosophia sacra et vere Christiana seu meterologia cosmica* (Francofurti, 1626), 54.

42 "ubi radii sapientiae directe descendentes, atque in chaos penetrantes, simul atque radii sursum reflectendo ob repercussionem more vibratali ascendentes explicantur." Robert Fludd, *Philosophia sacra*, 158.

He had not yet made the earth, nor the rivers, nor the poles of the world.

When he prepared the heavens, I was present: when with a certain law and compass he enclosed the depths:

When he established the sky above, and poised the fountains of waters:

When he compassed the sea with its bounds, and set a law to the waters that they should not pass their limits: when be balanced the foundations of the earth;

I was with him forming all things: and was delighted every day, playing before him at all times;

Playing in the world: and my delights were to be with the children of men. (Proverb 8: 22–31)

God's Wisdom in Fludd, as in Proverbs, is imbued with agency and power. It is through Wisdom that grace maintains its presence in the world, and it is through Wisdom that each creature realizes its being.

In *Mosaicall Philosophy,* a statement of his ideas he deemed so important that it was issued in both Latin and English editions, Fludd, mindful of the repercussions of pure nature theology and materialistic philosophies, articulates his position in the clearest terms:

But because some of the learned of this world may reply, that though this is true, that God by his divine Spirit or Word, did create all things; yet it followeth not, that he doth act immediately, and exist essentially in every thing. But after that this eternall Spirit of wisdom, had bestowed on each creature a peculiar vertue in its creation, then the creature can act of it self by a free-will, which is absolutely; and distinguished, and divided from the immediate act of God. I answer, that by our founded rules in Divinity, the true essence of the Deitie is individual, and therefore God doth impart no essentiall act or vertue unto any creature which can be discontinued or seperated from Himself.[43]

In asserting that "the true essence of the Deitie is individual" and that the individuality of the creature issues from that of the Cre-

---

43 Robert Fludd, *Mosaicall Philosophy*, 15.

ator, might it not be too farfetched to call Fludd an early modern proponent of a holistic, Christian personalism contra Descartes' more materialistic, egocentric personalism? As always, Fludd turns to scripture to uphold his claim, here citing (amongst a slew of other passages) St. Paul's assurance of God's continuing presence in Creation, "For of him, and by him, and in him, are all things" (Rom 11:36), a notion standing in stark contradistinction to Descartes' "Cogito, ergo sum." In one place, Fludd equates Wisdom with "spiritus ille Dei Catholicus omnia implens," "that Catholic spirit of God filling all";[44] and in another he connects Sophia to the quintessence of the alchemists, *A certain infinite power in things, which penetrateth and passeth through all things, ingendering every thing, and augmenting and nourishing them, and procreating like things of their like.*[45] He punctuates this idea with what follows:

> And verily, if you will be pleased to consider really what I have spoken before, you will remember how I told you, that the angelicall vertue proceeded from the archetypicall emanations, and are the types of the divine Idea. Again, that the aetheriall spirit was filled with the angelicall influences, which had their essentiall root from God. So that in verity, it is not the starry light which penetrateth so deeply, or operateth so universally, but that eternall centrall spirit, with which his divine and unresistable essence, penetrateth all things, both in heaven above, and in the earth and waters beneath.[46]

The "eternall centrall spirit" here is synonymous with Sophia since elsewhere he writes that "Sophia is the soul of the angels, the central spirit."[47] In Fludd's writing, then, as well as serving as an agent, Wisdom is that quality of divinity which God imparts to creation, the "eternall Sapience, which is the radicall

---

44 Robert Fludd, *Sophiae cum Moria*, 4.

45 Robert Fludd, *Mosaicall Philosophy*, 221. Quoting the alchemical tract *Scripta de Arte Chimia* (Francofurti, 1603).

46 Robert Fludd, *Mosaicall Philosophy*, 221.

47 "sapientia est angelorum dictorum anima, seu vita centralis." Robert Fludd, *Philosophia Sacra*, 200.

beginning, or unity of all things."[48] It is that by which God works in the world.

It would be easy, of course, to interpret Fludd's sophiology in terms of panentheism if not pantheism. But, as it is in panentheism, creation is not a part of God's essence in Fludd's thought; rather, God's presence is part of Creation. Fludd is no advocate of "creation spirituality" *avant la lettre,* and he readily acknowledges the existence of evil in the fallen world. Gassendi, in fact, ridiculed Fludd as being something of a Pollyanna when it comes to the created world, saying that "Robert sells you Sophia, while he ignores death."[49] Fludd, a physician, was certainly aware of the reality of death, and he was also aware of the presence of evil and death in Creation as a consequence of the Fall (Gen 3; Rom 6:23). His discussions of storms and illness in his works on medicine and meteorology attest to this.[50] Fludd's position, however, is that despite the fallenness of Creation, God's presence persists. And he has an arsenal of scriptures to back up his claim.

Often, and as we have already seen, Fludd describes Wisdom's participation in creation in terms of "light," and, more exactly, as a property of the "uncreated light" of Genesis 1. This is a concept both Henry and Thomas Vaughan would later adopt in their writings, for instance, as Henry does in the opening lines to "Cock-crowing":

> Father of lights![51] what Sunnie seed,
> What glance of day hast Thou confin'd
> Into this bird? To all the breed
> This busie Ray thou hast assign'd;
>   Their magetism works all night,
>   And dreams of paradise and light. (lines 1–6)

For Fludd, first of all, the uncreated light, the light of the first

48 Robert Fludd, *Mosaicall Philosophy*, 48.
49 "Robertus Sophiam tibi vendicat, cum Moriam tibi relinquat." Quoted in Robert Fludd, *Clavis Philosophiae et Alchymiae Fluddanae...* (Francofurti, 1633), 27. Original found in Petri Gassendi, *Theologi Epistolica Excercitatio...* (Parisiis, 1630), 10.
50 See, in particular, *Philosophia sacra.*
51 Note the allusion to James 1:17.

day, clothes Creation with the spirit, teaches the angels, and simply forms the name of God in the soul. As divine act, it is the source of both spiritual substance and spiritual illumination.[52] The uncreated light, then, is identical with Sophia, since "Wisdom was the first created" (Sirach 1:4).[53] This light is furthermore the "*immediatus voluntatis divinae,* seu *Dei patentis,*" "the absolute of the divine will, or an opening of God."[54] In *Philosophia Sacra* Fludd describes this phenomenon as that which provides, "DEI patentis soboles," "shoots of God's access."[55] But most importantly, this uncreated light is the source of life in the human person.[56]

This notion of the uncreated light, or the light of the first day, in Fludd has more than a little in common with twentieth-century Catholic theologian Hans Urs von Balthasar's contemplations on the idea of "splendor." Fludd sees the sun as emblematic, a very real *signatura,* of this splendor (which both he and von Balthasar term "glory"). Interestingly, Fludd takes as his scriptural basis for this insight St. Jerome's *mistranslation* of Psalm 18:6. Jerome's translation reads "*in sole posuit tabernaculum suum,*" "He has placed his tabernacle in the sun." A more accurate translation, however, reads "In the heavens, he has set a tent for the sun." Poorly translated or not, this is one of Fludd's favorite passages from scripture, and he cites it habitually.[57] Indeed, even though

---

52 "Hinc dicet Ecclisiasticus; *Sapientia est prima creatura. Eccl.* 1. & quod lux sit primo die create, & sic in uno, respect videlicet, vestimenti mundi spiritualis quod induit; dicitur angelus, respect animae simpliciter formalis seu nominis DEI magni in Angelo inscripit est Iehova, seu immediate DEI seu fontls lucis emanation in mundum, per quan eius spiritus in sola potential existens erat informatus." Robert Fludd, *Philosophia Sacra,* 54.

53 Cited by Fludd as "*Sapientia est prima creatura.*" *Philosophia Sacra,* 54.

54 Robert Fludd, *Integrum Morborum Mysterium, sive Medicinae Catholicae, Tomi Primi...*(Francofurti, 1633), 12.

55 Robert Fludd, *Philosophia Sacra,* 7.

56 "Inveniums igitur, debitam in sacris Scripturis inquisition facta, spiratorum, ex Deiforme illud spiraculum vitae procedebat, meram & purissimam esse lucem increatam." Robert Fludd, *Tractatus Theologo-Philosophicus...* (Oppenheim, [1617]), 23.

57 For example, in *Philosophia Sacra,* 55 and 190; *Tractatus Theologo-Philosophicus,* 18.

he knows that Jerome's translation was a cause for concern, Fludd holds to the passage, arguing "we must rather impute the errour unto the corruption or alteration of the Hebrew Text, being that the whole harmony of the Scriptures, and main subject of the Psalm in which it is recited, do tend and incline rather unto the construction of St. *Jerom*."[58] For Fludd, the more literal translation may have a claim for possessing more Hebrew in it, but Jerome's has more truth.

The sun-tabernacle, for Fludd, proves a signature for the way the created light of the fourth day (the sun) stands in harmony with uncreated light of the first. The light of the sun, according to Fludd, "doth participate with divinity."[59] Commenting on Psalm 19:1's assertion that "The heavens declare the glory of God and the firmament the works of his hands," Fludd explains that where the Psalmist "expresseth that the glory of the Creator which is in the creature doth reveal the Creator in the creature; but where the glory is present, the essence is not absent."[60] Fludd illustrates how this glory, or splendor, is a quality Adam possessed prior to the Fall, when our first ancestor's body was in a state of innocence characterized by great clarity and radiance. Fludd also points to the manner in which Moses's face shone after his encounter with Yahweh in the Burning Bush.[61] This quality remains in Creation still, in what Fludd describes as "This Spirit of a God-like Nature, this soul or body of the most chaste, the most beautiful of women, is a receptacle of brilliance, of divine wisdom, and the tabernacle of God's strength."[62] The disclosure of this splendor, for Fludd, depends on a sophianic movement. The Holy Spirit of wisdom, he writes, "must form that created spirit clothed in ineffable splendor, for therefore Wisdom seems to act with these

58 Robert Fludd, *Mosaicall Philosophy*, 61.
59 Ibid., 62.
60 Ibid.
61 Robert Fludd, *Tractatus Theologo-Philosophicus*, 29–31.
62 "Hic, inquam, Spiritus Naturae Deiformis, haec Psyches vel Physis, omnium foeminarum castissima & pulcherrima, est receptaculum fulgoris, divinae sapientiae & Jehovae virtutis tabernaculum." Robert Fludd, *Tractatus Theologo-Philosophicus*, 51.

words themselves."[63] And, lest any of his readers assume Fludd to be flirting with heresy here, he supports his thesis with scripture: "For [Wisdom] is more beautiful than the sun, and excels every constellation of the stars. Compared with the light she is found to be superior" (Wisdom 7:29).[64]

Fludd's idea of splendor possesses a haunting affinity with von Balthasar's use of the same term and which the latter employs as a key figure in his theological aesthetics. Though he does not quite associate it with Sophia, von Balthasar nevertheless recognizes a quality illuminating nature, works of art, scripture, or liturgy that awakens in the beholder a feeling of wonder or recognition of the numinous.[65] In these extraordinary moments, writes Balthasar,

> We are confronted simultaneously with both the figure and that which shines forth from the figure, making it into a worthy, a love-worthy thing. Similarly we are confronted with both the gathering

63 "quoniam spiritus ille sapientiae sanctus Spiritum istum creatum informans est splendore ineffabili indutus, quod etiam Sapiens hisce verbis asseuerare videtur." Robert Fludd, *Sophiae cum Moria Certamen*, 18.

64 Fludd's example is a little different from the Vulgate's Latin. Here is Fludd: "Sapientia est splendor lucis aeternae, sole speciosior, & supra omnem dispositionem stellarum luci comparaitor." Here the Vulgate: "est enim haec speciosior sole et super omnem stellarum dispositionem luci conparata invenitur prior." Fludd adds "Sapientia est splendor lucis aeternae"—Wisdom is the splendor of the eternal light. Interesting.

65 Though not his primary concern, Fludd is in agreement with von Balthasar in relation to Wisdom (read as splendor) and its presence in the liberal, healing, and mystical arts. He writes, "this eternall wisdom is the foundation or corner-stone, first, of the higher Arts, namely, of *Theology, Physick*, or the art of Curing, *Astronomy, Musick, Arithmetic, Geometry, Rhetorick*; and after that, how the *Meteoro-logicall* Science onely dependeth on his act; then how true *Morall* learning, and *Politick* government is derived from the instructions and directions of this onely wise Spirit. And lastly, how all *mysticall* and *miraculous Arts* and discoveries, are effected and brought to light by it, confirming that place in Scripture, where it is said, *Caeterae sunt ancillae hujus, All sciences are but the handmaids unto his wisdom.*" *Mosaicall Philosophy*, 17. It does not appear that Fludd's reference to scripture is a direct quote, but a tradition with roots in the classical period of reading the relationship of Sarah to Hagar in Genesis allegorically. See Malcom de Mowbray, "Philosophy as Handmaid of Theology: Biblical Exegesis in the Service of Scholarship," *Traditio* 59 (2004): 1–37, at 4–9 and 32–34.

and uniting of that which had been indifferently scattered—its gathering into the service of one thing which now manifests and expresses itself—*and* the outpouring, self-utterance of the one who was able to fashion by himself such a body of expression: by *himself*, I say, meaning "on his own initiative," and therefore with pre-eminence, freedom, sovereignty, out of his own interior space, particularity, and essence . . . we are brought face to face with both interiority and its communication, the soul and its body, free discourse governed by laws and clarity of language.[66]

Furthermore, the phenomenon von Balthasar considers here functions as an opening which facilitates transcendence's coming-into-immanence, which makes possible the possibility that "causes worldly beauty gradually to become metaphysical, mythical and revelatory splendor,"[67] or what John Milbank has described as the mystery by which the invisible appears through the visible.[68] Another way to describe this phenomenon (it is something to be witnessed, after all, not invented) is as Fludd's "shoots of God's access." For von Balthasar, this splendor is "the primal phenomenon"[69] and one which he associates with Aquinas's description of Being as "a 'sure light' for that which exists."[70]

For von Balthasar, as for Fludd, the recognition of splendor is not a problem of analysis but one of perception. "But what are we to say," asks von Balthasar, "of the person that ignores this form and tramples it underfoot, then to enter into relationships answerable only to his own psychology's principle of 'this far and no further'?"[71] Most post-Cartesian modes of inquiry have

66 Hans Urs von Balthasar, *The Glory of the Lord: A Theological Aesthetics. Volume I: Seeing the Form*, ed. Joseph Fessio SJ and John Riches, trans. Erasmo Leiva-Merikakis (San Francisco: Ignatius Press, 1982), 20. Emphasis in source.

67 Hans Urs von Balthasar, *The Glory of the Lord: A Theological Aesthetics. Volume V: The Realm of Metaphysics in the Modern Age*, ed. John Riches, trans. Oliver Davies et al. (San Francisco: Ignatius Press, 1991), 598.

68 John Milbank, "Beauty and the Soul" in *Theological Perspectives on God and Beauty*, eds. John Milbank, Graham Ward, and Edith Wyschogrod (Harrisburg, PA: Trinity Press International, 2003), 1–34, at 6.

69 Hans Urs von Balthasar, *The Glory of the Lord*, I, 20.

70 Ibid., 19.

71 Ibid., 27.

allowed the human capacity to perceive splendor to degrade and atrophy, a development that in its infancy Fludd opposed. Furthermore, von Balthasar, like his friend and teacher Henri de Lubac, dedicated himself toward resetting the pure nature debate and restoring a proper understanding of the supernatural to contemporary ways of knowing:

> The supernatural is not there in order to supply that part of our natural capacities we have failed to develop. *Gratia perficit naturam, non supplet.*[72] The same Christian centuries which masterfully knew how to read the natural world's language of forms were the same ones which possessed eyes trained, first, to perceive the formal quality of revelation by the aid of grace and its illumination and, second (and only then!), to interpret revelation.[73]

The problem, for von Balthasar, is one of perception, of *reading* the world, of reading phenomena. Additionally, we might say that what Fludd fought and what von Balthasar describes here is a kind of cultural malaise in perception, an acedia or indifference in one's engagement with creatures.

In *Summa contra Gentiles*, St. Thomas describes a phenomenon which fascinated both von Balthasar and Fludd:

> In things composed of matter and form, the form is said to be the principle of being, for the reason that it is the complement of substance, whose act being is: even as transparency is to the air the principle of being lightsome, in that it makes the air the proper subject of light.
>
> Wherefore in things composed of matter and form, neither matter nor form, nor even being itself, can be described as that which is. Yet the form can be described as that *whereby it is*, forasmuch as it is the principle of being: but the whole substance is *what is*: and being is that whereby the substance is called *a being.*[74]

Even here, the Angelic Doctor cannot resist the metaphor of light to best explain being. We can consider Fludd, then, not so much an anti-Scholastic as an anti-*Neo*-Scholastic in much the way of

---

72 A paraphrase of *Summa Theologiae*, I, I, 8 *ad* 2.

73 Hans Urs von Balthasar, *The Glory of the Lord*, I, 29.

74 Saint Thomas Aquinas, *Summa contra Gentiles*, trans. by the English Dominican Fathers (London: Burns Oates & Washbourne, Ltd., 1923), 2.54.

his countryman and contemporary Thomas Vaughan who once complained that "*the* School-men *have got the* Day, *not by* Weight *but by* Number."[75] Von Balthasar's invocation of Aquinas, however, contains more than a little of Heidegger, whose meditations on Being recalibrated both philosophy and theology in the twentieth century and after.[76] This is no surprise, since Heidegger, like Aquinas seven hundred years before him, begins with a grounding in theology and finds his philosophical voice by turning to Aristotle.[77] At its core, these thinkers agree, the phenomenon of revelation is a revelation of Being.

It is easy to see how this discussion of splendor could lead to a consideration of the glorified body of the resurrection, which St. Bonaventure describes as characterized by radiance (*claritas*).[78] Fludd, indeed, considers the glorified body in *Tractatus Theologo-Philosophicus,*[79] and it could certainly argued that Fludd's project, both as a natural philosopher and as a physician, was occupied with achieving as close an approximation as possible (this side of the *Parousia*) to realizing this ideal, much as scientists preoccu-

75 From Vaughan's Preface to *The Fame and Confession of the Fraternity of R:C:, Commonly, of the Rosie Cross* (1652) in *The Works of Thomas Vaughan*, ed. Alan Rudrum with the assistance of Jennifer Drake-Brockman (1984; reprt., Oxford: The Clarendon Press, 2010), 483.

76 Oliver Davies argues that Heidegger is second only to St. Thomas as an influence on von Balthasar's thinking—but a distant second. See his "Von Balthasar and the Problem of Being," *New Blackfriars* 79, no. 923 (Jan 1998): 11–17, at 11. On Heidegger's importance to postmodern religious thought see the chapter entitled "Martin Heidegger and Onto-theo-logy" in Christina M. Gschwandtner's *Postmodern Apologetics?: Arguments for God in Contemporary Philosophy*, Perspectives in Continental Philosophy (New York: Fordham University Press, 2013).

77 "In some regards, one could rightfully claim that it was [Heidegger's] reading of Aristotle that made it possible for him to redefine for himself the task of phenomenology." Walter A. Brogan, *Heidegger and Aristotle: The Twofoldness of Being* (Albany, NY: SUNY Press, 2005), 1.

78 St. Bonaventure, *Commentaria in quatuor libros sententiarum magistri, in Petri Lombardi* 4, d.44, q.2, a.4, sol. 1. See Ann W. Astell's discussion of Bonaventure's teaching on the radiance of the resurrection body in her *Eating Beauty: The Eucharist and the Spiritual Arts of the Middle Ages* (Ithaca, NY: Cornell University Press, 2006), 123–25.

79 Robert Fludd, *Tractatus Theologo-Philosophicus*, 89–126.

pied with palingenesis were.[80] Such a notion underlies Fludd's philosophy and how he envisions Wisdom's role in Creation. This idea also informs Fludd's fascinating considerations of wheat in *Anatomiae Amphitheatrum* (1633) wherein he argues that wheat is the vegetable equivalent of Sophia while mindful that the "true bread" ("verus panis") is Jesus.[81] Elsewhere in the same text, Fludd expresses awe before "the great mystery of the Blood of Christ" ("De magno sanguinis Christi mysterio").[82] The Eucharistic implications of his thought are clear and are of a piece with his sophiology. Indeed, his sophiology is a thoroughly sacramental epistemology.

Who (or What) is Fludd's Sophia?

God's Wisdom in Proverbs is a *person*. But is she, as many allege, a *personification*? Fludd certainly has an opinion on the subject, but his position is not as straightforward as it may appear from his published work. Indeed, Sophia's identity in Fludd raises more questions than it answers.

Fludd connects Wisdom to many biblical and extra-biblical figures in his published work. For example, in *Philosophia Sacra*, he associates the uncreated light with "ipse *Iehova seu Sapientia*," Jehovah himself, or Wisdom.[83] In the same text, however, Fludd describes Wisdom as synonymous with the kabbalists' angel Metatron as well as with the *Anima Mundi*, or Soul of the World, a notion extant from at least the time of Plato.[84] In *Clavis Philosophiae et Alchymiae Fluddanae* (1633), he connects Wisdom to "that great angelic spirit which preceded the Israelites in the

80 Palingenesis was the supposed possibility of resurrecting a plant or animal from its ashes. For some insight into the scientific and religious significance of the practice, see the chapter entitled "Love's Alchemist: Palingenesis and the Unconscious Metalepsis of Sir Kenelm Digby" in my book *Literature and the Encounter with God in Post-Reformation England* (Aldershot, UK: Ashgate Publishing, 2014).

81 Robert Fludd, *Anatomiae Amphitheatrum*, 15 and 21.

82 Ibid., 250.

83 Robert Fludd, *Philosophia Sacra*, 156.

84 Ibid., 67, 211, 255.

desert,"[85] pointing to Sirach 3 (a blunder for 24:7) and Wisdom 10:17 as proofs for his assertion.[86] And so it is with all of Fludd's published works. But more than any other figure in his published works, Christ is the one Fludd most identifies with Wisdom.

Identifying Christ with Wisdom, of course, is not an innovation of Fludd's, but a tradition going back to the time of the Fathers and their reading of 1 Corinthians 1:24, "But unto them that are called, both Jews and Greeks, Christ the power of God, and the wisdom of God." It is along these lines that in *De Trinitate* St. Augustine writes of Wisdom as found in scripture:

> Why, then, is scarcely anything ever said in the Scriptures of wisdom, unless to show that it is begotten or created of God?—begotten in the case of that Wisdom by which all things are made; but created or made, as in men, when they are converted to that Wisdom which is not created and made but begotten, and are so enlightened; for in these men themselves there comes to be something which may be called their wisdom: even as the Scriptures foretell or narrate, that "the Word was made flesh, and dwelt among us"; for in this way Christ was made wisdom, because He was made man. Is it on this account that wisdom does not speak in these books, nor is anything spoken of it, except to declare that it is born of God, or made by Him (although the Father is Himself wisdom).[87]

It seems here that Augustine has *two* wisdoms in mind: one that is created and one that is begotten. The begotten wisdom, in his description, is Christ; but he also complicates things when he says that "Christ was made man," suggesting, perhaps, that Christ is *also* created wisdom. On the other hand, even a cursory reading of Proverbs 8 and 9 and the introductory chapters of the books of

85 [Robert Fludd], *Clavis*, 18.

86 "I had my tent in the heights, and my throne was a pillar of cloud" (Sir 24:4). "To the holy people she gave the wages of their labours; she guided them by a marvellous road, herself their shelter by day—and their starlight through the night" (Wisdom 10:17).

87 Augustine, *De Trinitate*, 7.3.4 from *A Select Library of the Nicene and Post-Nicene Fathers of the Christian Church. Vol. III: St. Augustin on the Holy Trinity, Doctrinal Treatises, Moral Treatises,* ed. Philip Schaff (Buffalo, NY: The Christian Literature Co., 1887).

Wisdom and Sirach might compel some to reevaluate Augustine's suggestion that "wisdom does not speak in these books, nor is anything spoken of it, except to declare that it is born of God, or made by Him." But he emphasizes his point, "And therefore Christ is the power and wisdom of God, because He Himself, being also power and wisdom, is from the Father, who is power and wisdom." Even though Christ identifies Wisdom as feminine in Luke's Gospel, "wisdom is justified by all her children" (Luke 7:35—which could certainly trouble Patristic consensus a little), the Fathers are content to read Wisdom as synonymous with Christ, a tradition that continued well into the early modern period and persists today.[88]

For the most part in his published work, Fludd, who liked to think of himself as representative of what he considered Christian tradition, follows the model set by the Fathers. In *Mosaicall Philosophy*, he unabashedly declares Christ to be "the true Wisdome"[89] and later admonishes the Ethnick Philosophers for their neglect of "the divine wisdom Christ Jesus."[90] In *Summum Bonum*, Fludd also asserts the Christ-Sophia identity.[91] Furthermore, he writes that "the Spiritual Christ, the divine word, or eternall wisdome, is the true basis or foundation of the essentiall Philosophy, as is proved by the Apostle's testimony."[92] Throughout his works, Fludd announces his agreement with the patristic notion that Christ and Wisdom are one as a way to avouch for his own religious orthodoxy. But perhaps things are not as straightforward as they first appear. Elsewhere in *Mosaicall Philosophy*, however, Fludd claims that "this divine Word, is the root and fountain of this eternal Spirit of Wisdome."[93] The notion of "root or fountain" suggests—does it not?—that the Word may in

88 A classic text on the subject, though not without its faults, is Eugene F. Rice, Jr., *The Renaissance Idea of Wisdom* (Cambridge: Harvard University Press, 1958).

89 Robert Fludd, *Mosaicall Philosophy*, 28.

90 Ibid., 40.

91 Ioachim Frizium [pseudonym for Robert Fludd], *Summum Bonum...* (1629), 18 (mistakenly numbered "59").

92 Robert Fludd, *Mosaicall Philosophy*, 242.

93 Ibid., 20.

fact be *that from which Wisdom arises* while not maintaining una-
nimity with it. Jesus, for instance, may be the "seed of David" or
spring forth from "the root of Jesse," but he is not identical to
them. And, while Fludd's primary understanding of Wisdom as
an aspect of Christ is secure in his published work, he is not
entirely consistent about it.

In fact, upon occasion, Fludd, like Boehme, suggests that Wisdom is *feminine.* In the *Tractatus Theologo-Philosophicus,* Fludd
includes a section in which he speaks of Wisdom in feminine
terms, an anomaly in his voluminous published record:

> For this Soul is the friendly spirit of wisdom in the Word and most
> plentiful, most glorious strength of Jehovah. This is the most beau-
> tiful bride and sister of the spirit of discipline, who fills the orb of
> the earth, which is said to be an enclosed garden for the beloved
> and most wonderful bridegroom.[94]

This is one of the more astounding of Fludd's published statements concerning Wisdom. In it, he touches on the *Brautmystik*
of the medieval cloister and the Canticle of Canticles (indeed, he
quotes from the latter right after this passage). But it is not
uncharacteristic of his *unpublished* work, which discloses another
facet of Fludd's Sophia.

Sophia in Truth's Golden Harrow

A manuscript of Fludd's housed in the Bodleian Library (MS.
Ashmole 766) gives another perspective of his sophiology and
raises some important questions about the Sophia of his published work. It is written almost entirely in Fludd's hand (even
though he did employ an amanuensis), and the consonance
between the ideas present in the work and his published treatises
makes it apparent that he not only wrote down the work but is its
author as well.[95] Fludd entitles the work *Truth's Golden Harrow*

---

94 Robert Fludd, *Tractatus Theologo-Philosophicus,* 37.

95 See, in particular, C. H. Josten's introductory material to " *Truth's Golden
Harrow*: An Unpublished Alchemical Treatise of Robert Fludd in the Bodleian
Library," *Ambix* 3 (1949): 91–150, 91–101, at 91. Hereafter *Truth's Golden Har-
row.* Scot was a retainer of James I and inclined toward a strict Calvinism.

and it is, in the main, a response to Patrick Scot's *The Tillage of Light*, a work which argued that the claims of alchemy were in the main symbolic or metaphorical. Fludd viewed such an interpretation as materialistic and in denial of the spirit, neglectful of God.

First in the manuscript, Fludd describes the Elixir of the alchemists in feminine terms, pointing to those who look to "purchase but a vewe of her bright countenance, and to enjoy but the wayght of a grayne of mustard seed of her grace and perfection."[96] Fludd is not explicitly saying that the Elixir is Sophia, of course, but he is speaking of her in sophianic terms, "For such therfore and unto such was she sent downe from heaven: with them she delighteth and dwelleth."[97] The language here is an appropriation of Sophia's description of herself in Proverbs 8: "When he prepared the heavens, I was there . . . and my delights were with the sons of men" (Proverbs 8:27, 31). Subsequently, Fludd calls the Elixir "the true temple of wisdom" and further connects it to Sophia of Proverbs 9 as "the house of wisdome propped up with .7. pillers."[98] As he does in his published work, he anchors the power of Sophia in Christ, since "the forme or divine soule is the light shining out of darknes," an invocation of John 1:5.[99] But he moves from metaphor to literal forms of discourse when he writes, "Now it is certayne that this word and spirit of God is that first begotten wisdome the which dwelleth in the universall waters of this world as in the humble tabernacle of the created Nature."[100] These ideas, of course, are familiar in Fludd's work, but he does something in *Truth's Golden Harrow* that is not characteristic of his published writings. And it all comes down to a pronoun.

Fludd makes a move concerning gender in *Truth's Golden Harrow* similar to what we find in Boehme. "But this mental beame," writes Fludd,

---

96 *Truth's Golden Harrow*, 104.
97 Ibid.
98 Ibid., 108.
99 Ibid., 109.
100 Ibid., 110.

being the ofspring from immortall and divine parents gliding
downe into the dark hyle or chaos, very smal in substance, and yet
neverthelesse being all and on and every wher dispersed in the
world; turneth about by her power and vertue the vast and wide
cavity of the heavens, and preserveth them from ruin and corruption by her presence, for she is every wher present by changing and
fashioning her self into divers formes, for part of her is imployed
to give motion and lif to the stars, part instituteth the order of the
angels and againe part doth indue an elementary and earthly shape
which doth reciprocally embrase with a grievous tye or knot, in so
much that she beeing seperated from her immortall parents she
sucketh in dark oblivion, and so forgetting her self she admireth
the unpleasing earth, respects it with a blind solicitude and care,
and by that means is prone to affect corporall things, and to
incline it self unto human affairs.[101]

The operative terms here are "she" and "her." Interestingly, Fludd's
notion of Sophia as a "tye or knot" here bears more than a little
resonance with Henry Vaughan's exceedingly Marian poem, "The
Knot," which has clear sophianic overtones. The poems begins,

> Bright Queen of Heaven! Gods Virgin Spouse!
> The glad worlds blessed maid!
> Whose beauty tyed life to thy house,
> And brought us saving ayd.[102]

It may be construed that in *Truth's Golden Harrow* Fludd speaks
explicitly of the Elixir ("mental beame") as a thing unto itself, and
not necessarily of Sophia. But, for Fludd, the Elixir *is* Sophia, for
Sophia is that divine quality which inheres nature and makes
health and healing possible.[103]

A little further on in *Truth's Golden Harrow*, Fludd argues that
Sophia is a simultaneously physical and metaphysical phenome-

---

101 Ibid., 112.

102 Lines 1–4.

103 This is the thrust of Fludd's *Medicina Catholica, seu Mysticum Artis
Medicandi Sacrarium...* (Francofurti, 1629). Fludd's German counterpart,
Michael Maier (1568–1622) claimed to have discovered a universal medicine.
See Hereward Tilton. *The Quest for the Phoenix: Spiritual Alchemy and Rosicru-
cianism in the Work of Count Michael Maier (1569–1622)* (Arbeiten zur Kirch-
engeschichte, Band 88. Berlin: Walter de Gruyter, 2003), 76.

non: "though wisdome be the mark that Philosophers and Theosophists do ayme at, yet they consider her as she is in created nature as well subject to the sence as invisible, and consequently material."[104] He emphasizes Sophia as emissary of God, as divine quality, and as accessible to the sincere seeker. Above all in *Truth's Golden Harrow,* he emphasizes Sophia as a *person*:

> I will shew you heare what is the power of that hidden wisdome which inhabiteth, as is sayed, every creature more or less: and how by so much the more *she* aboundeth in any of them.[105]

> *She* maketh frends of God and prophets, for God loveth none but such as doth dwell with wisdome, for wisdome is brighter than the sonne.[106]

> Al perfection is from the spirit of wisdome, all things are sayed to be good for as much as they doe participat of *her* and in that respect each work of the creation wer by God him self affirmed to be good.[107]

And, as he reminds us, he has ample biblical precedent for speaking of Sophia in feminine terms:

> Salomon sayeth (speaking of the outward effects of wisdome) that *her* spirit howldeth in her left hand riches, but unto her right hand he attributeth longe lif and prosperity.[108]

The question is: why is Fludd's attribution of a feminine gender so explicit in *Truth's Golden Harrow* and, while not absent, subsumed into the masculine gender of Christ in the published work?

To be honest, Fludd does figure a feminine Wisdom in his published treatises—but almost exclusively (with a handful of exceptions) by way of citation of scripture where Wisdom's gender (especially in the Old Testament) is unerringly feminine. While it is true that the Patristic tradition generally agrees that the feminine gendering of Wisdom in the Old Testament is a rhetorical

---

104 *Truth's Golden Harrow,* 114.
105 Ibid., 130. My emphasis.
106 Ibid., 131. My emphasis.
107 Ibid., 137. My emphasis.
108 Ibid., 139. My emphasis. A reference to Proverbs 3:16.

move (personification), it tends to avoid the fact that gendering Wisdom as masculine can also be interpreted as metaphorical. What is so special about a feminine Wisdom? Why is a feminine Wisdom more effective a trope? The Fathers are silent on this topic, other than to say that God, when he is not masculine, not Father, is genderless.[109] But this, too, is problematic—though in ways the Fathers certainly would never have anticipated. For is not our postmodern culture's *laissez-faire* approach to gender a hideous caricature of the Fathers' occasionally referenced genderless God? As John Milbank has argued, a true "gender equality" is grounded in "the equality of Bride with Bridegroom" and "the essential significance of Biblical engendered typology" as well as "the Biblical and theological significance of sexual difference."[110] Our culture offers us a bewildering alternative to this model.

It may be argued that Fludd's published works, with only a few exceptions, appeared only in Latin, and that Latin, being a highly inflected language, does not have a need for personal pronouns which are generally implied and gender interpreted by context. Fludd, that is, may be implying Sophia's gender through the gender of *Sapientia*, which is feminine. Nevertheless, in the more explicit moments in his Latin writings (or at least most of them), as we have seen, Fludd genders Sophia as masculine and in relation to Christ. Yet, the evidence in *Truth's Golden Harrow*—a text written in English—overwhelmingly suggests that Fludd thinks of Sophia in feminine terms.

My claim is that in *Truth's Golden Harrow* Fludd lets his guard down. In his published work, he generally follows Patristic and Church tradition by gendering Wisdom ultimately as masculine

---

109 As St. Gregory of Nyssa does: "No one can adequately grasp the terms pertaining to God. For example, 'mother' is mentioned in place of 'father' (cant 3:11). Both terms mean the same because the divine is neither male nor female." *Commentary on the Song of Songs*, Homily 7.20. Quoted in Rosemary Radford Ruether, *Goddesses and the Divine Feminine: A Western Religious History* (Berkeley: University of California Press, 2005), 135.

110 John Milbank, "Sophiology and Theurgy: The New Theological Horizon," in *Encounter between Eastern Orthodoxy and Radical Orthodoxy: Transfiguring the World through the Word*, ed. Adrian Pabst and Christopher Schneider (Aldershot, UK: Ashgate Publishing, 2009), 45–85, at 83.

and associating it, in the main, with Christ. He did this, for one, to avoid controversy and because he liked to think of himself as a traditionalist (and his opponents as the innovators). It does not appear that Fludd ever intended to issue an edition of *Truth's Golden Harrow* in print. Attacking Patrick Scot, one of the King's inner circle, in the public forum of print would not have been a prudent political move (to be double-sure, he never mentions Scot by name in the manuscript). So, without the pressure of public discourse and the potential for disfavor to dissuade him, Fludd articulates his ideas with a greater degree of freedom in *Truth's Golden Harrow* than was possible in his published work. This is not to say that Fludd's association of Christ with Sophia was insincere. Rather, Fludd appears to have understood Wisdom in more nuanced terms than he thought the theologians of his religiously- and politically-volatile age were ready to encounter. His vision of Wisdom bears traces of Boehme's association of Christ with Sophia, as both uncreated and created Wisdom, and anticipates developments in sophiology that would not be more fully developed in the theology of exoteric Christianity for almost three centuries. It may be that Fludd stays away from unravelling the distinctions between *Sapientia creata* and *Sapientia increata*, but his main theological thrust is in preserving a holistic vision of the Creation as something in which and with which God continually participates by his Wisdom. That is, Fludd's attention is on the epistemological disruptions then arising in the intellectual life of Europe, the consequences of which he saw with remarkable clarity and prescience.

In both print and manuscript, Fludd refuses to divide perception of the world of nature from his perception of the world (and Word) of God. His disputes with Gassendi, Mersenne, Libavius, and others are anchored in his defense of just such a position. Fludd, in his allegiance to an essentially religious epistemology, maintains what philosopher William Desmond describes as the way "[b]eing religious reveals perhaps the most primal porosity of the human being: the nakedness of the soul before the divine."[111]

---

111 William Desmond, *The Intimate Strangeness of Being: Metaphysics after Dialectic*, Studies in Philosophy and the History of Philosophy 56 (Washington, DC: The Catholic University of America Press, 2012), 170.

Though the intellectual juggernaut of the West eventually left Fludd and his ideas behind—at least for a time—his worldview clearly requires a reconsideration as it embodies not only theological and philosophical implications, but also ways to reimagine science and our relationship to nature. For, as Bruce V. Foltz has observed, "the underlying religious sensibility of deep ecology calls for self-sacrifice and overcoming egoism and even a kind of mystical identification with the whole of nature, exhorting us to a higher calling."[112] The theological-philosophical mysticism of Robert Fludd, then, becomes for us not an esoteric oddity from the attic of intellectual history, but a worldview that asks us to reconsider our own assumptions about the Creation and the qualities of knowing.

112 Bruce V. Foltz, *The Noetics of Nature: Environmental Philosophy and the Holy Beauty of the Visible*, Groundworks: Ecological Issues in Philosophy and Theology (New York: Fordham University Press, 2014), 93.

Chapter Four

The Noble Failure of Romanticism &
Rudolf Steiner's Sophianic
Epistemology

Nah ist
Und schwer zu fassen der Gott
~ *Friedrich Hölderlin*[1]

OLLOWING THE AGE that witnessed Robert Fludd's defense of a sophiological vision of the created world, a variety of materialist epistemologies, hastened by Cartesian metaphysics and Baconian empiricism (among other contributing factors), began to secure dominance in all fields of intellectual inquiry. This was even the case in some quarters of theology, and religious tracts such as John Toland's *Christianity Not Mysterious* (1696) and Matthew Tindal's *Christianity as Old as the Creation* (1730) paved the way for rationalist approaches to religion perhaps most fully realized in the deism Immanuel Kant articulated in his influential *Religion within the Limits of Reason Alone* (1793). No doubt, nominalism and the theology of pure nature informed this development to a profound degree. The triumph of rationalism, at least at the cultural level, contributed to the rise of secularization in the way the life of faith was effectively privatized and the marketplace of ideas became a forum for philosophical, economic, and scientific debate, leaving

---

1 "Near is / and difficult to grasp, the God." Friedrich Hölderlin, "Patmos" from *Hyperion and Selected Poems*, ed. Eric L. Santer, The German Library 22 (New York: Continuum, 1994), lines 1–2.

religion to look on from the gallery. As Kate Rigby has argued, "the disenchanted world of modern science was one from which the divine had largely been expelled."[2] Such a development was not without significant psychological and epistemological ruptures.

One such rupture, and hardly one of the more extreme, was central to the utter madness that attended the French Revolution and came to flower in the Reign of Terror. A mind-numbing violence made palatable and efficient through the technological advances of science (e.g., the guillotine) and justified by reason then initiated a series of secularist revolutions, the violence of which—augmented by exponentially growing technological advances—"dwarfs the horrors of all earlier ages."[3] The rationality of the revolutionary ethos, rendered absurd in the *Culte de la Raison*, rather than reason (*ratio*) and the promise of *liberté, egalité, fraternité*, instead—quite literally—*willed* to posterity a legacy of terror, as revolution after revolution, having discarded even the possibility of a transcendent God, turned to violence and coercion to achieve its aims. Indeed, the Bolshevik Revolution sought to "transcend [a telling metaphor] the narrow confines of the French Revolution" and its Enlightenment aims and, furthermore, championed "humanity's final victory over nature, and its spread throughout the cosmos."[4] Most revolutions following that of 1789 disclose the same kind of hubris.

Initially inspired by the notions of freedom and rights promised by Enlightenment philosophies, with the French Revolution's turn to barbaric violence and the Napoleonic imperialism and despotism that followed, some European thinkers and poets began to reevaluate the enthusiasm for reason and the accompanying spiritual and moral sterility that marked the second half of the 18th century and the beginning of the 19th. The rise of technology, its contributions to unchecked Capitalism and its impli-

2 Kate Rigby, *Topographies of the Sacred: The Poetics of Place in European Romanticism* (Charlottesville, VA: University of Virginia Press, 2004), 21.

3 Charles Taylor, *A Secular Age* (Cambridge: Belknap-Harvard University Press, 2007), 687.

4 Dmitry Shlapentokh, *The French Revolution and the Russian Anti-Democratic Tradition: A Case of False Consciousness* (New Brunswick, NJ: Transaction Publishers, 1997), 214.

cation in the problems inherent to the Industrial Revolution also provoked this reconsideration of the culture's assumptions as it became increasingly clear that doing away with religion and the notion of original sin only rendered the sinfulness of a world without grace all the more apparent. When William Blake contrasted the "dark Satanic Mills" of industrialization with the idyllic vision of the boy Jesus standing upon England's "green & pleasant Land" he not only presented a striking poetic juxtaposition, he also marked the battle lines of a profoundly important clash of epistemologies.[5] Romanticism was, indeed, engaged in a war with materialism: a war fought, however, with only the subtle weapons of art and thought. Ernst Cassirer once argued that Romanticism's "poetical and esthetic conception was not equal to the task of solving the problems of political life,"[6] though it is hard to believe that the Enlightenment project has been any more successful—unless we accept that force trumps all. The conflict between Enlightenment and Romanticism (in a way a kind of secularist caricature of the nature/grace binary) is not limited to the political realm, but also touches on notions of the environment and stewardship. Indeed, as Bruce Foltz writes, "it was not romanticism, but the rationality specific to modern science and technology that led to the ongoing, probably intensifying, set of environmental crises that became evident in the last century."[7] This is clearly an historical moment in need of reconsideration.

In this chapter I will argue that Romanticism, particularly in some of its German manifestations, intuited—but was unable to realize—a sophiological understanding of Creation, society, and divinity. The movement ultimately failed, and it failed primarily in the way it distanced itself from traditional religious ways of being. Romanticism, after establishing a kind of religious self,

5 William Blake, *Milton*, 1.1–16, in *The Complete Poetry and Prose of William Blake*, ed. David V. Erdman, commentary by Harold Bloom, rev. ed. (Berkeley and Los Angeles: University of California Press, 1982).

6 Ernst Cassirer, *The Myth of the State* (New Haven: Yale University Press, 1946), 186.

7 Bruce V. Foltz, *The Noetics of Nature: Environmental Philosophy and the Holy Beauty of the Visible*, Groundworks: Ecological Issues in Philosophy and Theology (New York: Fordham University Press, 2014), 90.

provided that self no end, no teleology, no horizon. With no anticipation of the Parousia, the possibility of a kairotic immanence stagnated into an affective preoccupation with "perception, feeling, and activity,"[8] all good things, certainly, but not a substitute for religion. A religion based on the self, then, eventually becomes a religion of the self, and ultimately finds itself bogged down in the "spiritual but not religious" ethos characteristic of postmodern existential ennui. It is a religion of the present moment, invested with feelings and aestheticism, but the ideas of sacrificial love and ultimate truth are foreign to it.

I will further argue that the Austrian philosopher and seer Rudolf Steiner (1861–1925), who rose from a philosophical tradition grounded in German Idealism and the scientific writings of Johann Wolfgang von Goethe (both with strong ties to Romanticism), strove to envision a sophiology that is much in harmony with the Romantics' aesthetics, but that he was more successful than they were by anchoring his thought in a singular, albeit idiosyncratic, understanding of Christ's role in not only the salvation of humanity but in the salvation of the Creation itself. Steiner's eclectic epistemology is simultaneously scientific, artistic, and theological: a bold reimagination of the kinds of epistemological approaches engaged by Robert Fludd and Thomas Vaughan in 17th century England and Marsilio Ficino and Giovanni Pico della Mirandola in 15th century Florence. Steiner, though, was not interested in a retrieval along the lines of the nostalgic moves of Perennialism, but, instead, focused on the realization of new insights that could be simultaneously scientific, artistic, and theological. The (re)unification of science, art, and religion are necessary, he thought, to the regeneration of culture. He very nearly succeeded in uniting them. In some ways, indeed, perhaps he did.

Romanticism

While it has rightly been argued that Romanticism was reacting in defiance of the Enlightenment's totalizing reliance on reason as

8 Friedrich Schleiermacher, *On Religion: Speeches to Its Cultured Despisers*, trans. John Oman (New York: Harper & Brothers, 1958), 45.

the primary method to engage and subdue the world, its proper-
ties, and inhabitants, this reaction was certainly selective (the
focus on intuition, the emotions, and so forth). But the Romantics clearly interiorized some of the Enlightenment's aims. The
founding of the University of Berlin in 1809–1810 is emblematic
of this absorption of the Enlightenment ethos. The University of
Berlin, what has been called "the Romantic research university,"
helped to foster "the secularization of knowledge" that is now so
much a part of our own educational paradigm that we rarely give
it a second thought.[9] This new model for education encouraged
research in the sciences while it sequestered theology into its own
isolated department (a kind gesture—the *Philosophes* would have
banned it); it focused on the individual and looked to the state
for patronage.[10] This is still a fitting description of the modern
university; even, perhaps especially, tragically, the modern Catholic university.

Admittedly, the foundation of the University of Berlin was
rather late in the day for Romanticism. Napoleon, for one, had
crowned himself emperor in 1804, seriously compromising the
hopes projected on him as a Romantic hero and champion of
Revolution.[11] The poet Novalis (pseudonym of Georg Philipp
Friedrich Freiherr von Hardenberg), one the architects of German Romanticism, had died in 1801 at the age of twenty-eight,
preceding Friedrich Schiller's early death at forty-three by three
years. By the time the University was established, Goethe was
sixty, the radical Romantic philosopher Friedrich Schlegel had
converted to Catholicism, and the tremendously gifted poet
Friedrich Hölderlin had been institutionalized on account of
madness. The establishment of the University, then, might be
thought to serve as a fitting tombstone for the movement. Prior

9 Brad S. Gregory, *The Unintended Reformation: How a Religious Revolution
Secularized Society* (Cambridge: Belknap-Harvard University Press, 2012), 348.
10 Ibid.
11 Some of the English Romantic poets (Coleridge, Southey, Keats,
Landor, Wordsworth, Byron) were particularly enamored with Napoleon in
the late 1790s and first decade of the 1800s. See Simon Bainbridge, *Napoleon
and English Romanticism,* Cambridge Studies in Romanticism (Cambridge:
Cambridge University Press, 1995).

to Romanticism's untimely death, however, the movement was the source of a variety of inspiring insights concerned with being human in the world.

Romantic Natura: *Goethe's Union of Poetry, Science, and Religion*

Although Johann Wolfgang von Goethe (1749–1832) later repudiated some of the aims of Romanticism and turned toward a reimagined Classicism (*Klassik*), through his wildly successful novel *Die Leiden des jungen Werther* (1774, known in English as *The Sorrows of Young Werther*) and its introduction of the now stock image of the Romantic artist-hero too sensitive for coping with the harshness of a broken world, and due to his championing of the primacy of intuitive perception, he was in large measure central to the formation of Romantic aesthetics.[12] Goethe was a Romantic and a *Klassiker*, a poet and a scientist, a diplomat and an artist, a mystic as well as a skeptic, and, as a result of such a staggering and multifarious genius, it has been said that "There is no writer so paradoxical as Goethe."[13] This is true for literary critics, of course, as well as for historians of science, but it may be more accurate to read Goethe as a man bigger than our puny categories. Nevertheless, I find describing Goethe as a Romantic useful because his theories of perception—evident in his poetic as well as his scientific works—sets him in contrast to the materialist epistemologies of the scientific revolution and aligns him with the aims of the permutations of German Romanticism that followed. Furthermore,

12 See Gerhart Hoffmeister, "Reception in Europe and Abroad" in *The Cambridge Companion to Goethe*, ed. Lesley Sharpe (Cambridge: Cambridge University Press, 2002), 232–55, at 233. Gerhard Shulz suggests that debates regarding whether Goethe was either a "Romanticist" or "Classicist" are, in the main, "mostly unproductive." See his "From 'Romantick' to 'Romantic': The Genesis of German Romanticism in Late Eighteenth-Century Europe" in *The Literature of German Romanticism*, ed. Dennis F. Mahoney, The Camden House History of German Literature, Volume 8 (Rochester, NY: Camden House, 2004), 25–34, at 29.

13 Ronald Gray, *Goethe: A Critical Introduction* (Cambridge: Cambridge University Press, 1967), 3.

Goethe's poetics and scientific epistemology evidence a nascent, intuitive sophiological aesthetic as he strove to discover the phenomenon behind phenomena, what he called the *Urphänomen*.

The perception, the awareness, of something behind the appearances was not something Goethe *came to* in his life. Rather, it was something he *came with*. In his autobiography, he describes a level of awareness he possessed as a child, writing of his younger self in the third person:

> He came to the thought that he might immediately approach the great God of Nature, the Creator and Preserver of Heaven and Earth, whose earlier manifestations of wrath had long been forgotten in the beauty of the world, and the manifold blessings in which we participate while upon it. The way he took to accomplish this was very curious.
>
> The Boy had chiefly kept to the first article of Belief. The God who stands in immediate connection with nature, and owns and loves it as his own work, seemed to him the proper God, who might be brought into closer relationship with man, as with everything else, and who would take care of him, as of the motion of the stars, the days and seasons, the animals and plants. There were texts of the Gospels which explicitly stated this. The Boy could ascribe no form to this Being: he therefore sought Him in His works, and would, in the good Old Testament fashion, build Him an altar. Natural productions were set forth as images of the world, over which a flame was to burn, signifying the aspirations of man's heart towards his Maker.[14]

Goethe was not the first child to awaken to such intimations and was surely not the last. Indeed, such intuitions are common, as the English Romantic poet William Wordsworth (1770–1850) also shows in "Ode: Intimations of Immortality from Recollections of Early Childhood":

> There was a time when meadow, grove, and stream,
> The earth, and every common sight
> To me did seem

14 Johann Wolfgang von Goethe, *Autobiography: Truth and Poetry, from My Own Life*, vol. 1, trans. John Oxenford, revised (London: George Bell and Sons, 1897), 30.

> Apparelled in celestial light,
> The glory and the freshness of a dream.
> It is not now as it hath been of yore;—
> Turn wheresoe'er I may,
> By night or day,
> The things which I have seen I now can see no more.[15]

Predating the Romantics by a century, in his poetry Thomas Traherne articulates the same notion:

> And while my God did all his Glories show,
> I felt a vigour in my sense
> That was all Spirit. I within did flow
> With seas of life, like wine;
> I nothing in the world did know
> But 'twas divine.[16]

The faculty of perception illustrated in these passages, as Wordsworth laments, is something most people lose (or grow out of) as they migrate into adulthood. Goethe never lost this faculty, and his retention of it figures prominently in the range and depth of his accomplishments in poetry and science. Freud, of course, dismisses the phenomenon these poets describe as the "oceanic feeling" he attributes to a psychological mechanism connected to memories of well-being connected to breast feeding.[17] That is, for Freud, such a feeling is infantile and regressive, a condemnation he levelled at religion as well. But contra Freud (who confessed that he had never experienced this oceanic feeling), this eventamental and essentially religious way of perceiving the world, the poets would argue, is a more immediate, more unmediated, and purer form of perception than that of the founder of psychoanalysis.

Goethe's attentiveness to the world, and to the *Urphänomen* behind it, is characterized by an inherently sophianic mode of

15 William Wordsworth, *The Poetical Works* [vol. 4], ed. E. de Selincourt and Helen Darbshire (Oxford: The Clarendon Press, 1947), lines 1–9.

16 Thomas Traherne, "Wonder," lines 19–24, from *The Poetical Works of Thomas Traherne, 1636?–1674*, ed. Bertram Dobell, 2nd ed. (London: Published by the Editor, 1906).

17 Sigmund Freud, *Civilization and Its Discontents*, trans. James Strachey (New York: W. W. Norton and Company, 1961), 13. This is also the theme of Freud's essay *The Future of an Illusion*.

perception. Hans Urs von Balthasar has observed that Goethe, "unquestionably represents a last secular manifestation of the heritage of 'glory' which the history of western metaphysics has bequeathed to us,"[18] though this assessment should not be accepted uncritically. Indeed, it is not at all clear to what extent Goethe's metaphysics can be interpreted as purely "secular." Using words like "glory" or "splendor" to describe the poet-scientist's metaphysics surely troubles such a categorization to a significant degree. For Goethe, concepts were deadening; what lived were perceptions and he perceived splendor behind phenomena. And this splendor is gendered in Goethe, as is evident in the oft-quoted lines from the end of *Faust*: "The Eternal-Womanly/ Draws us above."[19] This splendor, furthermore, is grounded in a divine Mediatrix:

> And glorious, midway seen
> Star-crowned, yet tender,
> Heaven's own lofty Queen!
> It is Her splendor.[20]

It is *her* splendor. The Virgin Mother bears a distinctly salvific role in Goethe's play. Interestingly, Goethe employs a similar personification—if, indeed, it is a personification—in the preface to the first edition of his *Theory of Colours* (1810):

> The completeness of nature displays itself to another sense in a similar way. Let the eye be closed, let the sense of hearing be excited, and from the lightest breath to the wildest din, from the simplest sound to the highest harmony, from the most vehement and impassioned cry to the gentlest word of reason, still it is Nature that speaks and manifests her presence, her pervading life and the vastness of her relations.[21]

---

18 Hans Urs von Balthasar, *The Glory of the Lord: A Theological Aesthetics, Vol. 5: The Realm of Metaphysics in the Modern Age*, trans. Oliver Davies, Andrew Louth, Brian McNeil, John Saward, and Rowan Williams; ed. Brian McNeil and John Riches (San Francisco: Ignatius Press, 1991), 340.

19 Johann Wolfgang von Goethe, *Faust, Parts One and Two*, trans. George Madison Priest (New York: Alfred A. Knopf, 1950), lines 12110–1.

20 Goethe, *Faust*, 11993–6.

21 Johann Wolfgang von Goethe, *Theory of Colours*, trans. Charles Lock Eastlake (London: John Murray, 1840), xviii.

Goethe's epistemology is charged with an erotics not unlike that found in the *Brautmystik* ("bridal mysticism") of the medieval period and of the Song of Songs.[22] And, as the above lines from *Theory of Colours* show, *Faust's* Mater Gloriosa was no late innovation in Goethe's worldview and was integral to his thought more than twenty years earlier.

Critics have been at pains to distance Goethe from Catholic devotion to the Virgin, even suggesting that he "abandoned Christianity early in life in favour of a Hellenic neo-paganism,"[23] a rather extreme interpretation.[24] The last scene of *Faust*, finally finished when Goethe was eighty-one and following sixty years of labor, suggests a different story. His incorporation of the Virgin at the end of his *Meisterwerke*, which some suggest was inspired by Raphael's powerful *Sistine Madonna*,[25] is steeped in his notion of the archetype (*Urtypus* or *Urphänomen*).[26] For, indeed, the Mater Gloriosa of the play is nothing if not a figure of an archetypal, sophianic mother of mercy, what Hans Eichner has called

22 On the importance of erotics to Goethe's science, see Robert J. Richards, *The Romantic Conception of Life: Science and Philosophy in the Age of Goethe*, Science and Its Conceptual Foundations (Chicago: The University of Chicago Press, 2002), 326–27.

23 Colin Riordan, "Johann Wolfgang von Goethe, 1749–1832," in *Fifty Key Thinkers on the Environment*, ed. Joy A. Palmer, advisory eds. David E. Cooper and Peter Blaze Corcoran (London: Routledge, 2001), 64.

24 Robert J. Richards provides a more accurate observation of Goethe's religious sensibilities, writing that, though Goethe "broke from formal church ties during his Leipzig years [he] remained religious, though in a more generous sense. In the older Greek writers—Homer, Aeschylus, Sophocles—he found a poetically realized religion that cultivated the kind of feeling for the divinity of nature that he began to recognize as his own." See *The Romantic Conception of Life*, 336.

25 Hans Belting, *The Invisible Masterpiece*, trans. Helen Atkins (Chicago: University of Chicago Press, 2001), 63.

26 As we shall see, the *Sistine Madonna* bears a particularly important role in the religious awakenings and intuitions of several individuals, not to mention the Romantic poet Heinrich von Kleist. On Kleist's encounter with the painting, see Helmut J. Schneider, "Saint Mary's Two Bodies: Religion and Enlightenment in Kleist" in *Religion, Reason, and Culture in the Age of Goethe*, ed. Elisabeth Krimmer and Patricia Ann Simpson, Studies in German Literature, Linguistics, and Culture (Rochester, NY: Camden House, 2013), 141–65, at 144.

Goethe's artistic miracle: "the magisterial reappreciation of the Catholic archetype Mary" and a re-envisioning of the concept of grace.[27] Furthermore, the implied apocatastasis in the Mater Gloriosa's intercession as she saves the sinner Faust from damnation resonates deeply with the sophianic intuitions of the English Protestant mystic Jane Lead as well as with St. Thérèse of Lisieux's "blind hope in [God's] mercy."[28] Indeed, the concept of apocatastasis was popular with speculative theologians and thinkers of the period.[29] While it is true that Goethe could by no means be accounted a "traditional Christian"—his emphasis on the primacy of personal experience set him at odds with an ethos of receptive acceptance[30]—he was clearly drawn to the emotional aspects of Catholic piety as much closer to his own religious discoveries and intuitions, what he called "Christenthum zu meinem Privatgebrauch" ("Christianity for my own private use"),[31] than to either evangelical Protestantism or Pietism.[32] More than in the literary works, though, in his scientific writing Goethe anticipates a more fully realized—and revolutionary—sophianic epistemology.

27 Hans Eichner, "The Eternal Feminine: An Aspect of Goethe's Ethics," *Transactions of the Royal Society of Canada*, series 4, vol. 9 (1971): 235–44; in Gerald Gillespie, "Classic Vision in the Romantic Age: Goethe's Reconstitution of European Drama in *Faust II*" from *Romantic Drama*, ed. Gerald Gillespie (Amsterdam: John Benjamins Publishing Company, 1994), 379–98, at 396.

28 Hans Urs von Balthasar, *Theo-Drama: Theological Dramatic Theory, V: The Last Act*, trans. G. Harrison (San Francisco: Ignatius Press, 1998), 320.

29 Among those in whom Balthasar detects this inclination are S.W. Peterson; the Württemburg Pietists Bengel, Oetinger, and Hahn; the German Idealists; Friedrich Schleiermacher; and the twentieth-century theologians Albert Schweitzer, Ernst Troeltsch, Dietrich Bonhoeffer, and Karl Barth. See *Theo-Drama, V,* 318.

30 It is not without reason that Goethe's self-characterizations regarding religion have been called "notoriously contradictory and shifting." See Elisabeth Krimmer, "'Then Say What Your Religion Is': Goethe, Religion, and *Faust*" in *Religion, Reason, and Culture in the Age of Goethe*, ed. Elisabeth Krimmer and Patricia Ann Simpson, Studies in German Literature, Linguistics, and Culture (Rochester, NY: Camden House, 2013), 99–119, at 100.

31 From his *Dichtung und Wahrheit, Werke* 16: 677; quoted in Elisabeth Krimmer, "Then Say What Your Religion Is," 102.

32 Walter Naumann, "Goethe's Religion," *Journal of the History of Ideas* 13, no. 2 (April 1952): 188–99, at 198.

Goethe felt that his scientific writing was his most important contribution to culture, particularly his groundbreaking work *Theory of Colours* in which he boldly refutes Sir Isaac Newton's mechanistic optics.[33] Goethe rejected the notion that nature can be comprehended only through quantification and classification, but insisted that intuition (*Ahnung*) is primary to an understanding of the things of this world.[34] He articulates this in *Theory of Colours*, "The terms of the science of mechanics . . . always have something unpolished; they destroy the inward life to offer from without an insufficient substitute for it."[35] Goethe attends to what lives in phenomena, disclosing their inherent *zoē*, even in phenomena, like light or color, to which we might not ascribe *bios*.[36]

---

33 Goethe was particularly harsh with Newton, dismissing his optics as "contrafactual, a fairy tale, hocus-pocus, and word-rubbish." He had even more spleen to vent on Newton's followers. See Dennis L. Sepper, *Goethe contra Newton: Polemics and the Project for a New Science of Color* (Cambridge: Cambridge University Press, 1988), 3.

34 Colin Riordan, "Johann Wolfgang von Goethe, 1749–1832," 65.

35 Johann Wolfgang von Goethe, *Theory of Colours*, §752 (301).

36 My use of the terms *bios* and *zoē* is in consonance with the traditional Christian employment of the terms as seen, for instance, in C. S. Lewis's *Mere Christianity*, where *bios* is defined as the kind of life subject to decay and *zoē* is associated with the life-force which springs forth from God. See C. S. Lewis, *Mere Christianity* (London: Collins, 1967), 135. Considering the terms in the context of ancient Greek literature and philosophy, the Swiss mythologist Carl Kerényi affirms that *zoē* is for ancient Greece, as the term is also used in the New Testament, indicative of life "experienced without end [*aionion zoēn*, ζωὴν], an infinite life." See Kerényi's *Dionysos: Archetypal Image of Indestructible Life*, trans. Ralph Manheim, Bollingen Series LXV, 2 (Princeton: Princeton University Press, 1976), xxxvi. Such an understanding of *bios/zoē is* also implicit in Michel Henry's phenomenology as he articulates it in *I Am the Truth: Toward a Philosophy of Christianity*, trans. Susan Emanuel, Cultural Memory in the Present (Stanford, CA: Stanford University Press, 2003), especially chapter three, "A Truth Called Life." More recently, ostensibly deriving his understanding from Aristotle, Giorgio Agamben has distorted (and unfortunately popularized in academic circles) the postmodern understanding of the terms, inverting their meanings, calling *zoē* "bare life" and *bios* "the form or way of living proper to an individual or a group." See Giorgio Agamben, *Homo Sacer: Sovereign Power and Bare Life*, trans. Daniel Heller-Roazen (Stanford, CA: Stanford University Press, 1998), 1.

As was the case with Simone Weil long after him, in his method for engaging the world, Goethe was fundamentally concerned with attentiveness, allowing phenomena to exist in their own right.[37] Weil called this kind of attention a form of generosity. Goethe called it "reverence."

In *Wilhelm Meister's Wanderjahre* (*Wilhelm Meister's Apprenticeship*, 1821), Goethe describes his four categories of reverence:

> The religion which rests on reverence for that which is above us, we call the ethical one. . . . The second religion, which is founded on that reverence which we have for what is like ourselves, we call the Philosophic. . . . The third religion, based on reverence for that which is below us; we call it the Christian one . . . because it is the last one which humanity could and was bound to attain. . . . They together present the true religion; from these three reverences outsprings the highest reverence, reverence for one's self.[38]

Goethe, interestingly enough, finds these forms of reverence outlined in the Creed. Furthermore, as he writes, "the Christian religion having once appeared, can never disappear again; having once been divinely embodied, cannot again be dissolved."[39] Though, again, some critics have preferred to ameliorate what we can call Goethe's implicit Christianity,[40] his words here certainly complicate such claims.

Goethe's reverence becomes, in his scientific work, what he calls a "delicate empiricism" (*zarte Empirie*), a method of inquiry quite at odds with what he criticized as Newtonian science's "gloomy empirical-mechanical-dogmatic torture chamber."[41] By making observation his primary mode of intellectual inquiry,

37 Diogenes Allen and Eric O. Springfield, *Spirit and Community: Issues in the Thought of Simone Weil* (Albany, NY: State University of New York Press, 1994), 81.

38 Johann Wolfgang von Goethe, *Wilhelm Meister's Travels*, trans. and ed. Edward Bell (London: George Bell and Sons, 1885), 156–7.

39 Ibid., 156.

40 H.B. Nisbet, "Religion and Philosophy" in *The Cambridge Companion to Goethe*, ed., Leslie Sharpe (Cambridge: Cambridge University Press, 2002), 219–31, at 223.

41 Johann Wolfgang von Goethe, *Maxims and Reflections*, trans. Elisabeth Stopp, ed. Peter Hutchinson (London: Penguin, 1998), maxim 430 (55).

Goethe claims, the inquiry itself takes on a measure of holistic integration revolutionary in its ontological reciprocity:

> The human being knows himself only insofar as he knows the world; he perceives the world only in himself, and himself in the world. Every new object, clearly seen, opens up a new organ of perception in us.[42]

Heidegger would later go on to say that, rather than an organ, such attention opens up a new world. Goethe's delicate empiricism, then, proves to be a nascent form of what would become known in the twentieth century as phenomenology. Indeed, phenomenology is almost unthinkable without the contribution of Goethe. Goethe's science, indeed, was so revolutionary that we are only just now catching up with it. And, as von Balthasar has observed, such a stance begs a comparison with another intellectual revolutionary, St. Thomas Aquinas:

> [Goethe's] aim was to combine the cool precision of scientific research with a constant awareness of the totality apparent only to the eye of reverence, the poetic-religious eye, the ancient sense for the cosmos. But the scientists had gone over to his arch-enemy Newton, the Idealists preferred to deduce nature to an *a priori* system, or, if they were Romantics, to feel a vague irrational feeling of the whole. Goethe was just as much a lone fighter in his age as Thomas Aquinas had been when he sought to combine exact research and intellectual work with a reverentially pious perception of the divine in the cosmos. For without uniting the two, there can be no attitude objective enough to do justice to existence.[43]

Goethe's scientific method, as has been said of Romanticism writ large, can be seen as "a new wave of mysticism, like those that have arisen again and again in European history, renewing European thinking."[44] Connecting Goethe's science to mysticism should come as no surprise: both are grounded in contemplation, and both reach beyond the appearances. In the contemplative behold-

---

42 Johann Wolfgang von Goethe, *The Collected Works: Scientific Studies*, vol. 12 (Princeton: Princeton University Press, 1988), 39.

43 Hans Urs von Balthasar, *The Glory of the Lord: A Theological Aesthetics, Vol.* 5, 363.

44 Walter Naumann, "Goethe's Religion," 193.

ing of phenomena—whether of a plant or color in the case of Goethe, or of Christ in the case of a mystic—a reciprocity occurs, what I have called elsewhere "a double intentionality" and what John Panteleimon Manoussakis calls inverse intentionality, "a chiastic point where the two extremes cross paths."[45] As Brent Dean Robbins explains, "When we allow ourselves to be claimed by phenomena, we open ourselves to feel our relational obligation to them. In other words, we become morally engaged with them."[46] Goethe, in his scientific project, was deeply involved in a moral engagement with the world. He was committed to countering Cartesian and Newtonian approaches which treat matter as a thing at hand, something to be used, a methodology analogous to rape. Goethe's essentially erotic metaphysics would not allow him to treat the things of this world as objects of self-gratification.

Romantic Episteme: *Novalis's Marian Intuitions*

Like his contemporary Goethe and most other thinkers and poets associated with German Romanticism, Novalis positioned himself against the increasingly materialistic philosophies and science of his time. As Gabriele Rommel has observed in language that could also be applied to the opponents of pure nature in the 16th and 17th centuries, the Romantics felt deeply the "evident loss of a unified view of nature" which not only changed how nature was understood, but "altered human self-understanding" as well, leading to "the loss of a creative nexus between God, nature, and humanity."[47] In resonance with Goethe's scientific ethos, Novalis argued for "the *poeticization of the sciences*, where cognition is conceived as a historic-genetic process and becomes freed of all systematic constraints (whether through philosophy or natural

---

45 John P. Manoussakis, "The Phenomenon of God: From Husserl to Marion," *American Catholic Philosophical Quarterly* 78 no. 1 (2004): 53–68, at 62.

46 Brent Dean Robbins, "New Organs of Perception: Goethean Science as a Cultural Therapeutics," *Janus Head* 8, no. 1 (2005): 113–26, at 123.

47 Gabriele Rommel, "Romanticism and Natural Science" in *The Literature of German Romanticism*, ed. Dennis F. Mahoney, The Camden House History of German Literature, Volume 8 (Rochester, NY: Camden House, 2004), 209–27, at 211.

science) to thus offer a glimpse of the essence of things."[48] This Romantic philosophical *cri de coeur* is intrinsic to the movement, surfacing as well in the telling lines of Blake's *Jerusalem*:

> I must Create a System. or be enslav'd by another Mans
> I will not Reason & Compare: my business is to Create.[49]

Trained as a geologist, Novalis came to believe that "in matter itself is the ground of life."[50] This "life," however, is characterized not by *bios* but by *zoē* and is identical with that which he discloses in his poetry. Indeed, in his *Die Lehrlinge zu Sais* (written 1798–99), Novalis asserts that "Natural Scientists and Poets by force of speech have always seemed to be of one race."[51] But, in contradistinction to Goethe, Novalis, inspired in no small part by Schleiermacher, explores the possibilities of a renewal of religion through his own special type of Romantic contemplation. This impetus manifests itself most strongly through two of his most important works: the essay, *Die Christenheit oder Europa* (*Christianity or Europe*), and the extraordinary poetic sequence, *Hymnen an die Nacht*, known to readers of English as *Hymns to the Night*.

Christianity or Europe

From the time Novalis shared it with his colleagues in Jena, readers of *Christianity or Europe* have been struck—some would say "put off"—by the seeming nostalgia the work evokes for medieval European Catholicism. Even Novalis's friends and editors Ludwig Tieck and Friedrich Schlegel decided against including the essay in the first edition of his posthumously published *Schriften* (1802) for fear of how it might have been received in a German Romantic

---

48 Gabriele Rommel, "Romanticism and Natural Science," 217. Rommel's emphasis.

49 William Blake, *Jerusalem*, 10.20–1.

50 "In der Materie selbst liegt der Grund des Lebens." Fergus Henderson, "Novalis, Ritter and 'Experiment': A Tradition of 'Active Empiricism,'" in *The Third Culture: Literature and the Sciences*, ed. Elinor S. Shaffer (Berlin: Walter de Gruyter, 1998), 163.

51 Novalis, *The Disciples at Sais and Other Fragments*, trans. F.V.M.T. and U[na] C. B[irch] (London: Methuen & Co., 1903), 100.

milieu that had never completely freed itself from the anti-religious (and especially anti-Catholic) biases of the *Aufklarung*. The second and third editions (1805 and 1815) of the *Schriften* included only excerpts of the essay, a complete version not appearing in print until the fourth edition in 1826.[52]

The reason for Novalis's esteem for medieval Christianity is apparent from the essay's opening sentence. "Those were beautiful, magnificent times," Novalis writes, "when Europe was a Christian land, when *one* Christianity dwelled on this civilized continent, and when *one* common interest joined the most distant provinces of this vast empire."[53] As some critics have observed, Novalis's understanding of the period is not one typically shared by historians.[54] Even von Balthasar has maligned the era, joining in the chorus led by Jan Huizinga and others proclaiming that the "late Middle Ages is a time of darkness like few others" when "the radiance of the heavenly Jerusalem no longer breaks through the clouds to illumine God's earthly realm."[55] But such a jaundiced view, I think, is really informed by a Protestant—and then secular—desire to distance European culture from its Roman Catholic patrimony as well as by what has been called "the enormous condescension of posterity"[56] common to academic culture and not necessarily based on medieval realities. Novalis clearly believes that Christianity is essential to European

52 Frederick C. Beiser, note to *Christianity or Europe: A Fragment*, in *The Early Political Writings of the German Romantics*, ed. and trans. Frederick C. Beiser, Cambridge Texts in the History of Political Thought (Cambridge: Cambridge University Press, 1996), 61.

53 Novalis, *Christianity or Europe: A Fragment*, in *The Early Political Writings of the German Romantics*, 61. Emphasis in source.

54 Pauline Kleingeld, "Romantic Cosmopolitanism: Novalis's 'Christianity or Europe,'" *Journal of the History of Philosophy* 46, no. 2 (2008): 269–84, at 272.

55 Hans Urs von Balthasar, *The Glory of the Lord: A Theological Aesthetics*, *Vol.* 5, 11. See also J. Huizinga, *The Waning of the Middle Ages: A Study of the Forms of Life, Thought and Art in France and the Netherlands in the XIVth and XVth Centuries* (1924; reprt. New York: St. Martin's Press, n.d.).

56 E.P. Thompson, *The Making of the English Working Class* (1963; reprt. Harmondsworth: Penguin, 1986), 12.

unity, an issue still under debate today.[57] He does not turn to medieval Catholicism in order to dream himself into the past; he does it to provoke his contemporaries.[58] He's picking a fight.

He is also picking a fight with us. Indeed, Catholicism is almost nonexistent in the scholarly excavation of period.[59] Nevertheless, the Catholicism of *Christianity or Europe* is hardly implicit. Novalis celebrates, for instance, the fact that the medieval period "preached nothing but love for the holy, beautiful lady of Christianity," the Virgin Mary.[60] He likewise appreciates the ways in which royalty "submitted their disputes before the father of Christendom [the pope] and willingly laid down their crowns and splendour at his feet."[61] Furthermore, he decries division among Christians and the tragedy by which Reformers "separated the inseparable, divided the indivisible church, and impiously divorced themselves from the universal Christian union, through and in which alone genuine lasting rebirth was possible."[62] But Novalis is not simply a religious dreamer hankering for an idealized past that never really existed. He knows what the real problems are: (1) that Christendom's demise was hastened by "the pressure of commercial life" which led to war and even greater cultural schisms;[63] (2) the pressures of political support for breaking off from Rome;[64] and (3) the intervention of the state into religion.[65] "With the Reformation," Novalis writes, "Christianity was done for."[66] Of course, as was the case with many at the time

---

57 Gianni Vattimo, *After Christianity*, trans. Luca D'Isanto (New York: Columbia University Press, 2002), 74.

58 Pauline Kleingeld, "Romantic Cosmopolitanism," 273.

59 Timothy Webb, "Catholic Contagion: Southey, Coleridge and English Romantic Anxieties," in *Romanticism and Religion from Cowper to Wallace Stevens*, ed. Gavin Hopps and Jane Stabler (Aldershot, UK: Ashgate, 2006): 75–92, at 75.

60 Novalis, *Christianity or Europe*, 62.

61 Ibid., 63.

62 Ibid., 65.

63 Ibid., 63.

64 Ibid., 65.

65 Ibid., 67.

66 Ibid.

(and not a few Catholics), Novalis has harsh words for the Jesuits, but he also offers some otherwise remarkable insights.

Novalis is an accurate and close reader of his times. "The original personal hatred against the Catholic faith," he writes of the Enlightenment, "gradually became a hatred of the Bible, of Christian belief, and finally of all religion."[67] Furthermore, he condemns the "new philosophy" which "placed man of necessity at the top of the series of natural beings, and made the infinite creative music of the cosmos into the uniform clattering of a gigantic mill."[68] He also condemns Enlightenment atheism as a false religion, "this new church," and his criticisms could be equally applied to the New Atheists and others of the early 21st century: "the watchword of the educated was 'tolerance,' and . . . it was synonymous with philosophy."[69] He also damns mechanistic science for what he sees as its heresies. The architects of Enlightenment, he emphasizes,

> were constantly preoccupied with purging poetry from nature, the earth, the human soul and the sciences. Every trace of the sacred was to be destroyed, all memory of noble events and people was to be spoiled by satire, and the world stripped of colourful ornament. Their favourite theme, on account of its mathematical obedience and impudence, was light. They were pleased that it refracted rather than played with its colours, and so they called this great enterprise "Enlightenment." One was more thorough with this business in Germany: education was reformed, the old religion was given a new, rational and common sense meaning by carefully cleansing it of everything miraculous and mysterious; all scholarship was summoned to cut off taking refuge in history, which they struggled to ennoble by making it into a domestic and civil portrait of family and morals. God was made into the idle spectator of the great moving drama, performed by intellectuals, whom the poets and actors should entertain and admire at the end.[70]

None of this, according to Novalis, could amount to anything good.

67 Ibid., 69.
68 Ibid., 70.
69 Ibid., 71.
70 Ibid., 70–1.

Though it has been argued that Novalis adjusted his understanding of Catholicism in a way that it conformed to his own religious sensibilities, such an assertion, I think, does a great disservice
to the poet.[71] It seems to me that he understood Catholicism—
and his times—quite well. He clearly had an idiosyncratic—and
sometimes heterodox—way of explaining it, but his intuitions are
right on the mark. "Christianity has three forms," he writes:

> One is the creative element of religion, the joy in all religion.
> Another is mediation in general, the belief in the capacity of every-
> thing earthly to be the wine and bread of eternal life. Yet a third is
> the belief in Christ, his mother and the saints. Choose whichever
> you like. Choose all three. It is indifferent: you are then Christians,
> members of a single, ineffably happy community.[72]

Catholicism is universal, but it is not a homogenized singularity,
uniform in all aspects: "In my father's house there are many mansions." Novalis, indeed, may have understood the essence of
Catholicism much better than many purportedly Catholic theologians—in his era or ours.

As Charles Taylor has recognized, the medieval period was
organized around the notion of the parish, a nexus in which "the
social bond . . . was intertwined in the sacred, and indeed, it was
unimaginable otherwise."[73] The loss of the bond of the sacred
and the community is what the Romantics, and especially Novalis, lamented in the wake of Reformation and Enlightenment. It
is also what they tried to reimagine. "The old Catholic faith,"
Novalis writes in *Christianity or Europe*,

> the last of these forms, was applied Christianity come to life. Its
> omnipresence in life, its love for art, its deep humanity, the sanc-
> tity of its marriages, its philanthropic sense of community, its joy
> in poverty, obedience and loyalty, all make it unmistakable as gen-
> uine religion and contain the basic features of its constitution. It is

71 Veronica G. Freeman, *The Poeticization of Metaphors in the Work of Novalis*, Studies on Themes and Motifs in Literature 78 (New York: Peter Lang,
2006), 55.
72 Novalis, *Christianity or Europe*, 78.
73 Charles Taylor, *A Secular Age*, 43.

purified through the stream of time; and in indivisible union with the other two forms of Christianity it will bless the earth.[74]

What Novalis upholds here is a notion often interpreted as "cosmopolitanism," but perhaps a better description is "communitarian," as his vision begins at an interpersonal level of common prayer and human flourishing and his idea is explicitly set into a Christian framework. If he is interested in cosmopolitanism, it is in a very restricted sense. His religion, then, is not a desire for the past, but a present hope for the future. He articulates this hope in an altogether imaginative, even mystical, way in *Hymns to the Night*.

Hymns to the Night

Novalis composed *Hymns to the Night* between 1797 and 1800 following the death of Sophie von Kühn, the poet's fifteen-year-old fiancée. Critics and scholars have long speculated on what they take to be the fusing of young Sophie and the Virgin Mary in Novalis's psyche as given form in the poem. Some go so far as to suggest that the poet read "Sophie" as emblematic of the "Sophia" of Boehme's work, even positing that he saw the girl as Wisdom's incarnation.[75] It is easy to make too much of such an assertion, though the fact that Sophie died on the day of the year they had "playfully" set for their wedding—March 25th, the Feast of the Annunciation—certainly adds an element of wonder to the story. Indeed, Novalis himself died on this feast in 1801, which makes things even more interesting.[76] So does an entry from his journal recounting a visit to Sophie's grave on 13 May 1797:

> The hillock became a cloud of dust, and through the cloud I saw the glorified face of my beloved. In her eyes eternity reposed. I laid

74 Novalis, op. cit., 78.

75 Kristin Pfefferkorn, *Novalis: A Romantic's Theory of Language and Poetry* (New Haven: Yale University Press, 1988), 129. See also *The Birth of Novalis: Friedrich von Hardenberg's Journal of 1797, with Selected Letters and Documents*, trans. and ed. Bruce Donehower (Albany, NY: State University of New York Press, 2007), 2.

76 Ibid., 1.

hold of her hands, and the tears became a sparkling bond that could not be broken. Into the distance swept by, like a tempest, thousands of years. On her neck I welcomed new life with ecstatic tears. Never was such another dream; then first and ever since I hold fast an eternal, unchangeable faith in the heaven of Night, and its Light, the Beloved.[77]

This passage became the model for a number of moments in the *Hymns to the Night*, for example in the fourth hymn where he writes, "Far and exhausting to me this pilgrimage to the holy grave has been, and the cross oppresses. The crystal wave, unnoticeable by common senses, wells up in the mound's dark lap."[78] Throughout the poem, the real and the ideal, the personal-historical and the metaphysical are indistinguishable.

As *Christianity or Europe* can be taken as Novalis's theological poesis, the *Hymns* can be considered his mystical poesis. Novalis was more than aware of the potential synergies between poetry and mysticism, as he wrote in the *Fragments*: "The sense of poetry has much in common with the sense of mysticism. It is the sense of the peculiar, personal, unknown, mysterious to apparently end random necessity. It represents the unrepresentable being. It sees the invisible, feels the impalpable."[79] Poetry—and with it the ability to perceive the world poetically, to grasp beyond the appearances of phenomena—is for Novalis an inherently religious act. As Louis Dupré has observed, Novalis is engaged in "a quest for the invisible mystery that hides behind the visible world."[80] Dupré believes the reality Novalis seeks is "entirely spiritual," but I do not

---

77 Gisela H. Krenglinger, *Storied Revelations: Parables, Imagination, and George MacDonald's Christian Fiction*, Distinguished Dissertations in Christian Theology (Eugene, OR: Wipf and Stock, 2013), 74–5.

78 *Hymns to the Night*, trans. Dick Higgins, rev. ed. (New Paltz, NY: McPherson & Company, 1984), 19.

79 "Der Sinn für Poesie hat viel mit dem Sinn für Mystizism gemein. Er ist der Sinn für das Eigenthümliche, Personelle, Unbekannte, Geheimißvolle, zu *Offenbarende*, das Nothwendigzufällige. Er stellt das Undarstellbare dar. Er sieht das Unsichtbare, fühlt das Unfühlbare." Novalis, Fragment 187, from Novalis, *Werke*, vol. 4, ed. Gerhard Schulz (München: Verlag C.H. Beck, 1981), 561.

80 Louis Dupré, *The Quest of the Absolute: Birth and Decline of European Romanticism* (Notre Dame, IN: University of Notre Dame Press, 2013), 79.

think this is entirely accurate. Novalis's perception is sophianic; that is, he sees the world of the senses in participation with the divine reality undergirding it, a reality he attempts to disclose in his poetry. This participation rises to awareness only in the act of imagination, but it is not, therefore, only an imaginative act, an act of phantasy. Imagination, rather, is an interactive perception in Novalis, what he called "romanticizing," a commerce, a congress at the highest level with the things of this world. "The world must be romanticized," he writes. "Then one will again find the original sense. Romanticizing is nothing more than a qualitative involution."[81] Novalis is aware of a parousia behind appearances, a presence informing both the created world and the interior of his own being. But he is not an escapist.

As Kate Rigby has noticed, the consequence of materialism, the Cartesian *cogito*, is "self-alienation."[82] Novalis's countryman and fellow poet Hölderlin in his work beautifully articulates the existential repercussions of this self-alienation:

> Gods who are fled! And you also, present still,
> But once more real, you had your time, your ages!
> No, nothing here I'll deny and ask no favors.
> For when it's over, and Day's light gone out,
> The priest is the first to be struck, but lovingly
> The temple and the image and the cult
> Follow him down into darkness, and none of
> them now may shine.[83]

Novalis, for his part, offers a remedy.

Whereas in *Christianity or Europe* Novalis's remedy is rendered in a language of community and culture, in the *Hymns* he speaks a more private religious language: a language of contemplation leading to intimacy. It is a sensuous utterance, full of longing and characterized by eros. This remedy, first of all, resides in the night and the comfort the poet/speaker finds there.

---

81 Sketches 105, from Frederick C. Beiser (ed.), *The Early Political Writings of the German Romantics*, 85.

82 Kate Rigby, *Topographies of the Sacred*, 23.

83 Friedrich Hölderlin, "Germania," trans. Michael Hamburger, in *Hyperion and Selected Poems*, 211.

Praise the world queen, the high messenger of a holy word, a nurse of blessed love—she sends me you—tender, loved—Night's lovely sun—now I wake—for I'm yours and mine—you called Night to life for me,—humanized me—tear my body with spirit fire, so I can mix with you more inwardly, airily, and then the wedding night will last forever.[84]

The resonances with Goethe's "eternal feminine" and medieval Christendom's *Brautmystik* are rather obvious here. In addition, Novalis's appreciation for the writing of Boehme—particularly in terms of "the kiss"—also bears traces in the world of the poem.[85] As is the case with Goethe, Novalis's encounter with Raphael's *Sistine Madonna* in 1798—during the period he worked on the *Hymns*—surely holds some importance in the constellation of images invoked in the poem.[86] Novalis touches on this idea also in the *Geistliche Lieder* (*Spiritual Songs*), written during the same period as the *Hymns*:

> I used to see thee in my dreams,
> So fair, so full of tenderest beams!
> The little God in thine arms lying
> Took pity on his playmate crying:
> But thou with high look didst me awe,
> And into clouds of glory didst withdraw.[87]
>
> In countless pictures I behold thee,
>   O Mary, lovelily expressed,
> But of them all none can unfold thee
>   As I have seen thee in my breast!

---

84 Novalis, first Hymn, in *Hymns to the Night*, 13.

85 Kristine Hannak reports that Novalis checked out the entire nine-volume Amsterdam edition of Boehme from the Dresden library in November 1800 and that the poet "found a profound poetic inspiration in Boehme." See Kristine Hannak, "Boehme and German Romanticism" in *An Introduction to Jacob Boehme: Four Centuries of Thought and Reception*, ed. Ariel Hessayon and Sarah Apetrei, Routledge Studies in Religion (New York and London: Routledge, 2013), 162–79, at 165.

86 John O'Meara, *The Way of Novalis: An Exposition on the Process of His Achievement* (Ottawa, ON: Heart's Core Publications, 2014), 131.

87 Song 14 from Novalis, *Hymns to the Night and Spiritual Songs*, trans. George MacDonald (London: Temple Lodge Publishing, 1992), 51.

> I only know the world's loud splendor
> Since then is like a dream o'erblown;
> And that a heaven, for words too tender,
> My quieted spirit fills alone.[88]

The *Sistine Madonna*, of course, depicts the Virgin revealed from behind a veil, standing in clouds from which appear the faces of babies. The notion of the veiled Virgin especially appealed to Novalis who uses it in his tale *The Disciples at Sais* in the image of Isis. In that story, the protagonist, Hyacinth, meets an old Sybil in the forest who tells him how he is to be made whole. Hyacinth, weeping, tells his parents that he must leave them:

> If I try to think of the old days, mightier thoughts intervene. Peace is fled together with heart and love. I must go seek them. I would like to tell you whither, but I do not know. Thither where the Mother of All Things lives, the Veiled Virgin. My desire is aflame for Her. Farewell.[89]

Raphael's image, I think, was not simply one which Novalis evokes here, a source of inspiration, but, more importantly, he responded to it because it resonated with his own previously held intuitions. It is no surprise, of course, that critics in his own and subsequent ages have suspected him of Catholicism—though a good many modern critics try to deflect the label of Catholicism (which could taint their quasi-Enlightenment narrative) and explain that Novalis's Catholicism, if anything, is purely *symbolic*.[90] But even his friend Schleiermacher expressed disappointment in what he interpreted as Novalis's Catholic turn.[91] Nevertheless, Novalis's love for the Virgin, whatever the religious

---

88 Song 15 from Novalis, *Hymns to the Night and Spiritual Songs*, 53.

89 Novalis, *The Disciples at Sais and Other Fragments*, 116–7. The description is not unlike that revealed to Lucius in book 11 of Apuleius's *The Golden Ass*.

90 As both Pauline Kleingeld and Veronica G. Freeman do. See Kleingeld's "Romantic Cosmopolitanism," 272; and Freeman's *The Poetization of Metaphors in the Work of Novalis*, 55. It is doubtful that the poet would have accepted their assertions. He was interested in reality.

91 John H. Smith, "Living Religion as Vanishing Mediator: Schleiermacher, Early Romanticism, and Idealism," *The German Quarterly* 84, no. 2 (Spring 2011): 137–58, at 143.

context, is palpable. As he writes in *Pollen*, "Nothing is more indispensable to true religiosity than a mediator that binds us to the divine."[92] Novalis's mediator is clearly the Virgin. Indeed, the Virgin's humanity binds the divine and the natural orders in her role in the Incarnation, and the Incarnation makes possible the renewal of all things:

> Down now to the sweet bride, on
> To Jesus, to the beloved—
> Comfort, evening's darkling greys
> To the loving, to the grieving.
> A dream will break our fetters off,
> And sink us forever in our Father's lap.[93]

While many have said that the poet projected the Divine Sophia onto his dead fiancée, Sophie, it is probably more correct to say that Novalis projected Sophie onto the Divine Sophia, especially in the *Hymns*. For the alchemy of his poetry is such that the symbolic and the real meet in mutuality and equipoise at the horizon of the natural and the supernatural, of the physical and the metaphysical, of historicity and the *kairos*.

The Noble Failure

Despite Goethe's intuitive phenomenology and Novalis's rediscovery of a Marian spirituality, Romanticism ultimately failed as epistemology, or, as, it might be said in the words of Jacques Derrida, as "a religion without religion." It failed, I think, because it tried to reclaim what are essentially religious intuitions and religious ways of being though cut off from traditional sources of religion. Of course, Romanticism's religious sensibility did not entirely vanish from human culture and experience. We see the remnants of this Romantic urge to reinvent religion in, among other things, the "spiritual but not religious" ethos so prevalent in postmodern societies. Dupré detects this "idea of religion as a purely interior feeling, detachable from its symbolic expression"

---

92 Novalis, *Pollen,* in *The Early Political Writings of the German Romantics,* 22.
93 Novalis, *Hymns to the Night,* 43.

in the early Schleiermacher, though he recognizes that later the Romantic theologian regarded this early insight as a mistake.[94] Graham Ward, on the other hand, notices in Novalis a phenomenon that could easily be applied to even postmodern permutations of the Romantic religious sensibility. Taking the Novalis of the *Hymns* as his starting point, Ward writes,

> What emerges as religion is not a return to medieval orthodoxy, nor Protestant dogmatics, nor moral reasoning, but it is nevertheless a continuation—albeit with renewed energy—of the Christian religion's universalization. Religion from now on will define itself with respect to an experience of the unconditional; an experience recreated and performed through a new turn to allegorization that renders the materiality of the world resonant with what Novalis called a "magical idealism." The allegorization—understood both as an even transforming subjective perception of the world and as a literary form, a view of the world and a way of writing—accommodated a new religious syncretism.[95]

Religious syncretism, it could be argued, remains a hallmark of postmodern neo-Romantic spirituality. It is essentially a way to find a way of being mindful of transcendence and attentive to immanence in the midst of a cultural milieu very often schizophrenic in its values and a religious milieu seemingly more concerned with political positions and adherence to lists of proscribed behaviors and attitudes than in an encounter with divinity. In a way, it is difficult to blame those who choose this path.

Romanticism's fascination with religion—while simultaneously being separated from religious streams grounded in history—could not help but fail. As Kate Rigby has said, "in the end, though, it proved impossible to create fresh religion *ex nihilo*" and the majority of the Romantics returned to one or another variety of the old one.[96] This was the case with Friedrich Schlegel, Schleiermacher, Franz von Baader, and others, and clearly seems to

94 Louis Dupré, *Religious Mystery and Rational Reflection* (Grand Rapids, MI: Wm. B. Eerdmans Publishing Co., 1998), 7.

95 Graham Ward, *True Religion*, Blackwell Manifestos (Malden, MA: Blackwell Publishing, 2003), 77.

96 Kate Rigby, *Topographies of the Sacred*, 46.

be the direction in which Novalis was heading. It was, I contend, the universalizing idea of Christianity that drew the Romantics with its communitarian ideal, the return to the idea of a parish. This idea is nowhere more present than in the Catholic Church. As Gianni Vattimo writes,

> The Church is certainly an important vehicle for revelation, but it is above all the community of believers who, in charity, hear and interpret freely the meaning of the Christian message, mutually correcting and helping one another. It is an idea of Church, found in many Romantic thinkers such as Novalis and Schleiermacher, that is wrongly treated as a utopia to be dismissed with other theses of eighteenth- and nineteenth-century German idealism. Perhaps it is only by taking seriously this utopia that Christianity will be able to realize in the postmodern world its vocation as a universal religion.[97]

Vattimo elsewhere also thinks the Church would do well to embrace some aspects of secularism; but here he encourages secularism to embrace the Church. Vattimo, in other words, is a Romantic.

The cosmopolitan, some would say utopian, ideals of the Romantics, it could be argued, failed because they remained at an aesthetic, conceptual level without ever really becoming actualized. They were fables constructed to inspire the imagination without any accompanying knowledge of how to apply them to actual lived experience. A very late Romantic, however, did more than any of his predecessors in trying to realize in the world-as-we-know-it a project for cultural renewal that, while fantastic in its theoretical aspects, was startlingly effective in its practical application. That man was Rudolf Steiner (1861–1925).

Rudolf Steiner's Sophiology

Steiner, it could easily be argued, is one of the most fascinating geniuses of his era. He was a philosopher trained by, among others, the important thinker and psychologist Franz Brentano (1838–1917). In addition to Steiner, Brentano greatly influenced

---

97 Gianni Vattimo, *After Christianity*, 9.

subsequent streams of phenomenology, analytic philosophy, and psychology, including Edmund Husserl, Gilbert Ryle, and even Sigmund Freud. Steiner studied with Brentano just before Edmund Husserl did, and Brentano's influence, especially in terms of his notion of intentionality, manifests in both. In Husserl's work, phenomenology becomes more fully realized, a genuine movement, whereas Steiner investigates the possibilities in intentionality in his important book, *Die Philosophie der Freiheit* (1894; known in English by three different titles: *The Philosophy of Freedom*; *The Philosophy of Spiritual Activity*; and *Intuitive Thinking as Spiritual Path*). Steiner, while still in his early twenties, was chosen to edit Goethe's scientific writings for the Weimar edition. Goethe's influence on Steiner's thought was enormous.

For the first half of his career, Steiner drew on the traditions of German Idealism, though he also owed a debt to Romanticism, particularly Novalis's Marian intuitions and communitarianism. Having been born into a working class family, Steiner, though an important intellectual, never lost his appreciation for the lives of the common folk and for what he called the "peasant wisdom." Indeed, he saw more wisdom in the peasantry than he did in the rampant materialism he found among intellectual elites, certainly a Romantic sensibility. Around the turn of the century, however, Steiner unexpectedly turned to Theosophy, the highly intellectually suspect occult movement founded by Helena Petrovna Blavatsky and H.S. Olcott, and at that time directed by Annie Besant and C.W. Leadbeater.

Why Steiner turned to Theosophy is not at all clear. He was not impressed with his first encounter with the movement, A.P. Sinnet's book *Esoteric Buddhism*. He found the table-rapping and sensationalism of the then-vogue spiritualism equally repellent. Steiner, it is true, claimed a kind of clairvoyance achieved through thinking[98] (and not through what he called "atavistic clairvoyance"), and his insights led him to affirm the truth of the Eastern

---

98 As Jonael Schickler has written, Steiner's "phenomenology of thinking lays a basis for understanding the clairvoyance which grows out of it." See Jonael Schickler, *Metaphysics as Christology: An Odyssey of the Self from Kant and Hegel to Steiner* (Aldershot, UK: Ashgate, 2005), 139.

notions of karma and reincarnation—ideas certainly central to the quasi-Buddhism/Hinduism of Theosophy. But Steiner was no quasi-Buddhist/Hindu. Indeed, central to his own system (which, subsequent to his break with the Theosophical Society, would later be named Anthroposophy) is what he called "the Event of Golgotha" and the Incarnation of Christ. As Jonael Schickler has written, for Steiner Christianity was not to be understood as one religion among others (certainly the view of Theosophy) "but as a universal and defining spiritual-natural event for humanity; in short as an event with a profound inner logic."[99] Steiner, that is, though an esoteric thinker, was a thoroughly Christian one. In that way, he had much to offer Theosophy. All Theosophy, a tremendously popular phenomenon at the time, had to offer Steiner was an audience receptive to his esoteric ideas.

Though he had grown up in a nominally Catholic household—and spoke feelingly about his time as an altar boy in his local parish—Steiner, a man of his time, in the early part of his career was uninterested in religious questions and had only a passing knowledge of the Bible and theology. However, he came to understand the Incarnation of Christ, culminating in the death and resurrection of Jesus, as the most important event not only in the history of the human race but in the history of the earth and cosmos as well. This understanding came gradually, but it came completely, as Steiner writes in his *Autobiography*:

> During the period when my statements about Christianity so contradicted my later ones in literal content, a conscious knowledge of true Christianity began to dawn within me. Around the turn of the century this knowledge grew deeper. . . . This experience culminated in my standing spiritually in the presence of the Mystery of Golgotha in a most inward, profound and solemn festival of knowledge.[100]

Elsewhere, Steiner speculates that had not things turned out as they did in his biography, he would have become a Cistercian

99 Jonael Schickler, *Metaphysics as Christology*, 146.
100 Rudolf Steiner, *An Autobiography*, trans. Rita Stebbing (Blauvelt, NY: Rudolf Steiner Publications, 1977), 319.

priest. "For in the town where I spent my youth," he told an audience in Arnhem, The Netherlands, on 18 July 1924,

> the *Gymnasium* was only a few steps away from the *Realschule* and it was by a hair's breadth that I went, not to the *Gymnasium* but to the *Realschule*. If, however, at that time I had gone to the *Gymnasium* in the town, I should have become a priest in the Cistercian Order. Of that there is no doubt whatever. For at this *Gymnasium* all the teachers were Cistercians. I was deeply attracted to all these priests, many of whom were extremely learned men. I read a great deal that they wrote and was profoundly stirred by it. I loved these priests and the only reason why I passed the Cistercian Order by was because I did not attend the *Gymnasium*.[101]

It is evident in his voluminous writing and lecture transcripts that Steiner, a man who every afternoon at three o'clock would stop whatever he was doing to say the Lord's Prayer in Latin, is ever mindful of Christ.[102] But he did not merely hold the reality of Christ as a personal truth. Rather, he held it to be a tremendously scientific, existential, ontological, and teleological reality. As he spoke in a lecture in 1922:

> Humankind must become increasingly "Christened," through and through. This, above all, is important—that what we experience only here on Earth, *as human beings with other human beings*, be carried through the gate of death by means of Christianity. This is a most essential truth.[103]

Though it was of a highly idiosyncratic character, Steiner held his Christianity very sincerely.

---

101 Rudolf Steiner, *Karmic Relationships, Volume VI: Esoteric Studies*, trans. E.H. Goddard, D.S. Osmond, and M. Kirkcaldy (1971; reprt. Forest Row, UK: Rudolf Steiner Press, 1989), 137.

102 Rudi Lissau, *Rudolf Steiner: Life, Work, Inner Path and Social Initiatives* (Wallbridge, UK: Hawthorn Press, 1987), 40. He also recommended that children in Waldorf schools begin the day with the Lord's Prayer. See *Faculty Meetings with Rudolf Steiner, 1919–1922, Volume I*, trans. Robert Lathe and Nancy Parsons Whittaker (Hudson, NY: Anthroposophic Press, 1998), 38.

103 Rudolf Steiner, *Isis Mary Sophia: Her Mission and Ours: Selected Lectures and Writings*, ed. Christopher Bamford (Herndon, VA: Steiner Books, 2003), 237. Steiner's emphasis.

My purpose here, however, is not to interrogate Steiner's religious views, but his contributions to sophiology. I find the "heresy-hunting" approach to scholarship distasteful. What interests me in Steiner is how his intuitions concerning Christ led him to further, sophiological intuitions concerning nature and its relationship to the supernatural. In this way, he is not unlike Boehme or Fludd, who also came to insights in the main unexamined or neglected (if not ridiculed and dismissed) by what might be described as the materialist, pure nature metanarrative so familiar to us that it constitutes almost the entirety of the intellectual environment which we inhabit here in the West. Even many Catholic scholars—thinkers who (ostensibly) believe in the Real Presence of Christ in the Eucharist—tend to favor a materialist, pure nature metanarrative when it comes to the hard sciences. Can a person who believes bread and wine become the very Son of God in the Eucharist maintain any kind of intellectual integrity by dismissing the possibility of the numinous outside of a very restricted and provincial sense of what is termed "religious"? The divine interplay of being is done a disservice when cordoned off in the theology building—whether it be the theology building of the campus or that of the mind.

Fundamental to an understanding of Steiner's sophiological intuitions are the ideas he explores in a series of lectures given in Berlin between 6 February and 20 March, 1917 and published in English under the title *Cosmic and Human Metamorphoses*. Steiner, always mindful of the rhythms of human and cosmic life (the rhythms of the day, the seasons; the movements of the sun, moon, planets, and stars; the rhythms of aging, of human history), draws his audience's attention to three rhythms he connects to the "principles" of the Father, the Son, and the Spirit. It is not, however, always clear when Steiner speaks metaphorically and when he speaks literally. It may be that, like Novalis, he did not care for such distinctions, thinking them artificial and arising from the same binary way of thinking that paved the way for Cartesian dualism and materialism.[104]

---

104. As Christopher Bamford, editor and publisher of Steiner Books, in an extended form of his interview for Jonathan Stedall's documentary, *The*

In the lectures, Steiner first speaks of what he calls the possibility for three meetings each human person can—and does—experience with the Father, Son, and Spirit quite naturally and not necessarily connected to religious observance. He does not suggest that these meetings replace religious observance, but only that they occur as a natural occurrence of living a natural human life. That is, for Steiner, the Father, Son, and the Spirit are intimately and simultaneously intertwined with the cosmos and the human person. Christianity, therefore, is not merely a religion. Rather, Christianity is a biographical, physiological, and cosmological reality, a principle of the universe.

The first meeting, that with the Spirit, according to Steiner takes place in the rhythm of sleeping and waking. It is a daily rhythm and, in Steiner's understanding, the human soul meets the Spirit through the agency of the guardian angel (the "genius" is Steiner's term). He attends particularly to the ways in which materialism compromises and encroaches upon this meeting (and all of the meetings) and how a closer relationship to the natural world is more conducive to facilitating the meeting and its effects:

> [The first meeting] takes place quite simply in normal sleep, on almost every occasion, between sleeping and waking. With simple country people, who are nearer to the life of nature, and who go to bed with the setting of the sun and get up at sunrise, this meeting takes place in the middle of their sleeping time, which as a rule is the middle of the night. With people who have detached themselves from their connections with nature, this is not so much the case. . . . It all depends on whether the soul is refined enough, sufficiently acquainted with its inner life, to be able to observe these. This meeting with the genius is brought to the consciousness of every man in some form or other; but the materialistic surroundings of the present day which fill the mind with ideas coming from the materialistic view of the world and especially the life of today,

---

Challenge of Rudolf Steiner, observes, discerning metaphor and literal meaning in Steiner is clearly a matter of interpretation, something with which one struggles to come to terms. See "Christopher Bamford interviewed for the film *The Challenge of Rudolf Steiner*," www.youtube.com, at about 40:50.

permeated as it is by materialistic opinions, prevent the soul from paying attention to what comes as the result of the meeting.[105]

Steiner describes the second meeting in terms of the Son, an encounter with Christ. He sees this meeting unfolding over the course of an earthly year, and particularly in the way in which the cycle of the seasons meshes with the Christian year—from the fixed feast Christmas to the movable feast Easter, the fixed feast of St. John's Day to the movable feasts of Ascension and Pentecost. The relation between the natural realities of the earthly realm and the supernatural realities inherent in Christ's incarnation as reflected in the Church year is of paramount importance for Steiner. For Steiner, since Christ is "the directing and guiding principle" of the cosmos and that "through the Mystery of Golgotha, that Being whom we designate as the Christ has united Himself with the course of the Earth" it only makes sense to conclude that "in the course of a year, a man really goes through a rhythm which imitates that of the seasons of the year, in which he has a meeting and a union with the world of the Son."[106]

Finally, the human soul, in Steiner's exposition, arrives at an experience with the Father through the rhythm of "the patriarchal life of seventy years," particularly between the ages of twenty-eight and forty-two.[107] Unfortunately, the consciousness of this meeting is lacking for most people. Steiner is aware of this and offers a remedy:

> During a certain period of our life—the period of preparation—education ought, in the many different ways this can be done, to make the meeting with the Father-Principle as profound an experience as possible. One way is to arouse in a man, during his years of education, a strong feeling of the glory of the world, of its greatness, and of the sublimity of the world-process. We are withholding a great deal from the growing boy or girl if we fail to draw their

105 Rudolf Steiner, *Cosmic and Human Metamorphoses* (1926; reprt., Blauvelt, NY: Spiritual Research Editions, 1989), 25.

106 Rudolf Steiner, *Cosmic and Human Metamorphoses*, 63.

107 For those who die before this time, according to Steiner, the encounter comes at the moment of death. Rudolf Steiner, *Cosmic and Human Metamorphoses*, 29.

attention to all the revelations of beauty and greatness in the world, for then, instead of having a devoted reverence and respect for these, they may pass them by unobserved.[108]

This notion of reverence, which he had certainly found confirmed in Goethe, would become an important aspect of Waldorf education, still two years away from being established when Steiner gave this lecture.

The question, of course, is: is all this true? But perhaps that is the wrong question. Do we ask if a fairy tale is true, a poem, a painting? Is it not the case that with fairy tales and poetry and art that while they may or may not be "historically true" it is better to say that *there is truth in them*? I cannot prove—or disprove—that what Steiner says here is true. But what he says regarding these three meetings does provide us with a more fulfilling way to live a human life. Mindfulness that the numinous inheres and interacts with every aspect of human life and with the nature is a far more healthy way to engage the world than the deadened picture of the nature we have inherited from pure nature theology and its disastrous consequences. This holistic worldview, characterized by an assumption of God's presence and activity in the natural world, also argues for a deeper ecology than that we typically find in postmodern cultures. What Steiner articulates here is an essentially sophianic understanding of world process.

The curious thing, however, is that most of Steiner's explicit references to Sophia in his lectures are utterly disappointing. Early in what we could call his "esoteric career," Steiner, to his detriment, spoke in the language of the Theosophists and couched his discussions of Sophia in terms of occult correspondences and quasi-Gnostic revivalism. In 1908, for example, he spoke of the Virgin Sophia as "the purified astral body" and in 1913 in terms of Valentianian Gnosticism's Sophia as a cosmic being in captivity.[109] He also speaks of Sophia in relationship to the Egyptian goddess Isis in language clearly inspired by Novalis, and does so in the light of considering Raphael's *Sistine Madonna*,

---

108 Rudolf Steiner, *Cosmic and Human Metamorphoses*, 28.
109 Rudolf Steiner, *Isis Mary Sophia*, 74 and 186–7.

drawing a further line of contact with the Romantic poet.[110] Despite these derivative and not-very-convincing repackaged thoughts on Sophia, Steiner's work is nevertheless profoundly sophiological, and this is the case especially in the practical realms of education, agriculture, medicine, and economics.

Had he died before World War I, Steiner would probably be remembered primarily as the leader of an obscure offshoot of the Theosophical Society and for designing the first Goetheanum, his fascinating yet idiosyncratic contribution to the architecture of German Expressionism.[111] But he didn't die before World War I. Following the War, faced with the cultural, economic, and spiritual devastation that ravaged Europe, he almost singlehandedly introduced innovation after innovation into the realms of medicine, agriculture, education, economics, and the arts. He worked tirelessly—and probably worked himself, literally, to death—as he prepared the way for a profound regeneration of a holistic, multifaceted, integrated understanding of the relationship between the natural and supernatural orders. And, unlike many of his wilder intuitions concerning cosmology and esoteric Christianity, they were extraordinarily practical.

Interestingly, even these innovations would never have come about had Steiner not been asked to help with a variety of problems posed to him by concerned individuals in the wake of Europe's devastation. He seems to have never turned anyone down. When Emil Molt, owner of the Waldorf Cigarette factory, asked him to develop a system of education for the children of his workers, Steiner gave him—and the world—what has become known as Waldorf (or Steiner) Education, a remarkable system with schools now on every continent with the exception of Antarctica. In Waldorf schools, the arts imbue each subject and a profound sense of reverence (and joy) permeates each school day. Prayer and reverence are exceedingly important pedagogical tools

110 Ibid., 205.

111 An informative article on Steiner's contributions to architecture is David Adams, "Rudolf Steiner's First Goetheanum as an Illustration of Organic Functionalism," *Journal of the Society of Architectural Historians* 51, no. 2 (June 1992): 182–204.

for Steiner: "When you teach, you must bring the children into a prayerful attitude, beginning with the lowest grades. You need to slowly develop a strongly prayerful attitude in the children. Children need to find the mood of prayer. We need to carry out 'Not my will, but thine be done.' We must raise the children into divine experience."[112] In this spirit, Steiner wrote what he preferred to think of as "verses" (he expressly emphasized that they are *not* to be called "prayers")[113] which students in every Waldorf school recite at the beginning of each school day. They are beautiful meditations, reminders of what education is actually supposed to be about:

Verse for Grades 1–4

The Sun with loving light
Makes bright for me each day;
The soul with spirit power
Gives strength unto my limbs;
In sunlight shining clear
I reverence, O God,
The strength of humankind
Which thou so graciously
Hath planted in my soul
That I with all my might
May love to work and learn:
From Thee stream light and strength;
To Thee rise love and thanks.

Verse for Grades 5–12

I look into the world
Wherein there shines the Sun
Wherein there gleam the stars
Wherein there lie the stones;
Wherein the plants do live and grow,
The beasts do feel and move;
And man to spirit gives
A dwelling in his soul.

112 *Faculty Meetings with Rudolf Steiner,* 367.
113 "Never call a verse a prayer, call it an opening verse before school." Ibid., 20.

I look into the soul
That lives and moves in me:
God's spirit lives and weaves
In light of sun and soul,
In heights of worlds without,
In depths of soul within.
To Thee, o Spirit of God,
I turn myself in prayer,
That strength and grace and skill
For learning and for work
May live and grow in me.

As Heiner Ullrich has cogently observed, and as these verses illustrate, "Waldorf schools represented the first successful attempt at overcoming Enlightenment intellectualism in the German school system."[114] Indeed, I have often found myself perplexed that so many aspects of Catholic education, from the pre-kindergarten through college and university levels and even touching catechesis—and I've been through them all—are still so resolutely bound to the assumptions of Enlightenment pedagogy.

Likewise, when asked by Count Carl von Keyserlingk in 1924 to share his insights into agriculture at a conference in Koberwitz, Germany (now Kobierzyce, Poland) Steiner provided the Count and his fellow farmers with a series of eight lectures that laid the groundwork for what is now known as Biodynamic agriculture. Steiner's agricultural indications—as with all of his work—center on treating the matter at hand holistically, considering quality as well as quantity, form as well as force, spirit as well as matter. The farm, for Steiner, is an organism, a totality, and needs to be considered as such. That is, the farm should have animals, garden and field crops, bees and orchards, a water source, woods, and function without the spiritual and physical degradation brought on by the use of pesticides, herbicides, and antibiotics. Instead of chemicals, Steiner prescribed a set of "preparations" to be sprayed on crops or inserted into compost piles as substances intended to "enliven" the

114 Heiner Ullrich, *Rudolf Steiner*, trans. Janet Duke and Daniel Balestrini, Continuum Library of Educational Thought 11 (London: Continuum, 2008), 156.

soil and thus bring health and fecundity to not only the farm as an organism but to the food and animals raised on the farm as well. Some of the preparations—cow manure buried in the earth in a cow horn for six month, for instance, or yarrow flowers fermented in a stag's bladder in the sun for the summer and then buried in the earth for the winter—sound a bit unusual to say the least. Steiner was well aware of this, but held that his method is sound and that farmers would "get it." As he says in the agriculture course:

> What would result if our non-farmer friends now began to pass these things on, as a fresh and interesting chapter of anthroposophical teaching? The result would be what has occurred with many of our lecture-cycles. Others—including farmers—would begin to hear of these things from this and that quarter. As to the farmers—well, if they hear of these things from a fellow-farmer, they will say, "What a pity he has suddenly gone crazy!" Yes, they may say it the first time and the second time. But eventually—when the farmer sees a really good result, he will not feel a very easy conscience in rejecting it outright.[115]

In the past two decades, in fact, Biodynamic agriculture has revolutionized viticulture, rehabilitating the wine industry and vast acres of vineyard with its holistic approach to farming.[116]

Steiner, one of the pioneers of the organic movement, was also amazingly prescient about what would happen if beekeepers continued to feed their bees artificially, to treat their bees with chemicals, and work with the bee colony as one would any machine with replaceable parts (the practice of "requeening," for instance). Such a methodology, he said, would have dire circumstances:

> There is no way, based on the current situation with the artificial methods used in feeding and breeding bees, to predict what the significance of these procedures will mean for the future fifty or sixty years, or even a century from now. . . . Today [1923] it is impossible to object in any way to the artificial methods applied in beekeeping. This is because we live in social conditions that do not allow

115 Rudolf Steiner, *Agriculture: A Course of Eight Lectures*, trans. George Adams (1958; reprt., London: Rudolf Steiner House, 1974), 150.

116 See, for example, Mrill Ingram, "Biology and Beyond: The Science of 'Back to Nature' Farming in the United States," *Annals of the Association of American Geographers* 97, no. 2 (Jun 2007): 298–312, at 307.

anything else to be done. Nevertheless, it is important to gain this insight—that it is one matter if you let nature take its course and only help to steer it in the right direction when necessary, but it is entirely another matter if you apply artificial methods to speed things along. But I really don't want to take a strong position against what Mr. Müller [a beekeeper] has stated. It is quite correct that we can't determine these matters today; it will have to be delayed until a later time. Let's talk to each other again in one hundred years, Mr. Müller; then we'll see what kind of opinion you'll have at that point. This is something that can't be decided today.[117]

Faced with the ravages of pesticides, colony collapse disorder, varroa mites, and the very real possibility of the mass extinction of bees, it is not difficult to think what Mr. Müller would have to say today were he alive. As one observer has remarked, "For a 'crank,' some of Steiner's ideas seem remarkably persistent."[118]

These examples suffice, I think, to illustrate Steiner's implicitly sophianic epistemology, despite his (rather disappointing) explicitly gnostic pronouncements on Sophia. Steiner's worldview is saturated by a holistic ethos, one that is simultaneously conscious of the chemical, biological, and cosmological workings of nature and of the action of the divine working through them. Most people of faith, of course, would attest to God's presence in his handiwork, but for them this is typically a matter of belief. For Steiner, it is a scientifically verifiable fact, which is why he called his method "spiritual science." He refused to bow to the mechanistic and materialistic philosophy and science of his day, again and again upholding the truth that the supernatural is in constant commerce with the natural and that we can, indeed, perceive this living dynamic if only we train ourselves to perceive it. Like Blake, Steiner believed that "We who dwell on Earth can do nothing of ourselves, every thing is conducted by Spirits, no less than Digestion or Sleep."[119] But our inclination—is it not?—is to dismiss both Steiner and Blake as "cranks," even if we happen to be persons of faith. This is

117 Rudolf Steiner, *Bees*, trans. Thomas Braatz (Great Barrington, MA: Anthroposophic Press, 1998), 74–5.

118 Stephen Skelton, *Viticulture: An Introduction to Commercial Grape Growing for Wine Production* (London: SP Skelton, 2007), 197.

119 William Blake, *Jerusalem*, 3 (145).

a result, I contend, not of Steiner's or Blake's delusion, but of our, unconscious for the most part, assimilation of the mechanistic and materialistic commitments of Enlightenment rationality. This is not to say that science, in and of itself, is a wholly mechanistic, materialistic project. Goethe and Steiner certainly would not have conceded as much. Nor would quantum physics. But the temptation to Enlightenment-inspired, binary thinking so prevalent in our own culture would have us believe so. As Andrew Welburn has observed, "Science becomes materialistic, not when it seeks to understand the laws or regularities in nature, but when it comes to regard things, beings and people as only a product of regularities, only real in so far as they can be manipulated by control of their predictable behavior."[120] Clearly, as the thinkers I have examined in this chapter would argue, science, as long as it ignores spiritual realities and maintains an incomplete picture of the world and its processes, has yet to rise to its true vocation.

The sophiological intuition, as we have seen now in Fludd as well as the Romantics and Steiner, demands that we question this commitment to Enlightenment science and philosophies. It also compels us to reconfigure our understanding of the roles of art and faith in the striving for a worldview that encompasses—and affirms—the living, breathing dynamic between natural and supernatural realities. The Romantics, especially Goethe and Novalis, succeeded in the theoretical realm: they brought forth beautiful notions and sentiments in their attempts to reaffirm the role of the human being in an increasingly technological and oppressively rationalistic world, and Goethe's "soft empiricism" offered a method of contemplative inquiry. They failed, however, by their inability to show how their ideas might have some practical application in the world. Steiner, on the other hand, at least to some degree, succeeded in his project for cultural renewal, since he was able to put his ideas into practice. Steiner and the Romantics continue to provide a countermovement to the nominalist, materialist, and technological triumphalism we face in the early twenty-first century. They still speak to us.

120 Andrew Welburn, *Rudolf Steiner's Philosophy and the Crisis of Contemporary Thought* (Edinburgh, UK: Floris Books, 2004), 66–7.

Chapter Five

Russian Sophiology:
Poetics and the Agon with Reason

*She has come down to earth not for the first time
But crowding round her for the first time
Are her new heroes and champions…
And strange is the gleam of her deep eyes…*
          ⌒Alexander Blok[1]

*To representatives of the clergy Christianity had long become a matter of
everyday prose, whereas those who were in search of a new Christianity
wanted it to be poetry.*   ⌒Nikolai Berdyaev[2]

THE SEVENTEENTH CENTURY, as we have seen, marks an important watershed in the development of Western culture. The scientific revolution, impelled by Cartesian metaphysics, Baconian empiricism, and Hobbesian pessimism, challenged cultural assumptions about God's activity in the world and called into question the place of the human person in the cosmos. This resulted in what has been called "the exile of God" and an existential crisis for persons disenfranchised from a cosmic order grown foreign and increasingly "other." However, this was the same period in which Boehme's works began to circulate in various editions and translations, offering a counter narrative to the often cold and alienating conclusions of early modern scientism. Similarly, as we have seen, the Rosicrucian impulse as promoted

---

1 *Verses about the Beautiful Lady* 17, in *Poems of Sophia* by Alexander Blok, trans. and ed. Boris Jakim (Kettering, OH: Semantron Press, 2014), lines 9–12.
2 Nikolai Berdyaev, *The Russian Idea*, trans. R.M. French (1947; reprt. Hudson, NY: Lindisfarne Press, 1992), 241.

by Robert Fludd, Michael Maier, Thomas Vaughan and (a few) others also cautioned against adopting the new epistemologies void of an integral view of human and divine involvement with the cosmos. Nevertheless, it was scientism (along with the parallel cultural phenomena of materialism and Deism) that was ascendant. The ideas of Boehme, Fludd, Maier, Vaughan, and their ilk were soon dispatched to the sidelines of the master culture, dismissed as curiosities if not worse. As the intervening centuries have proved, religious belief itself would eventually be invited to follow.

The ideas of Boehme and his Rosicrucian compatriots may have been sidelined, but they were by no means eradicated. Indeed, they found their way into streams of esoteric Christianity which maintained a vibrant following, if small in numbers, well into the postmodern era. This was certainly the case with Steiner in the 20th century, but the Behmenist-Rosicrucian ethos was also fundamental to the thought of the impresario behind the legendary Salon Rose+Croix, the French writer and art critic Joséphin Péladan (1858–1918), as well as central to the philosophies of the esotericists Martinez de Pasqually (c. 1727–1774) and Louis-Claude de Saint-Martin (1743–1803). But these Behmenist and Rosicrucian permutations of much earlier religious sensibilities did not only influence esoteric, albeit often heterodox, believers. They also touched the religious mainstream.

Indeed, especially in the case of Boehme, esoteric Christian approaches influenced mainstream religious currents in the two centuries following the German mystic's death. Boehme's influence on the Anglican priest and non-juror William Law (1686–1761) is well attested, as is the debt owed Boehme by the German Catholic philosopher and theologian Franz von Baader (1765–1841). Arguably, though, Boehme's ideas were nowhere as influential as in Orthodox Russia. But that is not to say they were introduced to Russian religious life without stirring up a significant amount of controversy in the process.

In this chapter, I will argue that the Russian manifestation of sophiology in the late 19th and early 20th centuries illuminates the problems inherent when the sophianic intuition is forced into the parameters of formal, dogmatic theology. Sophia, as we have seen, inhabits a metaxological space characterized by poesis and intuition, theology and logic joined to a capacity to read from the books of both scripture and nature. Sophianic insight—though always informed by scripture, liturgy, and the traditions of the Church—is arrived at experientially, mystically, artistically and, as such, proves an uncomfortable fit in the strictures of theological examination. Furthermore, Sophia, I will show, points to the limits of theology, especially what I have called earlier the "left-brain" theology of the schools or what Hans Urs von Balthasar has accurately described as "theology at the desk," a method of religious inquiry juxtaposed to both mystical theology and "theology at prayer."[3] This horizon provides us with new possibilities of belief, compelling us to reexamine our traditions and received wisdom, not with a goal of transcending or abolishing them, but, by way of the phenomenological disclosure of the horizon itself, strengthening and renewing them. The gesture is one of illumination; it cannot be achieved from the vantage point of one's desk.

A Sophianic Seedbed

In 17th-century Russia, a new service found its way into the liturgical literature of the Russian Orthodox Church. *The Office of Sophia, Wisdom of God* was composed by the lay Muscovite theologian Prince Simeon Shachovskoy.[4] Essentially a meditation on Sophia in a variety of aspects—as the Theotokos, as the glorified Church, as the salvation of all men, as Christ, as creative power—the service was composed for use on August 15, the Feast of the Dormition (Assumption), and reputedly has as its inspiration the famous Novgorod icon of Sophia. The Russian Church,

---

3 Hans Urs von Balthasar, "Theology and Sanctity" in *Explorations in Theology*, vol. 1, trans. A.V. Littledale and Alexander Dru (San Francisco: Ignatius Press, 1989), 208.

4 See in particular T. Spasskij, "L'Office liturgique slave de la 'Sagasse de Dieu,'" *Irénikon* 30 (1957): 164–88. An English translation of the service, unfortunately, is not currently available in English. However, in his *The Pillar and Ground of Truth: An Essay in Orthodox Theodicy in Twelve Letters,* trans. Boris Jakim (Princeton, NJ: Princeton University Press, 1997), Florensky quotes from the Office on page 281 and discusses it in note 713.

taking as its model the extraordinary church of Hagia Sophia in Constantinople, had a history of naming churches in honor of Holy Wisdom and likewise was home to an iconographic tradition depicting Sophia personified as a winged figure characterized by a fiery luminescence. The service was revised by two Greek theologians, the brothers Ioannikios and Sophronios Likhoudes, in an attempt to bring the text more into conformity with the Church's traditional association of Sophia with Christ, but neither edition was ever officially included in the Menaion of the Russian Church.[5]

Though the proliferation of Sophia icons and churches in Russia certainly provided ample warrant for composing such a service, the timing is more than a little interesting. And here, again, the name of Jacob Boehme appears. Boehme's German works began to be published in the early 17th century and they were soon translated into other languages, particularly gaining a foothold in England due to the relaxed censorship laws during the Civil War. Manuscript copies of Boehme circulated throughout Europe—including Russia—though it would not be until the early 19th century that the cultural atmosphere would be ripe for issuing an edition of Boehme in Russian without fear of reprisal. Such danger was very real. A Behmenist circle existed in Moscow in the 1670s and 1680s under the leadership of the merchant Konrad Norderman; and in 1689 Quirinus Kuhlman, a Silesian Behmenist with ties to the Philadelphian Society in England, arrived in Moscow to spread Boehme's ideas. Both Norderman and Kuhlman, unfortunately, burned as heretics in Red Square on 4 October 1689 for promulgating those same ideas.[6] Nevertheless, Behmenist and Pietist spirituality eventually infiltrated even some quarters of Russian Orthodox theology, particularly in the seminaries of Ukraine, and by the mid-18th-century aspects of

---

5 John Meyendorff, "Wisdom-Sophia: Contrasting Approaches to a Complex Theme," *Dumbarton Oaks Papers* 41, Studies on Art and Archaeology in Honor of Ernst Kitzinger on His Seventy-Fifth Birthday (1987): 391–401, at 400.

6 Zdenek V. David, "The Influence of Jacob Boehme on Russian Religious Thought," *Slavic Review* 21, no. 1 (Mar 1962): 43–64, at 46.

Boehme's thought could be detected in the writings of Metropolitan Platon Levshin (1737–1812), Saint Tikhon of Zadonsk (1724–1783), and the poet, philosopher, and composer Gregory Skovoroda (1722–1794).[7] While *The Office of Sophia, Wisdom of God* does not mention Boehme by name (not that it would), the liquidity of the attributions of Sophia in the text clearly echoes the same religious aesthetic found in Boehme. This liquidity would become a characteristic of what would develop into the theology of what is now known as Russian sophiology; though, as we shall see, calling Russian sophiology "theology" is not without its problems.

The intimations of sophiology found in Russian ecclesial traditions and iconography invigorated by Boehme's sophianic sensibilities as they filtered into Russia prepared a seedbed for the incredible growth of sophiology in Russian philosophical and theological circles from the late nineteenth and through the twentieth century. Indeed, Orthodox theology continues to wrestle with questions posed by sophiology. Sophiology challenges the Eastern Church, anchored as it is in Holy Tradition and the teachings of the Fathers, and demands that theologians reconsider these traditions and teachings in the light of Sophia, a development as much a retrieval as it is an innovation.

Vladimir Solovyov

Though some idealistic scholars like to trace Russian sophiology to the existence of the traditions of sophianic iconography and naming churches in honor of Holy Wisdom, Russian sophiology proper begins with the philosopher, literary critic, poet, and lay theologian Vladimir Solovyov (1853–1900), though it is perhaps more accurate to say that his is the first of the Russian *sophiologies*. In Solovyov, all of the subsequent problems and possibilities of sophiology first find utterance. Without his voice, Sophia would have remained an esoteric sidebar to Western religious history, one characterized by Gnostic exoticism and the specialized interests of

7 Zdenek V. David, "The Influence of Jacob Boehme," 48–9.

the sporadic enthusiasts for Boehme's ideas. Solovyov brought Sophia and the problems of sophiology into the Church and compelled theologians—first in Russia but later in the Western Church as well—to take seriously the problematics of the Wisdom of God. Solovyov's sophiology is dynamic and plastic, possessing qualities logical and systematic as well as intuitive and aesthetic. This no doubt accounts for its difficulty.

Solovyov's sophiology—and this seems to be consistent with the sophiologies of his inheritors Pavel Florensky and Sergius Bulgakov—begins with a series of religious experiences, the first of which occurred on the Feast of the Ascension, May 1862, when the philosopher was nine years old.[8] During Divine Liturgy in the Chapel of St Tatyana at the University of Moscow, the congregation chanted the cherubikon: "Let us, who mystically represent the Cherubim, bringing the thrice-holy hymn to the life-creating Trinity, set aside all earthly care." As the deacon censed the church and the faithful, young Volodinka (the diminutive used by his family) fell into a swoon. The people disappeared. The hymn, like the music in dreams, fell below the threshold of his awareness. A woman of extraordinary beauty appeared holding a blue flower. She smiled and was gone.[9] Like the child visionaries of Fatima, Solovyov described a being of incredible beauty. Unlike them, he fell into a period of virulent atheism from the ages of thirteen to eighteen.

Following his foray into denial and atheism, Solovyov returned to belief. At university, he studied sciences before switching to

---

8 The story of Solovyov's visions of his Eternal Friend is oft repeated. See his nephew, Fr. Sergey M. Solovyov's account, *Vladimir Solovyov: His Life and Creative Evolution*, trans. Aleksey Gibson (Fairfax, VA: Eastern Christian Publications, 2000), 35–6 and 129–36; Paul M. Allen, *Vladimir Soloviev: Russian Mystic* (Blauvelt, NY: Steiner, 1978), 23–8 and 109–119.

9 Sergey M. Solovyov (35) reports that his uncle's first vision of Sophia was on the Feast of the Ascension in 1862, as does Paul Allen in *Vladimir Soloviev: Russian Mystic*, 23. The story is beautifully rendered in Solovyov's poem, "Three Meetings." See Boris Jakim's exquisite translation in Vladimir Solovyov, *Sophia, God, & a Short Tale about Antichrist: Also Including At the Dawn of Mist-Shrouded Youth* (Kettering, OH: Semantron Press, 2014).

arts, taking his degrees in philosophy. He also studied at the Moscow Religious Academy. Mindful of his experience of the Eternal Friend he had had as a child, Solovyov began to study all he could of Sophia. This brought the young philosopher to Swedenborg, to Boehme, to Baader, and to Gnosticism.[10] Solovyov's syncretistic manner of entertaining a diverse body of opinion and doctrine led the thinker to considerations of occultism, Hermeticsm, and kabbalah regarding Sophia. Hans Urs von Balthasar describes Solovyov's foray into such dangerous theological territory in this way:

> Because in reading all these and many others he fully appropriates them for himself, the muddy stream runs through him as if through a purifying agent and is distilled in crystal-clear, disinfected waters, answering the needs of his own philosophical spirit, which (in contrast to that of so many of his speculative compatriots) can live and breathe only in an atmosphere of unqualified transparency and intelligibility.[11]

In the course of his research, Solovyov undertook a trip to London to make use of manuscripts concerning Gnosticism and kabbalah in the British Museum. There he once again was granted a vision of his Eternal Friend who told him to meet her in Egypt. Solovyov obeyed, boarded a ship for Cairo, and then beheld her once more in the desert. He recorded these experiences with her in his autobiographical poem, "Three Meetings," though he never describes her by name: "eternal beloved, I will not name you, / But my tremulous song will reach your ears."[12]

Solovyov's poetic, intuitive, experiential Sophia, however, represents only one aspect of his sophiology and, as many have noticed, it is easy to read Solovyov as a sort of split personality, "critical ana-

10 For a thorough overview of Solovyov's "occult" sources, or at least those from beyond accepted Christian traditions, see Kristi A. Groberg, "The Feminine Occult Sophia in the Russian Religious Renaissance: A Bibliographic Essay," *Canadian-American Slavic Studies*, 26: 1–3 (1992): 197–240.

11 Hans Urs von Balthasar, *The Glory of the Lord: A Theological Aesthetics, Volume III: Studies in Theological Styles: Lay Styles*, trans. Andrew Louth, et al. (San Francisco: Ignatius Press, 1986), 292.

12 Vladimir Solovyov, "Three Meetings," in *Sophia, God, and a Short Tale about Antichrist*, lines 3–4.

lyst by day, visionary poet by night."[13] Bulgakov, who followed Solovyov's sophiology in so many other ways, nevertheless distanced himself from the latter trait, which he viewed suspiciously. While Bulgakov recognizes that Solovyov's philosophical and theological works concerning Sophia are "undoubtedly syncretistic," bearing elements derived from Gnosticism, Boehme and elsewhere, it is the sophiology in the poetry that really disturbs him. "In his poetry," Bulgakov writes, "Solovyov is indeed very far from the Orthodox conception of Sophia"[14]—a charge that would later come back to haunt Bulgakov when he defended his own sophiology from charges of heresy. Tellingly, prior to his ordination Bulgakov's feelings about Solovyov's philosophical writings as opposed to his verse were reversed. In his essay "The Poetry of Vladimir Solovyov" (1915), for example, Bulgakov had written that "it is becoming more and more evident that, in Solovyov's multistoried, intricate, and complex work, only the poetry is absolutely authentic, so that his philosophy can and must be checked against the poetry."[15] Despite Bulgakov's late misgivings about Solovyov's poetic intuitions of Sophia, he is not above acknowledging the thinker as his "philosophical 'guide to Christ'" as Bulgakov moved from his earlier Marxist and materialist worldview and toward the Orthodox Church and the priesthood.[16] Bulgakov, called by many the most important Orthodox theologian of the 20th century, was nevertheless censured by the Russian Orthodox hierarchy for his sophiology. We can read in his late-realized discomfort with Solovyov, then, a desire to appear congenial to Church discipline. It is not a very convincing performance.

Solovyov's theological and philosophical works treating Sophia are notorious for their conceptual fluidity and lack of a coherent

---

13 George M. Young, *The Russian Cosmists: The Esoteric Futurism of Nikolai Federov and His Followers* (Oxford: Oxford University Press, 2012), 96.

14 Sergei Bulgakov, *Sophia, the Wisdom of God: An Outline of Sophiology*, trans. Patrick Thompson, O. Fielding Clarke, and Xenia Braikevitc, revised (Hudson, NY: Lindisfarne Press, 1993), 9.

15 Sergius Bulgakov, "The Poetry of Vladimir Solovyov" in *The Religious Poetry of Vladimir Solovyov*, 154–8, at 155.

16 Sergei Bulgakov, *Sophia, the Wisdom of God*, 10.

center. In *Lectures on Divine Humanity* (1878–1881), for instance, he describes Sophia as "God's body, the matter of Divinity" which unites to the Logos in the divinization of the world.[17] However, in the same lecture cycle he also describes Sophia as "ideal or perfect humanity, eternally contained in the integral divine being, or Christ."[18] In *Russia and the Universal Church* (1889) he calls Sophia "the guardian angel of the world" and the agent of "pan-unity," another of Solovyov's key philosophical/theological insights.[19] Furthermore, he connects Sophia to Christ, the Virgin Mary, and to the Church. The language he uses to limn this is startling, as if words alone cannot contain the concept. Here is a particular example:

> [mankind's] reunion with God, though necessarily threefold, nevertheless constitutes only a single divine-human being, the incarnate Σοφία, whose central and completely personal manifestation is Jesus Christ, whose feminine complement is the Blessed Virgin, and whose universal extension is the Church.[20]

Throughout his life, Solovyov continued to refine his attempts to define Sophia. In his lecture on Auguste Comte (1898), for instance, he says,

> Sophia, the divine Wisdom, approximates now to Christ, now to Our Lady, thus not admitting of complete identification either with Him or with Her. . . . This great, royal and feminine Being, which is not God, not the eternal Son of God, not an angel, not a saint . . . is no other than the true, pure, and perfect humanity, the

---

17 Vladimir Solovyov *Lectures on Divine Humanity*, 108.

18 Ibid., 113.

19 Vladimir Solovyev, *Russia and the Universal Church*, trans. Herbert Rees (London: Geoffrey Bles, 1948), 167. Florensky, for one, even though he follows Solovyov in many regards, criticized this concept of Solovyov's as a badly veiled pantheism. On this point, he writes, "Our entire work, in its antinomian spirit opposes Solovyov's conciliatory philosophy." See *Pillar and Ground of the Truth*, 433. It may be that, like Bulgakov following his own ordination, Florensky was anxious to prove his doctrinal orthodoxy by distancing himself from Solovyov in a rather Oedipal gesture.

20 Vladimir Solovyov, *Russia and the Universal Church*, 176.

highest and all-embracing form and the living soul of nature and of the universe, united to God from all eternity and in the temporal process attaining union with Him and uniting to Him all that is.[21]

It is difficult to ascertain what Solovyov means here by "approximates." It seems that in statements such as these—and he makes a number of them—Solovyov the philosopher is subsumed by Solovyov the mystic.

And perhaps that is how it should be. Simon Frank, for one, argues that Solovyov never succeeded in elucidating his ideas about Sophia because "the task he set himself is essentially unrealizable":

> The difficulty lies, in the last resort, in the impossibility of explaining in rational and logical terms the relation between the Creator and the creature. Our apprehension of it must inevitably remain mystical, i.e. metalogical, and can only be expressed in categories that belong to the realm of the "unity of opposites."[22]

For this reason, Frank believes that the attempts to "rationalize" and systematize the idea of Sophia assayed by Fathers Bulgakov and Florensky "also fail to achieve their purpose in spite of all their subtlety."[23] This is an idea to which we shall return.

Philosopher William Desmond, who reads Solovyov's concept of "All-unity" as essential to an understanding of the Russian's conception of Sophia, poses another sort of question. "Does not the formulation of such a doctrine," Desmond asks, "testify to a power *between* God as the ultimate other and the finite between as the milieu wherein the community of the human and the divine is coming to be? Is not the doctrine of Sophia a pointer to a *middle between* utter transcendence and an otherwise godless immanence?"[24] Sophia, then, is for Solovyov the conduit between God

---

21 Vladimir Solovyov, *A Solovyov Anthology,* ed. S.L. Frank, trans. Nathalie Duddington (1950; repr., Westport, CT: Greenwood Press, 1974), 57–8.

22 S.L. Frank, Introduction to *Solovyov Anthology,* 12–3.

23 Ibid., 12; note 1.

24 William Desmond, *Is There a Sabbath for Thought?: Between Religion and Philosophy*, Perspectives in Continental Philosophy 45 (New York: Fordham University Press, 2005), 181.

and man, between supernature and nature, the vessel of the arrival of the Immanuel, the God-is-with-us. This despite the ascendance of scientific materialism and the coldness of its culture:

> No longer do kings look up at the sky
> And shepherds do not listen in the desert
> To the angels speaking about God.[25]

This metaxological aspect of Sophia is essential to understanding Solovyov's religious philosophy.

Solovyov's doctrine of Sophia, not surprisingly, has more often than not brought out some of the worst qualities of theologians. As David Bentley Hart observes, "The figure of Sophia, admittedly, arouses more than a little suspicion among even Solovyov's more indulgent Christian readers, and some would prefer to write her off as a figment of the young Solovyov's dreamier moods, or as a sentimental souvenir of his youthful dalliance with the Gnostics. To his less indulgent readers, she is something rather more sinister."[26] Solovyov has been accused of trying to introduce a fourth hypostasis into the dogma of the Trinity, of Gnosticism, and of occultism. As A.V. Kartashov, writes,

> The mystical horse on which Solovyov flies over the formidable abyss that exists between God and the world is the long-deserted and forgotten Sophia. Repeating thousand-year-old ancient attempts of the Hellenic philosophy, the biblical hokism, the rabbinical Cabala, and the wild Gnostic science-fiction writings, to fill by illusion the abyss between the Creator and His creatures, Solovyov chooses for this purpose . . . Sofia, and thus infects our religious-philosophical thinkers and poets for a long time. . . . No gradualness, no bridges of eons can possibly cross the ontological breach between two polarities [God and world].[27]

25 Vladimir Solovyov, "Immanuel" from *The Religious Poetry of Vladimir Solovyov,* lines 6–8.
26 David Bentley Hart, Foreword to Vladimir Solovyov, *Justification of the Good,* xxxix.
27 Qtd. in Archimandrite Alexander Mileant, *The Greatness of God and the Triviality of Gods,* trans. Ana P. Joyce and Barbara Olson, Missionary Leaflet #E66b (Los Angeles: Holy Protection Russian Orthodox Church). Brackets in source.

This kind of invective has also been employed against Bulgakov and Florensky.

Pavel Florensky

Pavel Florensky (1882–1937) is without question one of the most impressive figures in Russia's intellectual history.[28] A priest and theologian of the Russian Orthodox Church, Florensky was also a gifted mathematician, scientist, and electrical engineer, and his genius also made an impact in the realms of art history and linguistics. For good reason, he has been called "the Russian Da Vinci." So valuable were Florensky's formidable talents that, though a priest who never appeared in public in any but ecclesiastical garb, he was not forced to leave Russia in 1922 following the banishment of so many like-minded intellectuals (Berdyaev and Bulgakov among them), but was invited to stay in order to help design and implement Russia's electrical grid.[29] Eventually—and predictably—his priestly vocation became a hindrance to his work for the government and he was sent to a Siberian gulag in 1933 where he continued his scientific and pastoral work until he was martyred on 8 December 1937.[30]

Florensky's sophiology, as with those of Boehme, Solovyov, and so many others, begins with religious experience, particularly by religious experience as mediated through the natural world. In his memoirs he writes,

> I remember my childhood impressions, and I do not err in their regard: at the seashore, I felt myself face to face before a dear, soli-

---

28 The best biography of Florensky available in English to date is that of Fr. Robert Slesinksi, *Pavel Florensky: A Metaphysics of Love* (Crestwood, NY: St. Vladimir's Seminary Press, 1984). Also available, interesting but suffering from some serious critical bias, is Avril Pyman's *Pavel Florensky: A Quiet Genius: The Tragic and Extraordinary Life of Russia's Unknown Da Vinci* (New York: Continuum, 2010).

29 Robert Slesinksi, *Pavel Florensky*, 34.

30 Loren Graham and Jean-Michel Kantor, *Naming Infinity: A True Story of Religious Mysticism and Mathematical Creativity* (Cambridge: Harvard University Press, 2009), 143–5.

tary, mysterious, and endless eternity, from which all flows and in which everything revolves. It called me, and I was with it.[31]

Florensky in his experiences reveals an intuition that Goethe or Fludd would certainly appreciate, combining the offices of priest and scientist in a manner simultaneously attentive to both the supernatural and the natural, or, as Fludd might say, to the light of both the first and the fourth days of Creation. In a book written for his children, Florensky further articulates this sensibility:

> All my life I have thought, basically, about one thing: about the relationship of the phenomenon to the noumenon, of its manifestation, its incarnation. It is the question of the symbol. And all my life I have pondered one single question, the question of the SYMBOL.[32]

The symbol, the connective tissue, as it were, between the real and ideal, between flesh and spirit, makes knowledge possible and, more importantly, makes the awareness of God's presence possible. This is a thoroughly Christological notion, as St. Paul writes describing Christ as "the image of the invisible God" (1:15), both *signum* and *signatum*. Because of his recognition of a Christological/sophiological aspect to creation, Florensky (as have the other sophiologists) has been suspected of baptizing pantheism— the same fault with which he charged Solovyov.[33] Indeed, some theologians rush immediately to charges of pantheism whenever the question of perceiving God through nature is broached. God, with the exception of the singular event of the Incarnation, it should be noted, does not appear *in* nature (which would justify the charge of pantheism), but *through* nature (which does not). Sophia, according to the sophiologists, is intimately involved in the internal, intentional, act of perception and is simultaneously present in that which is perceived.

In 1914, Florensky published a revised and greatly expanded version of his Master's thesis which had been serialized in the short-lived journal *Voprosy religii* (*Questions of Religion*) in 1908.[34] *The*

---

31 Quoted in Robert Slesinksi, *Pavel Florensky*, 30.
32 Quoted in Avril Pyman, ibid., 9.
33 Robert Slesinksi, op. cit., 29–30.
34 Ibid., 40–1.

Pillar and Ground of Truth is an extraordinary work and has rightly been called "one of the most unusual books" of the 20th century.[35] Appearing at the nexus of Solovyian sophiology, Russian Symbolism, and the Russian religious renaissance—but also standing face-to-face with the repercussions of the Bolshevik Revolution—it is one of the most curious works extant in the literature of Orthodoxy. Written as a series of letters addressed to "My meek, my radiant friend!" the book is at turns mystical treatise, theological meditation (with copious footnotes), and early modern emblem book not unlike George Wither's *A Collection of Emblemes, Ancient and Moderne* (1635) or Daniel Cramer's *Emblemata Sacra* (1634). Florensky heads each chapter with a Latin motto and an emblem. Letter one (entitled "Two Worlds"), for instance, has as its motto "*Sic semper*" ("thus always") which is accompanied by an emblem of an obelisk flanked on the one side by the shining sun and on the other by a storm. The effect of Florensky's disparate rhetorical and epistemological commitments on the reader is pleasantly destabilizing. Florensky deconstructs the reader's reliance on conventional forms of religious discourse, preferring instead to have his text inhabit a metaxological space between theology, poetry, Church history, and aesthetics, between the exoteric and the esoteric, between objectivity and subjectivity.

For Florensky, the apprehension of reality is not gained by reliance on rationality. "Let me say it simply," he writes, "Blind intuition is a bird in the hand while reasonable discursion is a bird in the bush."[36] In his attempts to understand what it is to understand, Florensky entertains the notion of the *epoche*, the delay of judgment characteristic of phenomenological investigation. He thinks this a valuable methodology, but recognizes that the epoche is irresolvable. What he wants is something *provable*, which the epoche only defers (a phenomenon later significantly explored by Jacques Derrida). Florensky, then, strives for a kind of *coincidentia oppositorum* in his claim that "truth is intuition-discursion." "Truth is intuition that is provable," he argues,

---

35 Boris Jakim, Translator's Preface and Acknowledgements to Pavel Florensky, *The Pillar and Ground of Truth*, vii.

36 Ibid., 26.

i.e., discursive. In order to be discursive, intuition must be intuition which is not blind, not obtusely limited. It must be intuition that tends to infinity. It must be speaking, reasonable intuition, as it were. In order to be intuitive, discursion must not lose itself in boundlessness. It must be not only possible but also real, actual.

Discursive intuition must contain a synthesized infinite series of its own grounds, whereas intuitive discursion must synthesize its whole infinite series of grounds into a finitude, a unity, a unit. Discursive intuition is intuition that is differentiated to infinity, whereas intuitive discursion is discursion that is integrated to unity.

Thus, if the Truth exists, it is real reasonableness and reasonable reality. It is finite infinity and infinite finitude or—to use a mathematical expression—*actual infinity*, the Infinite conceived as integral Unity, as one Subject complete in itself. But complete in itself, Truth carries in itself the whole fullness of the infinite series of its grounds, the depth of its perspective. The Truth is a sun that illuminates both itself and the whole universe. Its abyss is the abyss of power, not of nothingness.[37]

Thrusting these antinomies at one another, in a kind of epistemological supercollider, Florensky seeks to create new theological elements, new discoveries, that shake the foundations of rationality which, nevertheless, issue from a form of reason grounded in experience. Florensky follows this method in a consideration of the Trinity.

For Florensky, the "Subject of the Truth is a Relationship of Three" and the *ousia* or essence of the Three is its hypostasis, its actuality, its becoming "real." This amounts, then, to a fourth hypostasis of the Trinity—each has its own hypostasis and this fourth arises from the synergy between the Three. He explains:

In the three hypostases, each is immediately next to each, and the relationship of two can only be mediated by the third. Primacy is absolutely unthinkable among them. But every fourth hypostasis introduces in the relation to itself of the first three some order or other, thus through itself placing the hypostases into an unequal activity in relation to itself, as the fourth hypostasis. From this one sees that with the fourth hypostasis there begins a completely new

37 Ibid., 33.

essence, whereas the first three were of one essence.

In other words, the Trinity can be without a fourth hypostasis, whereas the fourth cannot be independent. This is the general meaning of the number three of the Trinity.[38]

Though he avoids articulating it here as such, this fourth hypostasis is Sophia.

Pillar and Ground of Truth's tenth letter is devoted to the subject of Sophia, and here Florensky lays out most directly (for such an indirect text) his sophiology. As is the case with Solovyov, Florensky describes Sophia by a bewildering complex of associations and attributes. First of all, Sophia "is the Great Root of the whole creation. That is, Sophia is all-integral creation and not merely *all* creation. Sophia is the Great Root by which creation goes into the intra-Trinitarian life and through which it receives Life Eternal from the One Source of Life."[39] Furthermore, in her relationship to creation, "Sophia is the Guardian Angel of creation, the Ideal person of the world"[40] as well as "the Holy Spirit to the extent that He has deified creation."[41] Additionally, as we have seen with Boehme and Solovyov, Florensky connects Sophia to the Virgin Mary: "Virginity as the power on high that gives virginity. The bearer of Virginity, the Virgin in the strict and exclusive sense of the word, is Mary, Virgin full of grace, filled with grace by the Holy Spirit, Full of His gifts, and, as such, She is the True Church of God, the True Body of Christ. The Body of Christ came out of Her, after all."[42] Finally, in a stunning sorites, Florensky obliterates the realm of concepts in his clearest explication of Sophia and sophianicity:

> If Sophia is all of Creation, then the soul and conscience of Creation, Mankind, is Sophia *par excellence*. If Sophia is all of Mankind, then the soul and conscience of Mankind, the Church, is Sophia *par excellence*. If Sophia is the Church, then the soul and conscience of the Church, the Church of the Saints, is Sophia *par*

38 Ibid., 38.
39 Ibid., 237. Emphasis in Florensky.
40 Ibid.
41 Ibid., 253.
42 Ibid.

excellence. If Sophia is the Church of the Saints, then the soul and conscience of the Church of the Saints, the Intercessor for and Defender of creation before the Word of God, Who judges creation and divides it in two, the Mother of God, "Purifier of the World," is, once again, Sophia *par excellence.* But the true sign of Mary Full of Grace is Her Virginity, the beauty of Her soul. This is precisely Sophia.[43]

Throughout the rest of the letter, Florensky sustains his meditation on the Virgin's beauty. "Sophia is Beauty. . . . Only Sophia is essential Beauty in all of creation. Everything else is only tinsel and the superficial smartness of clothing, and this illusory glitter will be taken away from the person in the trial of fire."[44] Mary, that is, is sophianicity itself. "The Mother of God," writes Florensky, "stands at the boundary separating creation from the Creator, and since what is intermediate between the two is utterly unfathomable, the Mother of God is also utterly unfathomable."[45] Furthermore, "the Virgin Mary is unfathomable in Her superiority with respect to all of nature. She is higher than nature."[46] One proof of this superiority for Florensky comes by way of the Marian iconographic tradition. The icon—made of wood, oil, natural pigments, tempera—becomes a vessel of grace through Mary's immanence and "the sophianic beauty of the Virgin Mary" discloses itself through and in these natural materials:

> Every legitimate icon of the Mother of God, every "revealed" icon, i.e., an icon that is accompanied by signs and miracles and that has been approved and confirmed, so to speak, by the Virgin Mother Herself, that She has confirmed in its spiritual authenticity, is an imprint of only *one* of Her aspects, a luminous spot on earth from only one ray of the Virgin full of grace, only one of Her iconographic names.[47]

Could it not also be the case, then, that even in the numberless examples of individuals experiencing the numinous, the Glory of

43 Ibid.
44 Ibid., 254.
45 Ibid., 259.
46 Ibid., 266.
47 Ibid., 267. Emphasis in Florensky.

the Lord, through nature we also find disclosed an aspect Mary's sophianicity, performing a revelatory, medial role resonant with that she played in the Incarnation? It is worth noting that the natural world often plays a role in the religious experiences of visionary children: the Virgin appearing above a tree to the children at Fatima; St. Michael likewise appearing to St. Joan of Arc before a venerable oak; or even the Virgin's appearance to St. Bernadette Soubirous in a garbage dumb that eventually led to the discovery of a hidden spring famous throughout the world for its miraculous healings. Indeed, especially in the case of Bernadette, are these not sophiology's promises made manifest, the Wisdom of God shining through nature?

Florensky's sophiology—intuitive, aesthetic, grounded in religious experience—is not, as some suggest, a late-flowering Romanticism or the extravagances of a religious dilettante.[48] Rather, Florensky's masterwork is itself performative of sophianicity. As Brandon Gallaher has astutely written, "sophiology is driven by a desire to celebrate the diversity of reality precisely in its union with God and to do this it uses paradox, privileges ambiguity, and even sometimes revels—in an almost liturgical zeal to express the inexpressible—in outright contradiction."[49] Though an important intellectual and scientist, Florensky knew the limits of reason: that reason is by definition a limit. This is why he rejected reason as ultimate touchstone for discerning truth, not that it lacks usefulness as a tool for the proper task. Because he knew reason so well, Florensky—scientist, mathematician, engineer—nevertheless self-identified in terms rather foreign to typical characterizations of such left-brain occupations, writing in his memoir, "I have always been a symbolist."[50] *The Pillar and Ground of Truth*

48 Georges Florovsky, who tended toward nastiness in his dealings with those with whom he disagreed, dismissed *The Pillar and Ground of Truth* as "the book of a Westernizer who dreamily and aesthetically seeks salvation in the East." Quoted in Robert Slesinksi, *Pavel Florensky,* 47.

49 Brandon Gallaher, "The Christological Focus of Vladimir Solov'ev's Sophiology," *Modern Theology* 25, no. 4 (2009): 617–46, at 630.

50 Quoted in Richard F. Gustafson, Introduction to *The Pillar and Ground of Truth,* xi.

and its sophiology should not be read as Florensky's attempt to create a "system." He, certainly, would not have read it that way and theologians who attempt to read it as such do him a disservice. Rather, the work should be read as *poetry*, what Martin Heidegger had in mind when he wrote that "All reflective thinking is poetic, and all poetry in turn is a kind of thinking."[51] The sophiology of Florensky's friend and colleague Sergius Bulgakov, however, was an attempt at creating a systematic sophiology—but it, too, never strays far from *poesis*.

Sergius Bulgakov

Intellectually imposing, mystically inclined, and aesthetically intuitive, Sergius Bulgakov (1871–1944) created the most fully realized sophiology of the modern era, a feat made more remarkable by its presentation in the context of mainstream Russian Orthodoxy. With Boehme, Fludd, even Solovyov, sophiology could be marginalized as a fascination for mystically-inclined laymen or esotericists, and Florensky's *Pillar and Ground of the Truth* could be discounted as a work of youthful imagination or religious romanticism; but with Bulgakov, one of the preeminent Orthodox theologians of his day, sophiology becomes an issue for serious—and unavoidable—consideration. John Milbank, for one, has called Bulgakov (along with Henri de Lubac) "one of the . . . truly great theologians of the twentieth century,"[52] but even among his most ferocious, neopatristic Orthodox detractors Bulgakov's formidable theological acumen and impressive body of work elicits great respect. As no less a theologian than Alexander Schmemann has written of Bulgakov, "Whatever the ultimate fate of his sophiology, he himself will remain as a great and creative thinker who has contributed more than many others toward the direction and the ethos of modern Orthodox theol-

---

51 Martin Heidegger, *On the Way to Language*, trans. Peter D. Hertz (New York: Harper Collins, 1971), 136.

52 John Milbank, *The Suspended Middle: Henri de Lubac and the Debate concerning the Supernatural* (Grand Rapids, MI and Cambridge, UK: William B. Eerdmans Publishing Company, 2005), 104.

ogy."[53] Orthodox theologians may disagree with Bulgakov on various points, but they cannot ignore him.

Though from a family with a priestly lineage, Bulgakov, like Solovyov before him, rejected religion in favor of atheism in his youth, eventually becoming a leading member of the Marxist intelligentsia. Marxism, however, was not able to maintain its grasp on his capacious mind and a series of religious experiences drew him back to the religion of his fathers and, eventually, to the priesthood. These religious experiences brought Bulgakov to an explicitly sophianic understanding of the world. The first such experience was inspired, as might be expected, by the splendor of the natural world. In 1895, as he travelled across the steppes and took in a majestic view of the Caucasus at sunset, the young materialist and Marxist found himself confronted with an unexpected realization. "Suddenly, in that evening hour," he writes,

> my soul was joyfully stirred. I started to wonder what would happen if the cosmos were not a desert and its beauty not a mask of deception—if nature were not death, but life. If he existed, the merciful and loving Father, if nature was the vesture of his love and glory, and if the pious feelings of my childhood, when I used to live in his presence, when I loved him and trembled because I was weak, were true, then the tears and inspiration of my adolescence, the sweetness of my prayers, my innocence, and all those emotions which I had rejected and trodden down would be vindicated, and my present outlook with its emptiness and deadness would appear nothing more than blindness and lies, and what a transformation it would bring to me![54]

This experience, however, did not cause Bulgakov to rush to the nearest church and confess his sins. Rather, this was but the first stage in a somewhat drawn out process of conversion. Three years later his conversion further unfolded in Dresden, as Bulgakov

53 Alexander Schmemann, *Ultimate Questions: An Anthology of Modern Russian Religious Thought* (New York: Holt, Rinehart & Winston, 1965), 298.

54 Sergius Bulgakov, *A Bulgakov Anthology: Sergius Bulgakov 1871–1944*, trans. Natalie Duddington and James Pain, ed. James Pain and Nicolas Zernov (London: SPCK, 1976), 10–11.

contemplated Raphael's *Sistine Madonna* (what is the secret of this painting's sophianicity?!), an experience which moved him deeply:

> The eyes of the Heavenly Mother who holds in her arms the Eternal Infant, pierced my soul. I cried joyful and yet bitter tears, and with them the ice melted from my soul, and some of my psychological knots were loosened. This was an aesthetic emotion, but it was also a new knowledge; it was a miracle. I was then still a Marxist, but I was obliged to call my contemplation of the Madonna by the name of "prayer." I went to the Zwinger Gallery early in the mornings to pray and weep in front of the Virgin.[55]

Ten years later, after another religious experience connected with a visit to Hagia Sophia in Constantinople, Bulgakov finally returned to full communion with the Church and was ordained a priest in 1918. Four years into his priesthood, he was expelled from Russia, eventually landing in Paris as Dean of St. Sergius Orthodox Theological Institute.

Bulgakov's writings on Sophia are extensive. Even before his ordination, while still a professor of economics, he explored the sophianic applications of economics in his book *Philosophy of Economy* (1912).[56] Bulgakov, who would later write that "the Russian soul thirsts for wholeness of life, and above that for the wholeness of a religious outlook,"[57] considers the economy holistically as well—its materiality as well as its metaphysics. His rejection of Marxism is palpable in the book. "The purpose of economic activity," he writes, "is to defend and to spread the seeds of life, to resurrect nature. This is the action of Sophia on the universe in an

---

55 Sergius Bulgakov, *A Bulgakov Anthology*, 11. There seems to have been a long-running Russian fascination with Raphael's famous painting by the time Bulgakov arrived. See Irene Pearson, "Raphael as Seen by Russian Writers from Zhukovsky to Turgenev," *Slavonic and East European Review* 39, no. 3 (July 1981): 346–69.

56 Sergei Bulgakov, *Philosophy of Economy: The World as Household*, trans. and ed. Catherine Evtuhov (New Haven, CT: Yale University Press, 2000). Bulgakov's work in economics offers an important contribution to current discussion about Communitarianism and Distributism, providing a much-needed, Eastern Christian voice on the subject.

57 Sergius Bulgakov, "From Marxism to Sophiology," *Religion in Life* 1, no. 4 (1937): 361–8, at 361.

effort to restore it to being in Truth. . . . Economic activity overcomes the divisions in nature, and its ultimate goal—outside of
economy proper—is to return the world to life in Sophia."[58] This
is a far cry from both the Capitalist view that economy is simply
about the production and exchange of goods and services and the
Marxist position that views the economy in relation to time, management, and power. With Bulgakov, on the contrary, economics
involves human participation in redemption, both economic and
soteriological. It is with Bulgakov's more properly theological
works, however, that his systematic sophiology is laid out, though
his ostensible *theologoumena* (no matter what he told his critics, he
was really proposing a new doctrine, not a pious opinion) regarding Sophia brought him into open conflict with some factions of
the Russian Orthodox Church and even put him at risk of excom-
munication. It was a risk he obviously thought worth taking.

Bulgakov's sophiology in many respects intersects with those of
Solovyov and Florensky, so rehearsing those similarities here
would amount to overkill, but they are nevertheless impossible to
completely avoid. Like his fellow sophiologists, Bulgakov reads
sophianicity in the integral wholeness of creation, understands
Sophia as the *ousia* of the Trinity and a kind of fourth hypostasis,
and interprets the Virgin as the exemplar of both Sophia and
sophianicity. Yet what is important to notice in Bulgakov is the
emphasis he places on the two aspects of Sophia, as simultaneously
created and divine, as well as his flirtation with the notion of
Sophia as "world soul." To be sure, Solovyov and Florensky also
engage these discussions, but Bulgakov extends them consider-
ably; and, as with his writings on economy, his considerations bear
particular importance on matters concerning ecology.

Bulgakov, throughout his work, deals in antinomies in order to
explain what cannot be explained. Sophia's "two modes" in Bulgakov are an excellent example of this tendency. Bulgakov, as a
theologian, felt obligated to provide a theological framework for
expounding his sophiology and tried to provide "principles" by
which to justify his intuitions. "The principle we require," he
writes regarding the dual aspects of Sophia,

---

58 Sergei Bulgakov, *Philosophy of Economy*, 153.

is not to be sought in the person of God at all, but in his Nature, considered first as his intimate self-revelation, and second as his revelation in the world. And here we have at once Sophia in both its aspects, divine and creaturely. Sophia unites God with the world as the one common principle, the divine ground of creaturely existence. Remaining one, Sophia exists in two modes, eternal and temporal, divine and creaturely. It is of the first importance for us to grasp both the unity and the "otherness" in this unique relation of the creature to its Creator.[59]

Interesting here is the distinction between God and his Nature, this gap which allows for the being of Sophia. In God, eternally fertile, eternally creative, even a gap produces life. In her participation in God, then, Sophia is divine, in her interaction with creation, she is creaturely and, like Christ, fully at home in both. The distinction between the divine and creaturely Sophias, then, could be interpreted as only a matter of perspective/perception:

> It was pointed out above that the *connection* of God and the world is grounded in sophianicity. The Divine Sophia is one, although she has two forms of being, in God and in creation. She is one and the same "Beginning" of being, which exists in God's eternity and in creaturely becoming. In and through this "Beginning" the world has its reality, divine in its source but extra-divine and, in this sense, no longer divine in its own being. This connection includes not only the relation of the Creator to creation, that is, the *createdness* of the world, but also the very being of the world as its own life, in which sophianicity acts as the determining force in becoming, in the world process. . . . Sophianicity is not only the statics but also the dynamics of the world, not only being but also protection and becoming. In this (but precisely only in this) sense, the Divine Sophia is the Guardian Angel of the creaturely world.[60]

For Bulgakov, because the world's relationship to God is structured sophiologically, the Church itself "is the Divine Sophia and the creaturely Sophia united," as he explains:

59 Sergei Bulgakov, *Sophia: The Wisdom of God*, 74.

60 Sergius Bulgakov, *The Bride of the Lamb*, trans. Boris Jakim (Grand Rapids, MI and Edinburgh, UK: William B. Eerdmans Publishing Company and T & T Clark, 2002), 223. Bulgakov's emphasis.

Divinity, or Sophia, is both transcendent and immanent to creation. Sophia is the noumen, *to ontōs on*, the *Ding an sich* of creation, which, nevertheless, preserves its proper empirical or historical form—the phenomenal world. And this union of non-creatureliness and creatureliness, noumenality and phenomenality, also characterizes the Church as the divine in the creaturely, as the eternal and unchanging being of God in the temporal world, created out of "nothing." The divine is unchanging and eternal, while the creaturely is temporal and historical. In this sense, the Church, once again, is a synergism uniting heaven with earth.[61]

The divine/creaturely non-binary (to coin a phrase) compels Bulgakov to describe Sophia as the world soul.

The notion of a world soul (*anima mundi*) was current in speculative metaphysics from the earliest days of Christianity and arose from early Christian engagement with the thought of Plotinus, the *Corpus Hermeticum*, and other sources which could ultimately be traced back to Plato and before him to Pythagoras. The notion was not too foreign to the Greek Fathers, though the Latin Fathers were more suspicious of it. In the Christian West, the idea of a world soul had become something of an anathema beginning in 1121 when Abelard's thesis "Quod Spiritus Sanctus sit anima mundi" was condemned, a development further complicated by the rise of Scholasticism,[62] which rejected the idea as both too close to pantheism and closed to Christian revelation.[63] But, as Louis Dupré has observed, "the world soul showed an ineradicable tendency to reclaim its divine status."[64] Robert Fludd, as we have seen, attempted to resuscitate the concept for early modern metaphysics, but with the rise of the scientific revolution in the 17th century, the notion lost all credibility, certainly among scientists and natural philosophers, but also among a good many theologians.

61 Sergius Bulgakov, *The Bride of the Lamb*, 271.

62 Louis Dupré, *Passage to Modernity: An Essay in the Hermeneutics of Nature and Culture* (New Haven: Yale University Press, 1993), 59.

63 William A. Wallace, "Appendix 8. Hexaemeron: Medieval Background" to Thomas Aquinas, *Summa Theologiae, Volume* 10: *Cosmogony.* 1a 65–74 (1967; rcprt. Cambridge: Cambridge University Press, 2006), 218.

64 Louis Dupré, op. cit., 59.

For Bulgakov, the world soul is the creaturely Sophia. This quality of Sophia brings life to the universe; it is a principle of livingness. Like the light of the first day standing as the principle behind all light, Sophia informs all life in the cosmos, including the movements of planets, growth of stars, and so forth. "This creaturely Sophia," writes Bulgakov,

> as the heavenly face of the world's being, already contains the entire fullness of creation, just as the spring earth already contains all the seeds that will issue forth sprouts in their time. The creaturely Sophia connects and contains all. She is the universe containing *all* of creaturely being and linking it in a cosmic connection. In *this* sense, the creaturely Sophia is the *soul* of the creaturely world, its supracreaturely wisdom, the divine instinct of creaturely being, the guardian angel of creation, the very substance of creatureliness, submerge in nothing.[65]

Bulgakov, while straying from the tradition of those of the Fathers who wished to associate Sophia precisely as (only) Christ as Logos, stays closer to scripture, as, for example, we find in the Psalms: "How great are thy works, O Lord? thou hast made all things in wisdom: the earth is filled with thy riches" (104:24), not to mention the passages on Wisdom found in Proverbs, Sirach, and Wisdom. For Bulgakov, Sophia as world soul informs all of creation and "moves genera either like a dark instinct, the inner law of being in its different forms, or like the life of individuals who have spontaneity of movement, which is the lower kind of creaturely freedom and self-creativity."[66] Furthermore, "the world soul *becomes* together with the world itself, as if again arising out of nonbeing. From the state of sophianic potentiality, the world soul is actualized in creation."[67] For Bulgakov, then, Sophia is intrinsically involved in *theosis*, not only of the human person but of the cosmos as well. In Bulgakov, however, Sophia is not a demiurge, as so many Gnostic accounts would have it, but, instead, is the agent *through which* God creates the world and *by which* he governs and maintains his presence in it. Sophia, as

65 Sergius Bulgakov, *The Bride of the Lamb*, 64. Emphasis in Bulgakov.
66 Ibid., 102.
67 Ibid., 102. Emphasis in Bulgakov.

Bulgakov so often points out, has no being outside of the Trinity. But, the question is, does *anyone*? Sophia, sophianicity, in Bulgakov functions, ultimately, as the vessel of *theosis* and its corollary phenomenon, *sophianization*.

Theosis (or deification) is the process of human glorification; an incomplete glorification this side of the Parousia, to be sure, but a glorification nevertheless. St. Athanasius, writing on the Incarnation, puts it this way: "[God] became Man that we might be made God."[68] Theosis comes about by the individual's growth in holiness: the process of drawing closer to God, a product of the subtle and mysterious movements of grace. Theosis bears an important sacramental/incarnational stamp. As Bulgakov articulates it, "Grace is Divine-Humanity in the process of being accomplished, the Church *in actu*."[69] Central to theosis for Bulgakov is prayer, which he defines as "the direct contact between creation and divinity, the sacrament of the Name of God . . . the simplest and most typical case of the action of grace, for in it there takes place an encounter or a union between divinity and the creature in the Name of God."[70] The agent for this movement of grace, not unexpectedly, is Sophia, "the heavenly prototype of humanity, which is being actualized in creation."[71] Bulgakov furthermore ties this to a Trinitarian soteriology:

> Grace is the actualization of the Divine-humanity of which the seed was implanted in man by virtue of his creation in the image of God and which was accomplished through his communion with God in the Incarnation and the Pentecost. Grace gains this power in the gradual and unceasing approach towards one another of the divine and human nature. In grace, man knows and realizes the foundation of his proper being.[72]

Through the theosis of man, creation itself is also thereby sanctified. This amounts to the sophianization of nature.

---

68 Athanasius, *De Incanatione Verbi Dei*, trans. and ed. T. Herbert Bindley, 2nd edition (London: Religious Tract Society, 1903), 54.3.

69 Sergius Bulgakov, op. cit., 301.

70 Ibid., 308.

71 Ibid., 305.

72 Ibid.

Sophianization occurs in man for Bulgakov through grace, but the cosmos also participates in sophianization when the Glory of the Lord shines through it. This manifestation of splendor requires divine-human participation and particularly concerns man because "the world, with man at its head, is the creaturely Sophia."[73] This quality of splendor, indeed, is implicit in the Creation, revealing, in Bulgakov's words, "a mystery . . . in the fact that the creative powers of being, which have as their source the Absolute itself, were poured out into nothing."[74] God, that is, in an incredible antinomy, imparts being onto nothingness; the Creation is a mixture of nothingness and being (a notion in some resonance with Boehme). Furthermore, while acknowledging the absolute transcendence of God, Bulgakov nevertheless asserts that the energies or operations of Divinity spread out into creation and "are the same Divinity, one, indivisible, and everlasting. In this sense the energy of God in its every manifestation, like the operation of God, is inseparable from God, but what appears to the creature is God in creation, the very Absolute-Transcendent."[75] But sophianization, though accessible only in glimmers in consequence of the Fall, is only able to be actualized since the coming of Christ because "in Divine-humanity, through the incarnation of the Son and descent of the Holy Spirit, the world and man have received the fullness of sophianization. The Divine Sophia has united with the creaturely Sophia; creation has been completely deified in the union of the two natures in Christ by the Holy Spirit."[76] Sophiology, then, becomes truly the centerpiece of both a Christian ecology and an ecological Christology.

In 1932, Bulgakov published a curious article on the Western Christian mythos of the Holy Grail in the journal *Put'* (*The Way*). He subtitled the article "An Attempt at a Dogmatic Exegesis of

73 Ibid., 402.
74 Sergius Bulgakov, *Unfading Light: Contemplations and Speculations*, trans. and ed. Thomas Allan Smith (Grand Rapids, MI: William B. Eerdmans Publishing Company), 195.
75 Ibid., 215.
76 Sergius Bulgakov, *The Bride of the Lamb*, 403.

John 19:34," pointing to the passage of scripture in which Christ's side is pierced by the centurion's spear: "But one of the soldiers with a spear opened his side, and immediately there came out blood and water." Bulgakov's meditation on the Sacred Blood results in the exposition of a profound Christian truth essentially ignored by theologians until the late 20th century. Christ abides in the earth, argues Bulgakov, through the union of his blood and water with the soil on Golgotha, effecting a chemical union between the divine and the land; indeed, with the planet and by extension with the cosmos. The eucharistic overtones are obvious. "Between Christ's presence in the eucharistic blood," writes Bulgakov, "and His presence in the non-eucharistic blood, the blood of Golgotha, of the cross, there exists a distinction only according to the *mode* of this presence, that is, a modal, not an essential distinction."[77] As we have seen, Steiner came to a similar insight, an insight bearing a stunning degree of significance for any manner of authentic Christian ecology.

Bulgakov also considers the further ramifications of this notion and the importance of the poetic intuition in discerning religious truth. He, appropriately, speaks of this truth in terms of a *mystery*. Christ's presence in the earth, his abiding, writes Bulgakov,

> is not a sacrament, for sacraments, despite all their mysteriousness, are always known, since they are linked to a definite place and time. Rather, this abiding is a *mystery*, the world's great holy, divine mystery, the world's treasure, holiness, and glory—the HOLY GRAIL. . . .
>
> It is not surprising if this mystery, till now still unilluminated by the theological-dogmatic consciousness, has lived only in the obscure presentiments of Christian legend and poetry, in which the holy myth is clouded by human imaginings, by romantic reveries. But at the appropriate time this mystery can take center stage in the Christian world's consciousness, and then the holy treasure of Montserrat will catch fire with heavenly light and will lead the nations to meet the coming of Christ. The whole world is the Holy Grail, for it has received into itself and contains Christ's pre-

---

77 Sergius Bulgakov, *The Holy Grail and the Eucharist*, trans. Boris Jakim (Hudson, NY: Lindisfarne Books, 1997), 42.

cious blood and water. The whole world is the chalice of Christ's blood and water; the whole world partook of them in communion at the hour of Christ's death. And the whole world hides the blood and water within itself. A drop of Christ's blood dripped upon Adam's head redeemed Adam, but also all the blood and water of Christ that flowed forth into the world sanctified the world. The blood and water made the world a place of the presence of Christ's power, prepared for the world for its future transfiguration, for the *meeting* with Christ come in glory. . . . The world has become Christ, for it is the holy chalice, the Holy Grail.[78]

Bulgakov's attention to the "obscure presentiments of Christian legend and poetry . . . holy myth clouded by human imaginings, by romantic reveries" is crucial to understanding his theology. For is not his sophiology also touched by legend and poetry, human imaginings, and romantic reverie? Does Bulgakov not imply here that some truths are better left to poetic, intuitive, and contemplative inquiry and that rational theologizing by itself is insufficient to the task of comprehending (let alone explaining) the mysteries of God? Indeed, as Alexander Schmemann observed at the Bulgakov centenary in 1971, the great sophiologist's attempt at creating a "system" of his thought—while noble and inspiring—was not altogether successful.[79] It was, finally, a temptation for some kind of "scientific legitimacy" to which Bulgakov the professional theologian succumbed.

What results from Bulgakov's considerations of the earth's potential for sophianicity is a sacramental *telos*. Such an outlook has no room, obviously, to allow the possibility of *pura natura*, and Bulgakov—who was familiar with Western discussion of the issue—was completely hostile to the idea which he dismissed as "only an abstract concept, without any real application in human life."[80] This is so because, as he argues elsewhere, "*the world does not exist* in its own being and relativity. Only the Absolute exists.

---

78 Sergius Bulgakov, *The Holy Grail and the Eucharist*, 43–4. Emphasis in Bulgakov.

79 Alexandre Schmemann, "Trois Images," *Le Messager Orthodoxe: Centenaire du P. Serge Boulgakov* (1871–1971): *Etudes et Textes* 27, no. 1 (1972): 2–20, at 14–5.

80 Sergius Bulgakov, *The Bride of the Lamb*, 298.

The world was created out of nothing—Christian revelation teaches. Between God and creature, between the Absolute and the relative, there lay *nothing.*"[81] His teleology touches quite close to the thought of Henri de Lubac, who also found himself in clerical hot water for his stance against *natura pura*; and Bulgakov's teleology furthermore bears a striking resemblance to Teilhard de Chardin's notion of the Omega Point—which also got *that* theologian into trouble. As with Teilhard, creation, for Bulgakov, ends in its own theosis, to which man acts as a kind of midwife: "Creation follows a path toward the fullness of its sophianization, toward glory. On this path, man is the leader as the living image of God, as the hypostatic bearer of the creaturely Sophia."[82] But this *telos*, this eschatology, is unthinkable without the participation of the Virgin.

With Bulgakov, as with Solovyov and Florensky, Sophia *par excellence* is revealed in Mary, the Virgin Mother of God. In addition to the salvific role epitomized in her "Yes" and her simultaneously spiritual and *biological* unity with both the Holy Spirit and Christ, Mary is, Bulgakov argues, touched by the Divine Sophia while remaining herself the creaturely Sophia. Mary, in her sophianic role, dwells at the boundary between heaven and creation. As Bulgakov writes, "it is there, in heaven, that Her maximal deification in accomplished and the supreme goal of creation, its theodicy, is fulfilled."[83] "In Her there is revealed all the fullness of the glory of the world; now nothing can be added to it."[84] Indeed, she herself "is the glory of the world."[85] The Akathist Hymn to the Mother of God, a devotion used by the Eastern Church from at least the 6th century, pronounces this truth in similar terms:

> Rejoice, Vessel of the Wisdom of God!
> Rejoice, Treasury of His Providence!
> Rejoice, Reproof of foolish philosophers!

---

81 Sergius Bulgakov, *Unfading Light*, 186. Emphasis in Bulgakov.
82 Sergius Bulgakov, *The Bride of the Lamb*, 403.
83 Ibid., 413.
84 Sergei Bulgakov, *Sophia: The Wisdom of God*, 130.
85 Sergius Bulgakov, *The Bride of the Lamb*, 412.

Rejoice, for the eloquent become speechless
before you!

As the hymn articulates it so beautifully, rationality can become
its own prison. Something more is required.

⊕

The sophiologies of Solovyov, Florensky, and Bulgakov, interpen-
etrating at points, diverging at others, never achieving either consensus or center are emblematic of an intuitive approach to
questions of God. Not precisely theology, they possess elements
of poetry and mysticism, speaking in a language of images and
symbols, pointing to, rather than presenting, the truth. As Milbank has observed, Russian sophiology is both modern and postmodern, an "often somewhat surrealist thought [that] appears
much more at home in the world of difference, simulacra, life,
the event and question of mediation than any of the other early
twentieth-century theologies."[86] It is no wonder, then, that a
number of Russian Symbolist poets—Andrei Belyi, Alexander
Blok, Vyacheslav Ivanov, and Solovyov's nephew Sergei Solovyov
among them—took up the cause of sophiology following the ini-
tial inspiration of Vladimir Solovyov. Yet, neither was the poetic
intuition able to fully capture the essence of Sophia, to distill a
hypostasis of the hypostasis. The disclosure of Sophia, it seems,
lies in a *metaxu*, a space (that is no space) between theology and
poetry, a disclosure of presence but not of concept; a disclosure of
an ever-allusive multiplicity, of an ever-elusive individuality.

86 John Milbank, "Sophiology and Theurgy: The New Theological Horizon" in *Encounter between Eastern Orthodoxy and Radical Orthodoxy: Transfiguring the World through the Word*, ed. Adrian Pabst and Christoph Schneider
(Farnham, UK: Ashgate, 2009), 45–85, at 50.

Chapter Six

Catholic Sophiology: The Submerged Reality

Let all God's glory through,
God's glory which would go
Through her and from her flow
Off, and no way but so.
　～Gerard Manley Hopkins[1]

Seul en Europe tu n'es pas antique ô Christianisme
L'Européen le plus moderne c'est vous Pape Pie X
　～Guillaume Apollinaire[2]

P RIOR TO BOEHME in the Christian West, there was a kind of sophiology, but it was generally submerged, only shining out in glimmers and usually in the light of a poetic or mystical awareness. Sophiology, nevertheless, was something clearly lived, particularly in the beautiful ways in which the agricultural and liturgical cycles intertwined. St. John's fires throughout Europe, the blessing of ploughs on the Sunday before Plough Monday (a week after Epiphany) in England, Corpus Christi plays, and other celebrations all spoke to the participation of the divine in the unfolding year.[3] Such traditions acknowledge both

---

1 Gerard Manley Hopkins, "The Blessed Virgin compared to the Air we Breathe" in *Poems*, ed. Robert Bridges and W.H. Gardner, 3rd ed. (New York and London: Oxford University Press, 1948), lines 30–3.

2 Guillaume Apollinaire, "Zone," from *Selected Writings of Guillaume Apollinaire*, trans. and ed. Roger Shattuck (New York: New Directions, 1971), lines 7–8.

3 An excellent book on the subject is Ronald Hutton, *The Rise and Fall of Merry England* (Oxford: Oxford University Press, 1996).

divine interaction in nature and human participation in divine realities mediated through nature, but these traditions were hardly occasions of sour-faced shows of piety and sanctimoniousness. Indeed, some of the rituals and feasts tended to be observed with great merriment and the possibility for excess—which caused some religious elites no small amount of disapproval.[4] Indeed, some elite party-poopers sought to limit the carnival aspects of the Church year and, following the Reformation, the feasts and their traditions were severely curtailed if not eliminated altogether, eventually influencing even Catholic communities. Ben Jonson made a living ridiculing such sanctimoniousness in his plays, aiming his dangerous wit at Puritans. But, even in Catholic countries, elites disparaged the carnival aspects of folk religion.

During the period, the growing preference for reason over intuition—a development underfoot since the rise of Scholasticism—and the arrival of what Charles Taylor has described as a "new ethic of rational control"[5] made significant inroads on religion. The rationalistic approach to God advocated by the humanist Desiderius Erasmus (1466–1536) is symptomatic of this impulse.[6] Erasmus wished to cleanse Christianity of what he believed were the contaminations of superstition and popular and folk religion, an intellectual stance that lent a massive level of stimulus to reform due to his formidable intellectual reputation. For Erasmus, Catholicism had been soiled by clergy "enveloping the superstitious common folk (*plebecula*) with ceremonies, so that they were led by the nose, and never grow up into a true teaching of Christ."[7] In England, Erasmus' friend and colleague St. Thomas More maintained a similar view, and, like Erasmus, valued elite ethical and expressive elements of religion over popular

---

4 See Charles Taylor, *A Secular Age* (Cambridge, MA: Harvard-Belknap, 2007), 45–54.

5 Ibid., 134.

6 Susan E. Schreiner, *Are You Alone Wise?: The Search for Certainty in the Early Modern Era* (Oxford: Oxford University Press, 2011), 12.

7 Erasmus, *Enarratio in Ps.* 1, LBV, 179EF, quoted in James D. Tracey, *Erasmus: The Growth of a Mind*, Avaux d'Humanisme et Renaissance CXXVI (Geneva: Librairie Droz, 1972), 147.

forms of piety such as pilgrimages and the veneration of saints.[8] As Taylor has observed, Christian humanists "fell into the negative judgment that elites all too easily make on popular piety, seeing it from the outside, and missing all too often the spirit which animated it."[9] Erasmus and his humanist peers, then, turned to reason as the salvation of Christianity rather than to Christianity as the salvation of reason.

The rituals and celebrations of folk religion, of course, are not evidence of sophiology, properly understood, but they are sophianic in the way that they affirm the presence of God's wisdom in the conjoined agricultural-liturgical cycle. As late as the mid-19th century, for example, Catholics of Benbecula in the Hebrides would invoke the protection of their flocks and herds on the first of May from St. Michael, St. Columba, and St. Bride, as well as from the Virgin:

> Mary, though mother of saints,
> Bless our flocks and bearing kine,
> Hate nor scathe let not come near us
> Drive from us the ways of the wicked.[10]

At the beginning of August, after the grain harvest, the faithful would celebrate what was called Lammas in England, a word derived from the Old English *hlāfmæsse* or "loaf-mass." Folk customs like these disclose the inherent sacramentality of a time when our binary "secular-religious" was unthinkable. Indeed, postmodern Christianity, to its detriment, is characterized by a kind of internalization of this binary. Tragically, Wiccans and Neo-Pagans, sensing the loss of something sacred in a cultural milieu surreptitiously poisoned by Enlightenment values, have appropriated for themselves a host of (previously) Christian customs, stripping them of their Christian elements in the process. One can hardly blame them.

---

8 C. John Sommerville, *The Secularization of Early Modern England: From Religious Culture to Religious Faith* (New York: Oxford University Press, 1992), 34.

9 Taylor, *Secular Age*, 71.

10 Ronald Hutton, *The Stations of the Sun: A History of the Ritual Year in Britain* (Oxford: Oxford University Press, 1996), 222–3.

Elites of medieval Latin Christendom and later, generally removed from the sophianic aspects of agriculture, tended to seek wisdom elsewhere. The 17th century Anglican priest and poet Robert Herrick, who served a country parish (that had obviously held onto some of its pre-Reformation Catholic folk customs), clearly saw the value of folk religion as he wrote in the opening poem of his book, *Hesperides*:

The Argument of his Book

I Sing of *Brooks*, of *Blossomes*, *Birds*, and *Bowers*,
Of *April, May*, of *June*, and *July*-Flowers.
I sing of *May-poles*, *Hock-carts*, *Wassails*, *Wakes*,
Of *Bride-grooms*, *Brides*, and of their *Bridall-cakes*.
I write of *Youth*, of *Love*, and have Accesse
By these, to sing of cleanly- *Wantonnesse*.
I sing of *Dewes*, of *Raines*, and piece by piece
Of *Balme*, of *Oyle*, of *Spice*, and *Amber-gris*.
I sing of *Time's trans-shifting*, and I write
How *Roses* first came *Red*, and *Lillies White*.
I write of *Groves*, of *Twilights*, and I sing
The court of *Mab*, and of the *Fairie-King*.
I write of *Hell*; I sing (and ever shall)
Of *Heaven*, and hope to have it after all.[11]

So what we see here is a kind of disconnect between the somewhat atavistic, unconscious sophianic sensibilities of the general population during the Reformation/Enlightenment periods and a burgeoning and increasingly dogmatic rationality in elite circles. More than C. P. Snow's categorization of the two cultures of the humanities and the sciences, the folk and elite cultures of medieval and early modern Catholicism demarcate a much more significant cultural Rubicon.

That is not to say that Catholic high culture was devoid of any sophianic elements. Clearly, the rise of devotion to the Virgin during the medieval period speaks directly to a kind of submerged sophiology, glimmering beneath the surface of medieval

---

11 *The Complete Poetry of Robert Herrick*, ed. J. Max Patrick (New York: W. W. Norton & Company, 1968).

Christianity. The appearance and subsequent popularity of the Rosary during the period and, later, the devotion to the *Memorare* and *Angelus* illustrate this submerged sophiology that straddles the border between allegedly elite and popular Catholic sensibilities. In a more obviously high culture context, Dante lends this phenomenon beautiful utterance in St. Bernard's sublime prayer to the Virgin in the *Paradiso*, written in the early 14th century:

> Virgin Mother, daughter of thy son;
>> humble beyond all creatures and more exalted;
>> predestined turning point of God's intention.
>
> thy merit so ennobled human nature
>> that its divine Creator did not scorn
>> to make Himself the creature of His creature.
>
> The Love that was rekindled in Thy womb
>> sends forth the warmth of the eternal peace
>> within whose ray this flower has come to bloom.
>
> Here, to us, thou art the noon and scope
>> of Love revealed; and among mortal men,
>> the living fountain of eternal hope.
>
> Lady, thou art so near God's reckonings
>> that who seeks grace and does not first seek thee
>> would have his wish fly upward without wings.
>
> Not only does thy sweet benignity
>> flow out to all who beg, but oftentimes
>> thy charity arrives before the plea.
>
> In thee is pity, in thee munificence,
>> In thee the tenderest heart, in thee unites
>> All that creation knows of excellence![12]

A kind of sophiology clearly inhabits Dante's prayer, particularly in the way he connects the Virgin to grace and to the elevation of nature.

St. Thomas Aquinas also touches upon the subject of divine

---

12 Dante Alighieri, Canto 33 from *The Paradiso*, trans. John Ciardi (New York: New American Library, 1961) lines 1–21.

Wisdom. The Angelic Doctor, in his discussion of the first chapter of Wisdom, distinguishes between *Sapientia increata* (uncreated Wisdom) and *Sapientia creata* (created wisdom). "When we say 'Wisdom was created,'" he writes,

> this may be understood not of Wisdom which is the Son of God, but of created wisdom given by God to creatures: for it is said, "He created her [namely, Wisdom] in the Holy Ghost, and He poured her out over all His works" (Ecclus. 1:9, 10)[. . . .] The saying may also be referred to the created nature assumed by the Son.[13]

St. Thomas goes on to admit the details when parsing the scriptural connotations of the word "wisdom" (and even "Holy Spirit") are inexact at best. He even suggests that the Son is "created *and* begotten," [my emphasis] which cannot be correct, as it counters the most fundamental reading of the Creed: "begotten, not made."

In *Liber Meditationem,* a work spuriously attributed to St. Augustine, the unknown writer distinguishes between *Sapientia increata* and *Sapientia creata.* Of these Wisdoms the writer says, "just as the illuminating light is differentiated from the illuminated light, so great is the difference between You, the highest, creating Sapientia and that Sapientia which is created."[14] One could easily apply this distinction to the distinction between Christ and the Theotokos. But this, of course, moves us into dicey theological territory. But perhaps the most revelatory mode of what might be called a nascent Roman Catholic sophiology is found in the spiritualities of St. Francis of Assisi and St. Hildegard of Bingen.

The love St. Francis (c. 1181–1226) bore for the natural world and its creatures is well known. So easily is Francis associated with the wholesomeness of the natural world that in 1979 St. Pope John Paul II declared him the patron saint of ecology. Indeed, as seen in his writings, Francis agrees with God's affirmation in

13 *Summa* I, 1, article 3, English translation from *Basic Writings of Thomas Aquinas,* trans. Anton C. Pegis, (New York: Random House, 1945). Scriptural passage in original.

14 Qtd. in Thomas Schipflinger, *Sophia-Maria: A Holistic Vision of Creation,* trans. James Morgante (York Beach, ME: Samuel Weiser, 1998), 71.

Genesis that creation is good. He feels a kinship with nature, calling its inhabitants "brother" or "sister":

> Be praised, my Lord, for our Sister, Mother Earth,
> Who nourishes and governs us,
> And produces various fruits with many-colored flowers
>   and herbs.[15]

Nature for Francis acts as a window through which he sees God. Furthermore, as J. Donald Hughes observes, Francis was the "first to take literally the command to 'preach the gospel to all creatures,'" including sparrows and wolves, recognizing their intrinsic worth as grounded in God.[16] Paradoxically, it may have been Francis's attention to nature that inspired later members of the Franciscan Order to take up a "scientific" approach to nature and the making of knowledge.[17] The Franciscans Robert Grosseteste (c. 1175–1253) and Roger Bacon (1214–1294), for example, are known more for their attempts to understand and control nature along proto-Enlightenment lines than they are for trying to befriend nature in the manner of Francis. As we have seen in this study, the proponents of the various sophiologies from the 17th century onward were often deeply interested in science if not practicing scientists, though the work of these Franciscan scientists was, like nominalism and *natura pura*, inclined *away* from a holistic cosmological epistemology. The height of the irony, of course, is that William of Occam, one of the primary champions of nominalism and a precursor to *natura pura*, was a Franciscan.

St. Hildegard of Bingen (1098–1179), named a Doctor of the Church by Pope Benedict XVI in 2012, also stands out as an important figure in the submerged sophiology of the medieval Catholic Church. Feminist and New Age writers are fond of drawing attention to the Wisdom figure Hildegard describes from

---

15 "The Canticle of Brother Son," quoted in Roger D. Sorrell, *St. Francis of Assisi and Nature: Tradition and Innovation in Western Christian Attitudes toward the Environment* (New York and Oxford: Oxford University Press, 1988), 101.

16 J. Donald Hughes, "Francis of Assisi and the Diversity of Creation," *Environmental Ethics* 18 (Fall 1996): 311–20, at 315.

17 Ibid., 319.

her visions, but these seem to me to be more in conformity with medieval Catholic traditions of personifying Wisdom as female as opposed to an assertion of a feminine face of God, as some scholars like to argue. Instead, Hildegard's sophiological intuitions shine forth in her insights into medicine, music, and the natural world which, combined with her visionary experiences, offer a holistic, integrated cosmology. Nowhere is this sophiological intuition found in Hildegard more than in her notion of *viriditas*, or what might be translated as "greeningness."

Viriditas in Hildegard's writing indicates life in its purist, freshest, most exuberant form: a quality of life that is more than alive and that inheres the entire cosmos. As Joseph Baird and Radd Ehrman explain,

> The world in the height of the spring season is filled with *viriditas*, God breathed the breath of *viriditas* into the inhabitants of the garden of Eden, even the smallest twig on the most insignificant tree is animated with *viriditas*, the sun brings the life of *viriditas* into the world; and (in the spiritual realm) the prelate who is filled with *taedium* (weariness) is lacking in *viriditas*, the garden where the virtues grow is imbued with *viriditas*, the neophyte must strive for *viriditas*, and the holy Virgin is the *viridissima virga*.[18]

Viriditas, with its resonances with the language of Fludd in particular—its connections to the sun and the breath of God—is the key to Hildegard's nascent sophiology which is further confirmed by the way she praises the Virgin, the *viridissima virga*, as the emblem and repository of this deep livingness. Hildegard, in a hymn on virginity, voices her sophiology:

> O most noble greening power
> Rooted in the sun,
> Who, in dazzling serenity,
> Shine in a wheel
> That no earthly excellence
> Can comprehend.

---

18 Joseph L. Baird and Radd K. Ehrman, Introduction, *Letters of Hildegard of Bingen, Volume I*, trans. Joseph L. Baird and Radd K. Ehrman (Oxford: Oxford University Press, 1994), 7.

You are enfolded
In the embrace of divine offices,
You blush like the dawn
And burn like a flame of the sun.[19]

How often sophiology appears in souls occupied with both science and poetry. These kinds of sophiological intuitions are never far from the heart of Catholicism, whether medieval, early modern, or modern. The medieval theologian St. Bonaventure, the early modern Swiss physician Paracelsus, and the Jesuit poet Gerard Manley Hopkins (who knew how "The world is charged with the grandeur of God") clearly maintained an integral, holistic view of the cosmos. But with the pervasiveness of Scholasticism—and even more with its permutations known as Neo-Scholasticism or (Neo)Thomism—and confronted by the scientific revolution with the Enlightenment in its wake, these and other holistic epistemologies were increasing set to the side where they suffered from neglect. Until, that is, the mid-20th century. Then things got interesting.

The Turn Toward a (Post)Modern Catholic Sophiology

The return of an explicitly Latin Catholic sophiology in the 20th century coincided with the appearance of the *Ressourcement* movement, also known as *Nouvelle Théologie*, which effectively hit the reset button for Catholic theology. *Ressourcement,* accomplishing in theology what Edmund Husserl did in philosophy, returned to "the things themselves," the sources at the foundation of Christianity: the scriptures and the Fathers. As the movement rediscovered (in a sense) the Greek Fathers its proponents drew closer to Eastern theology which had not been encumbered by the institutional duty to defend Scholasticism and Neo-Scholasticism. Indeed, the commitment to return to the sources encouraged theologians to look beyond the excrescence of commentary accumulated over at least eight hundred years and begin anew. Perhaps

19 Hymn 56 from Hildegard of Bingen, *Symphonia: A Critical Edition of the* Symphonia Armonie Celestium Revelationum, ed and trans. Barbara Newman, 2nd ed. (Ithaca, NY: Cornell University Press, 1998), 218. My translation.

as much as Vatican II, *Ressourcement* opened the windows of the Church to let in a little fresh air. Primary to this development is the thought of Henri de Lubac and his interrogation of *natura pura*, and from his inspiration and that of others a new era of Latin Catholic theology began. But such a renewal was hardly welcomed with a universal embrace from the theological establishment.

Pierre Teilhard de Chardin's "The Eternal Feminine"

A seminal document in the return of Catholic sophiology is Pierre Teilhard de Chardin's poetic meditation "The Eternal Feminine." Fr. Teilhard (1881–1955), a paleontologist as well as a priest, is yet another sophiologist inhabiting the space shared by science, poetry, and religion, and in "The Eternal Feminine" he beautifully articulates a scientific-religious poesis. Many of his statements in the short piece resonate with earlier sophiologies. He opens with what amounts to a paraphrase of Proverbs 8, "When the world was born, I came into being"[20] and his meditation oscillates between poetic scientific observation and scriptural exegesis:

> Follow with your eye the vast tremor that runs, from horizon to horizon, through city and forest.
>
> Observe, throughout all life, the human effervescence that works like leaven in the world—the song of the birds and their plumage—the wild hum of insects—the tireless blooming of the flowers—the unremitting work of the cells—the endless labours of the seeds germinating in the soil.
>
> I am the single radiance by which all this is aroused and within which it is vibrant.[21]

Furthermore, Teilhard anchors this notion of Sophia in Christ as the source of all things good:

> Christ has given me salvation and freedom.
>
> When he said: *Melius est non nubere*, men took it to mean that I was dead to eternal life.

20 Pierre Teilhard de Chardin, *Writings in Time of War*, trans. René Hague (New York: Harper & Row, Publishers, 1965), 192.
21 Ibid., 193–4.

> In truth, by those words he restored me to life, with Lazarus—
> with Magdalen—and set me between himself and men as nimbus
> of glory.[22]

In addition, as almost all sophiologists have done, he reads the
Church as sophianic and the Virgin as sophianicity itself:

> Lying between God and the earth, as a zone of mutual attraction, I
> draw them both together in a passionate union.
>   —until the meeting takes place in me, in which the generation
> and plentitude of Christ are consummated throughout the centu-
> ries.
>   I am the Church, the bride of Christ.
>   I am Mary, the mother of all humankind.[23]

These words, when Teilhard finished the poem at Verzy on 25
March 1913, the Feast of the Annunciation, were not original
insights. We have seen iterations of them in Boehme, in Fludd, in
Novalis, in the Russians, but they were pretty radical in the
hyper-neo-Thomist atmosphere of the early-20th-century Catholic Church.

In fact, Teilhard's ideas were seen as dangerous and he was censured, forbidden to either teach or publish, beginning in 1925. Following his death, Fr. Teilhard's critics unleashed even more venom
on his legacy, first with a *Monitum* (warning) the Holy Office
issued concerning his work on 30 June 1962, demanding that they
be removed from seminary libraries lest they endanger the minds
of youth. Acknowledging the popularity Teilhard's books were
gaining due to the publication of popular, secular editions of his
work (in a staggering number of translations into many, many languages), the Holy Office nevertheless cautioned that his "works
abound in such ambiguities and indeed even serious errors, as to
offend Catholic doctrine."[24] De Lubac, in fact, wrote three books
defending Teilhard's theology, one of them on "The Eternal Feminine." Mindful of the charges of heresy leveled at Bulgakov in the

22 Ibid., 197.
23 Ibid., 200–1.
24 Quoted in Gereon Wolters, "The Catholic Church and Evolutionary
Theory: A Conflict Model," *Scientific Insights into the Evolution of the Universe
and of Life: Pontifical Academy of Sciences, Acta* 20 (2009): 450–70, at 459.

Orthodox Church, de Lubac attempted to deflect the same kinds of criticisms of his friend's work. "We should not seek here," writes de Lubac, "for anything analogous to Bulgakov's sophiological theories. Wisdom is not a hypostasis which, in its created aspect, is realized in the Virgin. As in the liturgy, it is a symbol."[25] De Lubac, I think, is being a little disingenuous here. While it cannot be discerned that Teilhard is suggesting a "fourth hypostasis" in the poem, calling the eternal feminine simply a "symbol" hardly does justice to either the poem or Fr. Teilhard. I am reminded of a passage from one of Flannery O'Connor's letters wherein she responds to a Big Intellectual's opinion that the Eucharist is a symbol and "a pretty good one": "Well, if it's a symbol, to hell with it."[26] The symbolic language of liturgy, indeed, and the supreme mystery of the Eucharist, in particular, complicate the distinctions between allegedly "symbolic" and "real" modes of being to a significant degree which is, as we have seen, one of the fundamental insights of sophiology. Among de Lubac's rhetorical purposes, however, one was not to get Teilhard's theories *accepted*. Rather, he was trying to get them *read*.

In recent years, the anxiety Teilhard once provoked has diminished, and even Benedict XVI has expressed admiration for him,[27] though he is still viewed as a heretic by some arch-conservative Traditionalists. Be that as it may, what is important, though, is Teilhard's commitment to a thoroughly Catholic (in every sense of the word) vision of the cosmos. As de Lubac writes:

> God's universal presence—his immanence, active immanence in the world—whose part in cosmic evolution was one of Père Teilhard's favourite themes, was for him what it was for the whole of Christian tradition, the necessary corollary of God's transcendence.[28]

25 Henri de Lubac, *The Eternal Feminine: A Study on the Poem by Teilhard de Chardin followed by Teilhard and the Problems of Today*, trans. René Hague (New York: Harper & Row, Publishers, 1970), 95.

26 Flannery O'Connor, *The Habit of Being: Letters*, ed. Sally Fitzgerald (New York: Vintage Books, 1980), 125.

27 Among other places, in Joseph Cardinal Ratzinger [Pope Benedict XVI], *The Spirit of the Liturgy* (San Francisco: Ignatius Press, 2000), 28–9.

28 Henri de Lubac, *The Eternal Feminine*, 161.

Teilhard's cosmology also offers a point of access for Orthodox theologians who, lacking the expectations and Neo-Scholastic biases particular to some quarters of Catholic theology, have felt more of an affinity for his ideas than have many of Teilhard's Catholic critics.[29] As Orthodox theologian Andrew Louth has noted, *ressourcement* theology, though primarily a Catholic phenomenon, can indeed be understood as a collaborative project between Catholics and Orthodox.[30] Fr. Teilhard's work provides an important point of access for such a dialogue. Teilhard, however, was not alone in asserting a form of Catholic sophiology.

Thomas Merton and Sophiology

The convert Thomas Merton (1915–1968), a poet as well as a priest, also asserts a sophiological theology in some of his later work.[31] Not surprisingly, Merton had been immersing himself in the Fathers and in contemporary Russian Orthodox theology—particularly in Berdyaev and Bulgakov—and he was stirred. First of all, he admired the theological courage displayed by these Russians. "In their pages," he writes,

> for all the scandals one may fear to encounter, shines the light of the resurrection and theirs is a theology of triumph.
>
> One wonders if our theological consciousness is not after all the sign of a fatal coldness of heart, an awful sterility born of fear, or of despair. These two men have dared to make mistakes and were to be condemned by every church, in order to say something great and worthy of God in the midst of all their wrong statements. They have dared to accept the challenge of the sapiential books,

29 Orthodox theologian John Meyendorff, for example, expresses admiration for Teilhard in *Living Tradition* (Crestwood, NY: St. Vladimir's Seminary Press, 1978), 96.

30 Andrew Louth, "French *Ressourcement* Theology and Orthodoxy: A Living Mutual Relationship?" in *Ressourcement: A Movement for Renewal in Twentieth-Century Catholic Theology*, ed. Gabriel Flynn and Paul D. Murray with Patricia Kelly (Oxford: Oxford University Press, 2012): 495–507, at 507.

31 The most comprehensive text on this subject to date is Christopher Pramuk, *Sophia: The Hidden Christ of Thomas Merton* (Collegeville, MN: A Michael Glazier Book/Liturgical Press, 2009).

the challenge of the image of Proverbs where Wisdom is "playing in the world" before the face of the Creator.[32]

Merton, by rediscovering the Fathers and discovering the Russians (is this not *ressourcement?*) also discovered an integral vision of Catholicism unattainable within the strictures of a Latin Catholicism more or less entrenched in its allegiance to St. Thomas Aquinas and generally ignorant (and suspicious) of the Christian East—whether Catholic or Orthodox.

Merton understood that a Christianity divided is a Christianity weakened and dissipated. Therefore, an ecumenical sensibility inhabits Merton's thought—but an ecumenism that is more than ecumenism (and in this he has much in common with Solovyov). This was a bigger project than the facile "Kumbaya" spirituality of which Merton's detractors usually accuse him. His view, rather, is Christological, supra-ecclesial:

> If I can unite *in myself* the thought and the devotion of Eastern and Western Christendom, the Greek and the Latin Fathers, the Russians with the Spanish mystics, I can prepare in myself the reunion of divided Christians. From that secret and unspoken unity in myself can eventually come a visible and manifest unity of all Christians. If we want to bring together what is divided, we can not do so by imposing one division upon the other or absorbing one division into the other. But if we do this, the union is not Christian. It is political, and doomed to further conflict. We must contain all divided worlds in ourselves and transcend them in Christ.[33]

Merton, not surprisingly, arrives at an essentially Mariological understanding of Sophia. He gives utterance to this in his prose poem, "Hagia Sophia," a meditation based on the structure of the Liturgy of the Hours:

> It is she, it is Mary, Sophia, who in sadness and joy, with the full awareness of what she is doing, sets upon the Second Person, the Logos, a crown which is His Human Nature. Thus her consent

---

32 Thomas Merton, *A Search for Solitude: Pursuing the Monk's Life*, ed. Lawrence S. Cunningham (San Francisco: Harper, 1997), 85–6.

33 Thomas Merton, *Conjectures of a Guilty Bystander* (Garden City, NY: Doubleday & Company, Inc., 1966), 12. Emphasis in Merton.

opens the door of created nature, of time, of history, to the Word of God.[34]

Merton's insights here are not the kind that one simply derives from study, whether it be of the Fathers, the Russians, the Spanish mystics, or, even, scripture. Instead, Merton's insights, as Christopher Pramuk observes, are really the fruit of Merton's studies as they are rooted in contemplation and, I would add, liturgy.[35] Without prayer and liturgy, sophiology is just another dry theologically-constituted academic endeavor, one among many. A true sophiology, as we have seen, is one that arises through a contemplative engagement with the world which is why it has so often proved accessible to the interplay of poetic and scientific awareness.

Hans Urs von Balthasar's Half-Submerged Sophiology

In his theological aesthetics, Hans Urs von Balthasar (1905–1988) also embodies a form of Catholic sophiology, though he is careful to let it hover near the surface of his thought, at a point wherein it is never quite revealed though never completely submerged. He was careful to avoid the kind of controversy that impacted both de Lubac and Teilhard and their ability to teach or publish. Nevertheless, von Balthasar recognized the danger implicit in the estrangement between theology and mysticism and tried to rectify it, or at least to begin rectifying it. Indeed, he thought of his own substantial theological edifice as incomplete unless read in relationship to the mystical writings of his friend and associate Adrienne von Speyr, considering their work a symbiosis.[36] The sophianic qualities of von Balthasar's thought, ever mindful of

34 Thomas Merton, "Hagia Sophia" reproduced in Christopher Pramuk, *Sophia*, 300–5, at 305.

35 Christopher Pramuk, *Sophia*, 132.

36 See, for instance, Johann Roten, SM, "The Two Halves of the Moon: Marian Anthropological Dimensions of the Common Mission of Adrienne von Speyr and Hans Urs von Balthasar," in *Hans Urs von Balthasar: His Life and Work,* ed. David L. Schindler (San Francisco: Communio Books and Ignatius Press, 1991), 65–86.

mystical and poetic ways of knowing, as Adrian Walker argues, "[give] us the eyes to wonder at *physis* again and the resources to stand up for its integrity."[37] They are particularly evident in his conceptions of *glory* and *splendor.*

Glory, for von Balthasar, is first and foremost "the divinely beautiful: *doxa*," and therefore truth (*alatheia*) itself.[38] Beauty, however, as von Balthasar understood it, was (and is) in danger of vanishing from serious intellectual consideration, effectively abandoned to cosmetic performativity and solipsistic subjectivity. Even in the 1960s, von Balthasar was acutely sensitive to the diminished status of the concept of beauty among the learned classes, not only in aesthetics and literature, but even more disturbingly in philosophy and theology. At times, his words take the form of a lament:

> That which deserved the name of glory in the sphere of metaphysics has been lost to view. Being no longer possesses any radiance, and beauty, banished from the transcendental dimension, is confined to a purely worldly reality.[39]

The repercussions of such a loss are profound:

> No longer loved or fostered by religion, beauty is lifted from its face as a mask, and its absence exposes features on that face which threaten to become incomprehensible to man. We no longer dare to believe in beauty and we make of it a mere appearance in order to more easily dispose of it. Our situation today shows that beauty demands for itself at least as much courage and decision as do truth and goodness, and she will not allow herself to be separated and banned from her two sisters without taking them along with herself in an act of mysterious vengeance. *We can be sure that whoever sneers at her name as if she were an ornament of a bourgeois*

37 Adrian J. Walker, "Love Alone: Hans Urs von Balthasar as a Master of Theological Renewal," *Communio* 32 (Fall 2005): 1–24, at 23.

38 Hans Urs von Balthasar, *Love Alone*, trans. Alexander Dru (New York: Herder and Herder, 1969), 46.

39 Hans Urs von Balthasar, *The Glory of the Lord: A Theological Aesthetics, Vol. 5: The Realm of Metaphysics in the Modern Age,* trans. Oliver Davies, Andrew Louth, Brian McNeil, John Saward, and Rowan Williams; ed. Brian McNeil and John Riches (San Francisco: Ignatius Press, 1991), 597.

The pronoun shift here—the movement from "it" to "she"—is particularly intriguing in the light of sophiology. Some could argue, of course, that von Balthasar is drifting into metaphor, the realm of poetry; that this is simply a rhetorical flourish, an ornament. But, as I have been arguing, it is precisely in the attenuations of rigid conceptuality brought about by a poetic intuition that Sophia appears. The shift is deliberate. Von Balthasar's gesture is more daring than one might at first think: it is actually performative of sophiology itself in the way Sophia guards the threshold, the shift or transition, between transcendence and immanence.

The experience of beauty, furthermore, stands for Balthasar as an event when a "Thou meets me as an Other."[41] Such an experience should not be confused with "worldly beauty," however—von Balthasar is fully aware of this kind of beauty—and he goes on to trace the contours of revealed beauty:

> When one experiences startling beauty (in nature or in art) then phenomena normally veiled are perceived in their uniqueness. What confronts us is overpowering, like a miracle, and only as a miracle can it be understood; it can never be tied down by the person having the experience.[42]

Furthermore, an eros attends the phenomena because "even in nature eros is the chosen place of beauty. The object we love—no matter how deeply or superficially—always appears wonderful and glorious to us."[43] The idea that beauty in things can be veiled requires some examination here, as it is in this that Balthasar's theology becomes sophiological. The veiled-revealed language regarding beauty that Balthasar employs here coheres with the

---

40 Hans Urs von Balthasar, *The Glory of the Lord: A Theological Aesthetics, Vol. 1: Seeing the Form*, trans. Erasmo Leiva-Merikakis, ed. Joseph Fessio and John Riches (San Francisco and New York: Ignatius Press and Crossroad Publications, 1982), 18. My emphasis.

41 Hans Urs von Balthasar, *Love Alone*, 44.

42 Ibid.

43 Ibid., 45.

same concepts we have seen in the more explicit sophiologies of Boehme, Fludd, the German Romantics, Steiner, and the Russians. The *boundary* (as is the attendant notion, the *form*) is an important concept for von Balthasar. The point of access for the Beautiful's arrival is not an accident; it is integral to the experience of beauty and to Creation itself. The boundary—between nature and grace, philosophy and theology, spirit and matter, the divine and the human—is the exact nexus at which the beautiful appears.[44] The revelation of beauty is—and, indeed, can be—nowhere else. The experience of beauty, then, echoes theophany, it echoes Incarnation which itself "perfects the whole ontology and aesthetics of created Being."[45] Von Balthasar draws a further analogy:

> Both the person who is transported by natural beauty and the one snatched up by the beauty of Christ must appear to the world to be fools, and the world will attempt to explain their state in terms of psychological or even physiological laws (Acts 2:13). But *they* know what they have seen.[46]

This is "art," and, not surprisingly, for von Balthasar, the profoundest example of this art is disclosed by the Virgin,

> the "Handmaid of the Lord," in whom the feminine and bridal plasticity of the Daughter of Zion is totally recapitulated and who represents to us the highest paradigm of what is meant by "art of God" and by "well-structured sanctity": in each of these cases we confront life in the Holy Spirit, hidden life which is inconspicuous, and yet *so* conspicuous that its situations, scenes, and encounters receive a sharp, unmistakable profile and exert an archetypal power over the whole history of faith.[47]

A sophiological sensibility, again, shows itself to be indispensable from veneration of the Virgin Mother of God.

Closely tied to von Balthasar's concept of "glory" is his notion of "splendor." As with Bulgakov's thoughts concerning "theosis"

---

44 Hans Urs von Balthasar, *The Glory of the Lord,* Vol. 1, 34.
45 Ibid., 29.
46 Ibid., 33.
47 Ibid., 36. Emphasis in Balthasar.

and "sophianization," they are almost interchangeable. Splendor, for von Balthasar, is that which shines through phenomena and reveals the Beautiful. It is unthinkable apart from the form through which it shines. In the presence of splendor, "We are confronted simultaneously with both the figure and that which shines forth from the figure, making it into a worthy, a love-worthy thing."[48] Furthermore, "We see the form as the splendor, as the glory of Being."[49] But this splendor is not of itself *visible*. We come to it through the spiritual senses: "In order to read even a form within the world, we must see something invisible as well, and we do in fact see it."[50] *We do in fact see it.* A bold claim. Divine splendor, in addition, simultaneously reveals and conceals: "The superabundant power of the light and meaning of love, as it shines forth in the form, causes it to become necessarily a form of veiling—just because it reveals that which is utmost, the ineffable."[51] The English metaphysical poet Henry Vaughan, drawing on Dionysius the Areopagite (as well as Boehme), expresses a similar sentiment:

> There is in God (some say)
> A deep, but dazling darkness; As men here
> Say it is late and dusky, because they
> See not all clear;
> O for that night where I in him
> Might live invisible and dim.[52]

Yet, for all of von Balthasar's sophiological inclinations, he tends to distance himself from sophiology. And when he speaks directly on Sophia, he does so from behind ample cover. For instance, in the first volume of *Glory of the Lord,* his discussion of Sophia

48 Ibid., 20.

49 Ibid., 119.

50 Ibid., 444.

51 Hans Urs von Balthasar, *The Glory of the Lord: A Theological Aesthetics, Vol. 2: Studies in Theological Style: Clerical Styles,* trans. Andrew Louth, Francis McDonagh, and Brian McNeil (San Francisco: Ignatius Press, 1984), 11.

52 Henry Vaughan, "The Night" from *The Complete Poetry of Henry Vaughan,* ed. French Fogle (New York: New York University Press, 1965), lines 49–54.

comes in the context of discussing the Wisdom literature of the Bible, though what he has to say is telling. He particularly attends to Sophia's "self-contemplation" as a model for "inspired contemplation [which] casts an aesthetic light backwards (and also forwards) over salvation-history."[53] He has little affection for Boehme, whose writing he dismisses as "a misuse of the mystical tradition,"[54] and even less for English Behmenists (like Jane Lead) and German Pietism.[55] But he does display admiration for Bulgakov (albeit with a caveat about the Russian's "sophiological excesses")[56] and he is fascinated by Solovyov. In the chapter on Solovyov in volume three of *Glory*, for instance, von Balthasar offers a thorough précis of Solovyov's sophiology—but pulls back from making an assessment. "What (to introduce the term that now becomes necessary)," he asks,

> is God's *Sophia*? Is it the plenitude of the modes in which his essence can be imitated . . . coming to light through his power and freedom? or is it the plenitude of possibilities realized through his free power and grace, possibilities that are (eschatologically) linked with the form of preexisting ideas? The question is of some importance for aesthetics; from the viewpoint of the aspirations of reality, does the Beautiful lie in the sphere of ideal being only? or does ideality eternally include reality in itself? *For Solovyov, however, the question can be left as insoluble.*[57]

53 Hans Urs von Balthasar, *The Glory of the Lord*, Vol. 1, 43.

54 Ibid., 49.

55 Hans Urs von Balthasar, *Theo-Drama: Theological Dramatic Theory, V: The Last Act,* trans. G. Harrison (San Francisco: Ignatius Press, 1998), 318–9. His main criticism is that such non-professional attempts at theology were generally not "undergirded by a sufficiently deep, Trinitarian theology" (319).

56 Hans Urs von Balthasar, *The Glory of the Lord: A Theological Aesthetics, Vol. 7: The New Covenant,* trans. Brian McNeil (San Francisco: Ignatius Press, 1989), 213. In his *The Anatomy of Mis-Remembering: Von Balthasar's Response to Philosophical Modernity, Volume 1: Hegel* (New York: Herder & Herder, 2014), Cyril O'Regan names Bulgakov as one of von Balthasar's "fathers." See 305–21.

57 Hans Urs von Balthasar, *The Glory of the Lord: A Theological Aesthetics, Vol. 3: Studies in Theological Style: Lay Styles,* trans. Andrew Louth, John Saward, Martin Simon, and Rowan Williams, ed. John Riches (San Francisco: Ignatius Press, 1986), 307–8. My emphasis.

The question can also be left as insoluble for von Balthasar. He never answers it.

And who can blame him? Mid-20th-century Catholic theologians with a penchant for rocking the Neo-Thomistic boat found themselves in a potentially hostile work environment, as Teilhard and de Lubac knew only too well. Von Balthasar, politically but prudently, tried to avoid making too many waves, choosing instead to submerge ideas that might give suspicious Neo-Thomists reason to attack him (not that many of them would have been his match). This is not to say that I think he was a closet sophiologist, only that his thinking is inherently sophiological. Von Balthasar was a theologian and a priest who had to find a way to get along in the Church if his very important contributions to theology could find a proper audience. Another Catholic contemporary of his—a layman, a convert, and a Russian—did not live with the same realities and was able to write more freely on the subject. His name was Valentin Tomberg.

Valentin Tomberg and the Return of Esoteric Catholicism

Arguably, one of the more remarkable contributions to Catholic thought of the last fifty years is the book originally written in French but known to readers of English as *Meditations on the Tarot: A Journey into Christian Hermeticism*. Despite its similarities to Pavel Florensky's *The Pillar and Ground of the Truth*, Tomberg's *Meditations on the Tarot* is, nevertheless, a book like no other book. Rather than a manual of cartomancy, what the reader finds in this remarkable text is a series of what the author calls "spiritual exercises," profound meditations reaching into the iconography of the Marseilles Tarot, images, like those of the Dance of Death, with roots deep in medieval Catholicism. But, due to its unique and idiosyncratic nature (as is all too obvious from its title), the book has proved problematic for some. For others, however, it has provided an otherwise unexpected gateway into the eternally new Catholic mystery.

Like Florensky's book, *Meditations on the Tarot* has an epistolary structure: a series of letters addressed to the reader, the "Dear Unknown Friend." The author, too, prefers to remain anonymous and tells us in the foreword that by such anonymity the reader "will know . . . that the author of these Letters has said more about himself in these Letters than he would have been able to in any other way."[58] Despite his intentions, though, not long after his death in 1973, the author was identified as Valentin Tomberg, a Russian expatriate living in England.

Tomberg was born in St Petersburg in 1900. His mother was shot during the October Revolution, and soon thereafter he, his father, and his elder brother fled to Estonia, settling in the city of Tallinn. For the adult part of the first half of his life, Tomberg (a cradle Lutheran) became conversant with the various esoteric and occult currents then present in Russia, including a connection to a group studying the tarot under the guidance of Professor Gregory Ottonovitch Mebes at Pages College, St Petersburg.[59] Tomberg, a polyglot who knew at least nine classical and modern languages, was, as *Meditations* shows, thoroughly familiar with the literature of Western occultism and various schools of Eastern spirituality. In the early 1920s Tomberg encountered Anthroposophy and Rudolf Steiner and devoted the next fifteen years or so to the study of Steiner's thought.

Tomberg rose to prominence as a lecturer on anthroposophical topics and his lectures touched on a wide array of subjects: Russian spirituality, mysticism, yoga, and his esoteric meditations on Christ influenced in great part by Steiner's Christology. Perhaps his most interesting writings from this period are his three books examining the Bible from an anthroposophical perspective. His insights in these works, if not always compelling, are usually interesting, and his genius for meditation sometimes results in astounding observations. Occasionally, Tomberg's anthroposophical insights seem prescient. In his book on the Old Testament, for example, Tomberg unpacks the symbology of the worship of

58 *Meditations on the Tarot: A Journey into Christian Hermeticism,* trans. Robert Powell (Warwick, NY: Amity House, 1985), x.

59 Tomberg was not a formal member of this group, but became acquainted with its teaching following its dissolution following the rise of the Bolsheviks. He describes his relationship to it in the twenty-first chapter of *Meditations on the Tarot.*

Baal/Moloch in words that are disturbingly relevant in ways today that he could not have consciously anticipated:

> The details of that dark cult cannot be discussed with decency; suffice it to say that all its detail was so planned as to banish everything spiritual, everything holy from the relationship of father, mother, and child. Sex-life was to be torn loose from its divine source, and to become a prey to demonic forces; birth was to be mechanized. This was to be attained by killing all the first born—a purposeful measure designed to destroy the conscious, loving expectation of the soul descending among men, and to replace it by an unconscious, mechanical production of human beings.[60]

Though he did not live to see the slaughter of innocents that has become the abortion culture, that he missed the deconstruction of the family inaugurated by the sexual revolution and the call for "rights" to marriage that followed, and that he did not get to witness the increasing commodification of birth through what has been called "the fertility-industrial complex," Tomberg would surely recognize the destructive spiritual forces currently at work, the reality of our continuing struggle "against the cosmic powers of this present darkness."

Tomberg left the Anthroposophical Society sometime in late 1939 or early 1940 while he and his family were living in Holland. As World War II spread, Tomberg and his family found themselves in a camp for displaced persons where he met a pair of priests and became convinced that he should enter the Church (his wife, Maria, was already Catholic). Tomberg, as he would later write, recognized that the Church possesses "the fullness of manifested unity" protected under the "divine magical power of [the] keys."[61] Soon afterward, he and his family found themselves in Cologne as refugees. While in Cologne, Tomberg earned a Ph.D. in law, writing his dissertation, *Degeneration und Regenera-*

---

60 Valentin Tomberg, *Anthroposophical Studies of the Old Testament*, 2nd ed. (Spring Valley, NY: Candeur Manuscripts, 1985), 11. Reprinted with Tomberg's studies of the New Testament and the Apocalypse as *Christ and Sophia: Anthroposophical Meditations on the Old Testament, New Testament & Apocalypse*, rev. R.H. Bruce (Great Barrington, MA: Steiner Books, 2006).

61 *Meditations on the Tarot*, 108 and 120.

tion der Rechtswissenschaft (Degeneration and Regeneration of Jurisprudence), on Thomistic understandings of rights and law. And while his departures from perceived anthroposophical ortho-doxies raised the ire of a good many anthroposophists, Tomberg's turn to Catholicism went further, rendering him a *persona non grata* in most anthroposophical quarters.[62]

Following his conversion and the end of the war, Tomberg and his family settled in England where he lived a life of relative obscurity, working for the BBC utilizing his formidable language skills to monitor broadcasts out of the Soviet Union. Tomberg devoted much time to prayer and contemplation, working on *Meditations* from about 1961 until he finished the work on or about the Festival of the Holy Trinity, 21 May 1967. He also pro-duced another book for a Catholic readership, unfinished at his death and written in German; it was published posthumously as *Lazarus, komm heraus!* (*Lazarus, Come Forth!*) in 1985.[63]

After his turn to Catholicism, Tomberg wished to distance himself from Anthroposophy. When anthroposophist Willi Seiß wrote him in 1970 about his anthroposophical studies of the Bible from the early 1930s, Tomberg made his feelings on the topic quite clear:

> The author of the "Studies" concerning the Bible and the Gospel was a man who had made it his task to save Rudolf Steiner's life work—spiritual science[64]—from eradication and sclerosis by bringing it back to its central focus. However, the "inner descen-dent" of this same person today believes there is no "spiritual science" and never can be. Because even a "spiritual science" based on its central focus can only add momentum to the mill of death. It will unavoidably become intellectualized and "fossilized"....
> Nothing lies further from me today or would be more tiring than

62 Perhaps the most extreme anthroposophical critic of Tomberg is Sergei O. Prokofieff, who has written two anti-Tomberg (and viciously anti-Catholic) polemics: *The Case of Valentin Tomberg: Anthroposophy or Jesuitism?* (Forest Row, UK: Temple Lodge Press, 1998) and *Valentin Tomberg and Anthroposophy: A Problematic Relationship* (Forest Row, UK: Temple Lodge Press, 2005).

63 Published in English as both *Covenant of the Heart* (1994) and *Lazarus, Come Forth!* (2006).

64 Steiner's description of Anthroposophy.

to see the ashes of the anthroposophical past raised up . . . shield me from discussions about the "Studies," methods of work, and similar things, which are now totally alien to me.[65]

Tomberg had grown to understand spiritual initiatives outside of the greater body of the Church as sterile, cut off from the source of life. As he writes in *Meditations*,

Dear Unknown Friends—you who are reading these lines written by a Hermeticist in 1965, after nearly fifty years of endeavor and experience in the domain of Hermeticism—I beg you not to regard what is written here as a vow made for the future current of Hermetic historicism, but rather as a testament making you who read these lines a trustee of the task in question—without reserve, but, however, with your consent. If you consent, do all that you judge to be proper, but one thing I implore you not to do: to found an organization, an association, a society, or an order which is charged with the task in question. For the tradition lives not thanks to organizations, but rather in spite of them. One should content oneself purely and simply with friendship in order to preserve the *life* of a tradition; it is not necessary to entrust it to the care of the embalmers and mummifiers *par excellence* that organizations are, save for that founded by Jesus Christ.[66]

His Catholic works were clearly written by a different man, one transformed in the Blood of the Lamb. Furthermore, Tomberg achieves something almost unthinkable: the rehabilitation and restoration of esotericism under the protective mantle of the Church, placing it exactly where it belongs. As he writes,

The way of Hermeticism, solitary and intimate as it is, comprises authentic experiences from which it follows that the Roman Catholic Church is, in fact, a depository of Christian spiritual truth, and the more one advances on the way of free research for this truth, the more one approaches the Church. Sooner or later one inevitably experiences that spiritual reality corresponds—with an astonishing exactitude—to what the Church teaches: that there are guardian Angels; that there are saints who participate actively in

65 The letter is quoted (and translated) in full in Prokofieff's *Valentin Tomberg and Anthroposophy*, 2–3.
66 *Meditations on the Tarot*, 569. Emphasis in source.

our lives; that the Blessed Virgin *is* real, and that she is almost precisely such as she is understood, worshipped and portrayed by the Church; that the sacraments *are* effective, and that there are seven of them—and not two, or three, or even eight; that the three sacred vows—of obedience, chastity and poverty—constitute in fact the very essence of all authentic spirituality; that prayer is a powerful means of charity, for beyond as well as here below; that the ecclesiastical hierarchy reflects the celestial hierarchical order; that the Holy See and the papacy represent a mystery of divine magic; that hell, purgatory and heaven *are* realities; that, lastly, the Master himself—although he loves everyone, Christians of all confessions as well as all non-Christians—abides with his Church, since he is always present there, since he visits the faithful there and instructs his disciples there. The Master is always findable and meetable there.[67]

Tomberg has drawn only marginal attention from Catholic circles, though that is not to say that his Catholic readership has been negligible. Though von Balthasar provided a thoughtful introduction for the 1983 German edition of *Meditations* in which he calls the author a "thinking, praying Christian of unmistakable purity,"[68] very little attention has been paid to Tomberg's work in either Catholic or secular academic milieux. With the exception of a handful of recent articles (mostly focused on Balthasar), some interesting observations by Stratford Caldecott, and a few book reviews from the 1980s, Tomberg and his fascinating book remain anonymous. Nevertheless, *Meditations* "can be read as an intervention to arrest the progress of the modern West's state of spiritual amnesia," a West in many regards desiccated by centuries of rationalizing the sublime and unconsciously interiorizing the false natural-supernatural binary.[69] Tomberg, like Fludd before him, pushes back against this ethos. Though *Meditations* has sold surprisingly well, it was not written with a broad audience in mind.

---

67 *Meditations*, 282. Emphasis in source.

68 Hans Urs von Balthasar, Afterword, *Meditations on the Tarot*, 3rd English edition (New York: Tarcher/Putnam, 2002), 659.

69 Kevin Mongrain, "Rule-Governed Christian Gnosis: Hans Urs von Balthasar on Valentin Tomberg's *Meditations on the Tarot.*" *Modern Theology* 25: 2 (April 2009): 285–314, at 286.

Finally, what is perhaps the most important—though almost completely undocumented—aspect of Tomberg's Catholic works is the role they have played in bringing some of their readers to (or back to) the Church.

At several points in his Catholic works, Tomberg makes a case for a Catholic sophiology, sometimes implicitly and, at others, quite explicitly. One of the themes in *Meditations*, as in sophiology, is the relationship between art, science, and religion and the destruction wrought when they are walled off from one another. Tomberg is sensitive to the losses incurred by the scientific revolution and does not cede victory to the Enlightenment. His language here closely approaches that of Fludd, Goethe, and Steiner. "Now the ideal of Hermeticism," he writes,

> is *contrary* to that of science. Instead of aspiring to power over the forces of Nature by means of the destruction of matter, Hermeticism aspires to conscious participation with the constructive forces of the world on the basis of an alliance and a cordial communion with them. Science wants to *compel* Nature to obedience to the will of man such as it is; Hermeticism—or the philosophy of sacred magic—on the contrary wants to purify, illumine and change the will and nature of man in order to bring them into harmony with the creative principle of Nature (*natura naturans*) and to render them capable of receiving its willingly bestowed *revelation*. The "great work," as an ideal, is therefore the state of the human being who is in peace, harmony and collaboration with life.[70]

Furthermore, for Tomberg, the "synthesis of science and religion is not a theory, but rather the inner act of consciousness of adding the spiritual vertical to the scientific horizontal or, in other words, *the act of erecting the bronze serpent*."[71] Even more, though, does Tomberg assert an explicitly Catholic sophiology in the book.

Central to Tomberg's conversion to Catholicism—and implicit to his sophiology—was a religious experience concerning the Virgin while he was in living in the Netherlands during World War II. He was investigating the appearances of the Virgin there as "*de Vrouwe van alle Volkren*" ("The Lady of All Nations"), and he

---

70 *Meditations on the Tarot*, 68. Emphasis in source.
71 Ibid., 216. Emphasis in source.

reports in *Meditations* that he came to the conviction that both the seer (now known to be Ida Peerdeman) and that which she saw were authentic. Later experiences, "of a more personal nature," further confirmed his belief.[72] While living in Holland, though still five years prior to his formal entrance into the Church,[73] Tomberg, moved by his experience with the Lady of All Nations, composed a prayer that he and some associates used at the time:

> Our Mother,
> You who are in the darkness of the underworld,
> May the holiness of your name shine a light anew on
>   our remembering,
> May the breath of the awakening of your kingdom
>   warm all homeless wanderers.
> May the resurrection of your will enliven eternal faithfulness
>   unto the depths of matter.
> Receive today the living remembrance of you from human hearts,
> Who pray you to forgive the sin of forgetting you,
> And are ready to fight against the temptation in the world
> That has led you to existence in the darkness,
> That through the deed of the Son, the immeasurable pain
>   of the Father be stilled
> In the liberation of all beings from the misfortune of your
>   withdrawal.
> For yours are the homeland, the generosity, and the mercy
> For all and everything in the Circle of All. Amen.[74]

This prayer, with its evocation of the Gnostic mythos of Sophia's captivity by the demiurge, undoubtedly bears the imprint of Tomberg's anthroposophical period. Steiner, too, composed a verse, very similar in tone:

> Isis-Sophia
> Wisdom of God
> Lucifer has slain her,
> And on wings of cosmic forces

---

72 Ibid., 280. In May 2002, the appearances were approved as of supernatural origin by the Holy See.

73 Christopher Bamford, Introduction to *Christ and Sophia*, xxvii.

74 Quoted in Christopher Bamford, Introduction to *Christ and Sophia* by Valentin Tomberg, xxvii–xxviii.

> Carried her away into the depths of space.
> Christ-Will
> Working in us
> Shall tear her from Lucifer
> And on grounds of spiritual knowledge
> Call to new life in human souls
> Isis-Sophia
> Wisdom of God.[75]

It is not clear whether or not Tomberg later in life embraced the ideas embedded in his prayer. It is not, for example, reproduced in any of his works intended for publication. In both *Meditations* and *Covenant of the Heart* (written 20+ years after he entered the Church), he does offer the esoteric complement to the invocation of the Trinity in the construct of "the Mother, Daughter, and Holy Soul"—which would have offered an opportune moment for introducing the prayer—so it may be that he rethought things.

What did remain important to Tomberg from the period of his conversion and his encounter with the Lady of All Nations is his agreement with that revelation's emphasis on Mary's roles as "*Co-creatrix, Co-redemptrix, Co-sanctificatrix, Virgo, Mater, Regina.*"[76] Drawing on the sophiological tradition going back at least to Boehme, Tomberg anchors his assertions in the notion of *virginity*:

> This formula summarizes the thoughts relating to the principle of virginity. Here is the place to point out that principles do not exist separately from the beings who incarnate and manifest them. Principles as such are always *immanent*. This is why the reality of the principle of the Divine is God; the reality of the principle of the divine Word is Jesus Christ; and the reality of fertile and productive virginity is Mary-Sophia. Mary-Sophia represents, i.e. incarnates and manifests, the principle of virginity, that of non-fallen Nature, that of natural religion, and that of Force. . . . She is the central individuality—the "queen"—of the whole domain in question. She is the conscious, individual soul who is the concrete ideal—the "queen"—of virginity, motherhood, and creative-pro-

75 Rudolf Steiner, *Isis Mary Sophia: Her Mission and Ours: Selected Lectures and Writings*, ed. Christopher Bamford (Herndon, VA: Steiner Books, 2003), 214.

76 *Meditations on the Tarot*, 279. Emphasis in source.

ductive or queenly wisdom. . . . There is not a shadow of a doubt for anyone who takes the spiritual life of mankind seriously, even if he is short of authentic spiritual experience, that the Blessed Virgin is not an ideal only, nor a mental image only, nor an archetype of the unconscious (of depth-psychology), nor, lastly, an occultist *egregore* (a collective astral creation of believers), but rather a concrete and living individuality—like you or I—who loves, suffers, and rejoices.[77]

The "creative-productive wisdom" Tomberg highlights here is not to be taken lightly. Indeed, it is the source of the *élan vital* that allows even civilizations to thrive. And, as happens often with Tomberg, he definitively diagnoses the problem in a thoroughly important cultural and historical context:

> The Virgin, the Force of our Arcanum, is the principle of springtime, i.e. that of creative *élan* and spiritual flourishing. The prodigious flourishing of philosophy and the arts in ancient Athens took place under the sign of the Virgin. Similarly, the flourishing of the Renaissance at Florence was under the vernal sign of the Virgin. Also, Weimar at the beginning of the nineteenth century was a place where the breath of the Virgin perceptibly moved hearts and minds. . . . The sickness of the West today is that it is more lacking creative *élan*. The Reformation, rationalism, the French revolution, materialistic faith of the nineteenth century, and the Bolshevik revolution, show that everywhere mankind is turning away from the Virgin. The consequence of this is that the sources of creative spiritual *élan* are drying up, one after the other, and that an increasing *aridity* is showing up in all domains of the spiritual life of the West. It is said that the West is growing old. But why? Because it lacks creative *élan*, because it has turned away from the source of the creative *élan*, because it has turned away from the Virgin. Without virginity there is no springtime; there is neither freshness nor youth.[78]

Tomberg would weep to see the spiritual condition of the West fifty years after he wrote these words. But he would not be surprised.

---

77 Ibid., 279–80. Emphasis in source.
78 Ibid., 291–2. Emphasis in source.

Finally, the Virgin is for Tomberg not only the vessel of the Incarnation (the preeminent evidence of the sophianicity of the world), but she is even more that which renders the Trinity comprehensible. His utterance here combines several languages: of mysticism, of Hermeticism, of Holy Scripture:

> It is she—the "Virgin of Light" of the *Pistis Sophia*, the Wisdom sung of by Solomon, the *Shekinah* of the Cabbala, the Mother, the Virgin, the pure celestial Mary—who is the soul of the light of the three luminaries, and who is both the source and aim of Hermeticism. For Hermeticism is, as a whole, the aspiration to participation in knowledge of the Father, Son and Holy Spirit, and the Mother, Daughter and Holy Soul. It is not a matter of seeing the Holy Trinity with human eyes, but rather of seeing with the eyes—and in the light—of Mary-Sophia. For just as no one comes to the Father but by Jesus Christ (John 14:6), so does no one understand the Holy Trinity but by Mary-Sophia. And just as the Holy Trinity manifests itself through Jesus Christ, so *understanding* of this manifestation is possible only through intuitive apprehension of what the virgin mother of Jesus Christ understands of it, who not only bore him and brought him to the light of day, but who also was present—present as mother—at his death on the Cross. And just as Wisdom (Sophia)—as Solomon said—was present at the creation [Proverbs 8:27–31; 9:1], so Mary-Sophia was present at the redemption and "was at work beside him," and "built her house . . . set up her seven pillars," i.e., she became Our Lady of the seven sorrows. For the seven sorrows of Mary correspond, for the work of redemption, to the seven pillars of Sophia for the work of creation. Sophia is the queen of the "three luminaries"—the moon, the sun and the stars—as the "great portent" of the Apocalypse shows. And just as the *word* of the Holy Trinity become flesh in Mary-Sophia—the *light*, i.e., threefold receptivity, the threefold faculty of intelligent reaction, or *understanding*. Mary's words: *mihi fiat secundum verbum tuum* ("let it be done to me according to your word"—Luke 1:38) are the key to the mystery of the relationship between the pure act and pure reaction, between the word and understanding—lastly, between Father, Son and Holy Spirit on the one hand and Mother, Daughter and Holy Soul on the other hand. They are the true key to the "seal of Solomon"—the hexagram.[79]

---

79 Ibid., 547.

Father

Daughter   Holy Soul

Son   Holy Spirit

Mother

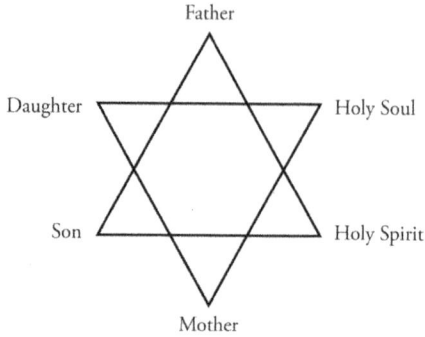

Tomberg describes this construct as "the luminous Holy Trinity," defining it as "the unity of the threefold *Fiat* and the threefold *mihi fiat secundum verbum tuum* which reveals itself in *natura naturans*, in the world created before the Fall; and in the triune divine *spirit* and the triune *soul* of the world manifesting in the *body* of the world—in *natura naturata*."[80]

I don't think Tomberg intended for his luminous Holy Trinity to be adopted as a new dogma of the Church. Rather, what he creates here is, first of all, an extrapolation of the notion of the fourth hypostasis put forth by the Russian sophiologists. He draws out their ideas and gives them symmetry. Secondly, what he offers is not theology so much as it is an artistic work, a kind of poetry. As Martin Heidegger has written, "*All art*, as the letting happen of the advent of the truth of what is, is, as such, *essentially poetry*."[81] Tomberg's paradigm, then, may or may not be "true" in a doctrinal sense, but there is truth in it: it discloses truth. Tomberg's esoteric and contemplative engagement, then, welcomes us to a poetic meeting—which is, nevertheless, *not* metaphorical—with Christ and Sophia.

Finally, in his sophianic speculations Tomberg does not simply apply esoteric paradigms to Church teaching. Instead, he attempts to illuminate Church teaching by way of his contemplative engagement with its truths. Among other things, what he finds valuable in the luminous Holy Trinity is what it says about divine

80 Ibid., 548.

81 Martin Heidegger, *Poetry, Language, Thought*, trans. Albert Hofstadter (New York: Harper & Row, 1971), 72. Heidegger's emphasis.

parenthood and parental love and the Decalogue's mandate "Honor thy father and mother." Parental love, for Tomberg, is "love bestowed by father *and* mother" and renders "the human being capable of comprehending or having a presentiment of divine love in a natural way by means of analogy."[82] Human familial love, then, resonates with and participates in the divine parental love. And implicit to the notion of parenthood is the reality of gender difference. Divine maternity, therefore, is no less important than divine paternity:

> The one and the other are equally necessary and equally precious. The one and the other render us capable of raising ourselves to the Divine. The one and the other signify to us the means of entering into a living relationship with God, which means to love God, who is the prototype of all paternity and all maternity.[83]

Tomberg furthermore argues that "all fatherhood has its origin and foundation in God" and that Mary, the Mother of God, is "the symbol and archetype of maternal love."[84] Such an understanding, I think, can help to counteract the sometimes overwrought "masculinity" of theological discourse which tends to subsume Sophia into the Logos in an entirely unconvincing attempt to keep theology tidy—and male—despite the fact that Sophia is spoken of in *explicitly* feminine terms in the Old Testament. As John Milbank argues while discussing Bulgakov's sophiology, we should reject such a move (a move which Milbank believes Bulgakov mistakenly takes) and, rather, "link gender equality to the equality of Bride with Bridegroom, thereby not abandoning the essential significance of Biblical engendered typology, nor the Biblical and theological significance of sexual difference."[85] For, as we have seen in our own times, divorcing the concept of marriage from Biblical typology can have disastrous consequences.

---

82 Valentin Tomberg, *Covenant of the Heart*, 185. Tomberg's emphasis.

83 *Meditations on the Tarot*, 550.

84 Valentin Tomberg, *Covenant of the Heart*, 185–6.

85 John Milbank, "Sophiology and Theurgy: The New Theological Horizon" in *Encounter between Eastern Orthodoxy and Radical Orthodoxy: Transfiguring the World through the Word*, ed. Adrian Pabst and Christoph Schneider (Farnham, UK: Ashgate, 2009), 45–85, at 83.

Though Tomberg's Hermeticism might make some wary, if not downright anxious, it is true—actually, more than true—that Catholicism is quintessentially what Charles Taylor calls a "multi-speed religion," and the more esoteric Catholic expressions of Tomberg and others can surely claim as rightful a place in this religious landscape as those accorded Catholic Worker activists, SSPX traditionalists, or members of Opus Dei. The Church accommodates an almost bewildering variety of rites and even theologies, and the superabundance of liturgical expressions found in the Latin Rite and the Eastern Rites attests to a "multi-speed" ethos. This is to say nothing of the myriad varieties of lay, domestic, and clerical manifestations of the Church—all of which could be almost infinitely subdivided. If it is true (and it is) that "in my Father's house there are many mansions" (John 14:2) there must surely be one for the Catholic Hermetic tradition of Valentin Tomberg, a humble example of the infinite generosity through which God provides his children every possible means of access to him, infinitely accommodating himself to nuances of their language, understanding, and perception.

The Submerged Reality

Elements of sophiology can be found in many other Catholic thinkers and mystics, of course. Louis Bouyer, who met Bulgakov in the 1930s and was deeply influenced by the Russian's thought, possesses a deeply sophiological sensibility.[86] The writing of the Carmelite phenomenologist St. Edith Stein (Teresia Benedicta of

---

86 See in particular Louis Bouyer, *The Seat of Wisdom: An Essay on the Place of the Virgin Mary in Christian Theology*, trans. A.V. Littledale (New York: Pantheon Books, 1962). Davide Zordan suggests that Bouyer "rectified" Bulgakov's sophiology, rendering it "less dualistic and more biblical." This may or may not be true, but it is true that Bouyer, as did Bulgakov in his denominational context, tried to push his speculations to their limit, while still refraining from trespassing ecclesial approval. See Davide Zordan, "De la Sagesse en théologie: Essai de confrontation entre Serge Boulgakov et Louis Bouyer," *Irénikon* 79, no. 2–3 (2006): 265–86, at 282. On Bouyer's friendship with Bulgakov and influence on von Balthasar, see Keith Lemna, "Louis Bouyer's Sophiology: A Balthasarian Retrieval," *The Heythrop Journal* 52, no. 4 (June 2011): 628–42.

the Cross) also contains moments of sophiological insight and this is also the case with Catholic phenomenology in general, starting with Franz Brentano and leading, among others, to Max Scheler (and Stein) as well as to Dietrich von Hildebrand, and more recently to Jean-Luc Marion and Jean-Louis Chrétien. Phenomenology arrives at this insight through attention to things-in-themselves. As Stein writes,

> This world with all it discloses and all it conceals, it is just this world that also points beyond itself as a whole to him who "mysteriously reveals himself" through it. It is *this* world, with its referrings that lead us out beyond itself, that forms the intuitive basis for the arguments of natural theology.[87]

Despite Tomberg's aspirations and insights such as Stein's, sophiology remains a submerged reality in Catholic theology, liturgy, and life. It takes more than a book or school of thought; it takes a paradigm shift. It may be, however, that such a shift is not impossible. Indeed, it is time to acknowledge the obvious shortcomings of the scientific revolution and Enlightenment which influence even the Church. Indeed, the "logical conclusions" of Enlightenment thinking are now bearing fruit throughout what used to be called Western Civilization (which impacts the entire planet) so much so that we no longer can be certain what nature is, what a family is, what rights are and from where (or whom) they are derived, what gender is, or, indeed, what a human person is. Sophiology answers all of these questions, and it does so by describing how in ever new and multifarious ways the holy Presence of God inhabits his creation.

> For in her is the spirit of understanding: holy, one, manifold,
>   subtile, eloquent, active, undefiled, sure, sweet, loving that
>   which is good, quick, which nothing hindereth, beneficent,
> Gentle, kind, steadfast, assured, secure, having all power, over-
>   seeing all things, and containing all spirits, intelligible, pure,
>   subtile.

87 Edith Stein (Sister Teresa Benedicta of the Cross, Discalced Carmelite), *Knowledge and Faith*, trans. Walter Redmond (Washington, DC: ICS Publications, 2000), 99. Stein's emphasis.

For Wisdom is more active than all active things: and reacheth everywhere by reason of her purity.

For she is a vapour of the power of God, and a certain pure emanation of the glory of the almighty God: and therefore no defiled thing cometh into her.

For she is the brightness of eternal light, and the unspotted mirror of God's majesty, and the image of his goodness.

And being but one, she can do all things: and remaining in herself the same, she reneweth all things, and through nations conveyeth herself into holy souls, she maketh the friends of God and prophets.

For God loveth none but him that dwelleth with Wisdom.

For she is more beautiful than the sun, and above all the order of the stars: being compared with the light, she is found before it.

For after this cometh night, but no evil can overcome Wisdom.[88]

88 Wisdom 7:22–30.

Conclusion:
Towards a Poetic Metaphysics

For someone who penetrates the interior essence of Life, the enigmatic content of Christianity is suddenly illuminated in a light of such intensity that anyone perceiving it in this light finds himself profoundly unsettled. ⌒Michel Henry[1]

Whoever wants to become a Christian must first become a poet.
⌒Elder Porphyrios[2]

I F THIS BOOK has proved anything, it has proved that an authentic, complete sophiology has yet to be realized. Many reasons exist for this, but, ironically perhaps, the most significant impediments are the various attempts to turn sophiology into a theology or doctrine. It is true that without the heroic efforts of Solovyov, Bulgakov, and von Balthasar (among others), sophiology as it is currently understood would never have entered into the consciousness of contemporary Catholic, Orthodox, and Protestant schools of theology. The real presence of Bulgakov, in particular, persists throughout the postmodern theological landscape. On the other hand, the sophiologies of Boehme, Fludd, and even Tomberg, I think, have proved more successful as *sophiologies*, while almost entirely unsuccessful as theologies or natural science. Sophiology, even more than theology (at least in the manner in which it is practiced now), upholds the notion that while rationality (and this is clearly a product of the Scholastic

1 Michel Henry, *I Am the Truth: Toward a Philosophy of Christianity*, trans. Susan Emanuel, Cultural Memory in the Present (Stanford, CA: Stanford University Press, 2003), 53.
2 Quoted in Bruce V. Foltz, *The Noetics of Nature: Environmental Philosophy and the Holy Beauty of the Visible*, Groundworks: Ecological Issues in Philosophy and Theology (New York: Fordham University Press, 2014), 116.

tradition) can be a useful tool for understanding God, something more is required. If the "dark glass" about which St. Paul wrote stands between our perception and the reality of God, then Scholastic rationality has inserted itself as a screen, a veil, between immediate perception and St. Paul's darkened glass. A true sophiology avoids this often clumsy apparatus and the contention that invariably arises through theological dialectics and turns, instead, to perception itself as the source of knowing. This epoche, this reliance on the pureness of perception, is the grounding by which phenomenology so often stumbles upon insights so congruous with sophiology. Indeed, it is only when they feel pressed to provide explanations for their insights in order to prove they are "philosophers" that phenomenologists sell their birthright for a plate of beans. For, more than anyone, sophiologists and phenomenologists rightly deserve the title "lovers of Wisdom."

Both sophiology and phenomenology begin in contemplation, the disposition which renders insight into the sophianicity of the phenomenal world possible. The simple activity of contemplation also makes awareness of God possible as the noumenon behind phenomena. Indeed, it is no surprise that so many phenomenologists—including Max Scheler, Edith Stein, Adolf Reinach, Hedwig Conrad-Martius, Dietrich von Hildebrand, to which one could add both Karol Wojtyla and Rudolf Steiner—came to religious conversions through their phenomenological inquiries. From such an engagement, a holistic view of the cosmos naturally arises. As Paul Evdokimov has written, "contemplative knowledge of God (*theognôsis*) integrates scientific, philosophical, and artistic data; by making them partake of its own reality, it makes them 'the eye' through which one views the Truth."[3] Sophiology, then, is a matter of perception.

Finally, sophiology remains incomplete because we have yet to say exactly what (or who) Sophia is, and this indecision surely indicates not a problem of perception so much as one of *self*-perception. More than a few people throughout history, following

---

3 Paul Evdokimov, *Woman and the Salvation of the World: A Christian Anthropology on the Charisms of Women*, trans. Anthony P. Gythiel (Crestwood, NY: St. Vladimir's Seminary Press, 1994), 11.

the Wisdom literature, have claimed that Sophia is most surely a *person*, and furthermore claim to have *met her*. This was the case with Jane Lead, with Vladimir Solovyov, and, I suspect, with both Jacob Boehme and Sergius Bulgakov. What do we do with this information? Dismiss these individuals as temporarily (if not permanently) insane? This seems neither fair nor honest. Interpret their experience as "dreams" or "metaphors"? Just as is the case with Marian visionaries, Sophianic visionaries assert that the subjects of their experiences were real persons, not dreams, not metaphors. Sophiologists also speak of Sophia as a quality of the Creation, as that which makes possible both the reception and the perception of grace and is that which God "poured forth upon all his works" (Sirach 1:8) and governs all things. In the Bible, Sophia is both person and quality.

While certainly not a feminist theologian, I do wish to resist the suggestion that Sophia is synonymous with the Logos and therefore with Christ. First of all, this does not seem to be what the Bible says at all (outside of a couple of New Testament passages which do not appear to be written in the context of the Wisdom literature). Some of the Fathers, certainly, wanted Sophia to be male; but there may be, indeed, more than a little residual misogyny in statements that dress Sophia in male attire, divine or not. As Paul Evdokimov reminds us, once upon a time Christian theologians seriously questioned whether or not women had souls, so a default association of Sophia with the Logos should come as no surprise.[4] And, as we have recently been made all too aware, gender differences are important—and they are important metaphysically as well. In words of startling prescience, Evdokimov describes our current situation:

> The modern, profoundly masculine world, where the feminine charism plays no role whatsoever, is more and more a world without God, for it has no mother and God cannot be born in it. It is typical that in such an atmosphere, homosexuality asserts itself openly. This disease of psychic splitting—a failure in the integration of the soul's male and female elements—reveals a male who resides either entirely in his subconscious, in the feminine part of

4 Ibid., 253.

his soul, which leads him to the masculine, or entirely on the surface, where he is polygamous—the infinitely vitiated Don Juan
mentality. Such are the most symptomatic signs of a psychic state
that has lost all its sensitivity toward archetypal feminine value that
of the Virgin-Mother. A too-masculine world disregards its eternal
origins; the clear fountain of virginal purity, and the maternal
womb that receives the Word, and brings it forth to make of men
His servants.[5]

Though Evdokimov wrote these words in 1958, his observation
retains its validity. Our culture, despite decades of feminism and
the participation of women in all realms of influence and power,
has yet to come to terms with the vocation of gender. Indeed, as
many have observed, one, unintended, outcome of feminist revolution has been to neutralize gender difference to the point where
gender itself is now nearly as changeable as any dramatic persona,
a tragic realization of Judith Butler's political and philosophical
project. Additionally, fertility, traditionally the province of both
the eternal and the temporal feminine, is now treated as a medical
condition and not as something to be safeguarded and treasured.
And, finally, sexuality has been stripped of its sacramental dimensions and diminished as a subconscious eruption of a search for
validation confused as self-expression. Sophiology, on the other
hand, honors gender difference, fertility, and sexuality as expressions of the sacred, of an integral cosmology. In this cosmology,
Sophia offers us an alternative to a culture that has made a New
Order out of disorder.

This is why I have been arguing throughout this book that
sophiology needs to be considered not as theology and not as science but as a poetic *metaxu* uniting the two. The absence of a
healthy sophiology, I contend, has resulted in the dire situation in
which we now find ourselves and our culture. The poetic engagement with Creation offered by sophiology simultaneously opens
the way to a science more concerned with care than domination,
an art renewed and redeemed in the presence of the Beautiful,
and a secure return of cosmology to religion. We need a poetic
metaphysics. This way leads to freedom.

5 Ibid., 251–2.

Conclusion: Towards a Poetic Metaphysics

Down now to the sweet bride, on
To Jesus, to the beloved—
Comfort, evening's darkling greys
To the loving, to the grieving.
A dream will break our fetters off,
And sink us forever in our Father's lap.[6]

6 Novalis, *Hymns to the Night*, trans. Dick Higgins (New York: McPherson & Company, 1984), 43.

Bibliography

Adams, David. "Rudolf Steiner's First Goetheanum as an Illustration of
Organic Functionalism." *Journal of the Society of Architectural Histori-
ans* 51, no. 2 (June 1992): 182–204.
Agamben, Giorgio. *Homo Sacer: Sovereign Power and Bare Life.* Trans.
Daniel Heller-Roazen. Stanford, CA: Stanford University Press, 1998.
Dante Alighieri. *The Paradiso.* Trans. John Ciardi. New York: New
American Library, 1961.
Allen, Diogenes and Eric O. Springfield. *Spirit and Community: Issues in
the Thought of Simone Weil.* Albany, NY: State University of New
York Press, 1994.
Allen, Paul M. *Vladimir Soloviev: Russian Mystic.* Blauvelt, NY: Steiner,
1978.
Apollinaire, Guillaume. *Selected Writings of Guillaume Apollinaire.* Trans.
and ed. Roger Shattuck. New York: New Directions, 1971.
Astell, Ann W. *Eating Beauty: The Eucharist and the Spiritual Arts of the
Middle Ages.* Ithaca, NY: Cornell University Press, 2006.
Bainbridge, Simon. *Napoleon and English Romanticism.* Cambridge Stud-
ies in Romanticism. Cambridge: Cambridge University Press, 1995.
Balthasar, Hans Urs von. *Explorations in Theology, Volume I.* Trans. A.V.
Littledale and Alexander Dru. San Francisco: Ignatius Press, 1989.
———. *The Glory of the Lord: A Theological Aesthetics, Volume I: Seeing
the Form.* Ed. Joseph Fessio, S.J. and John Riches, trans. Erasmo Lei-
va-Merikakis. San Francisco: Ignatius, 1982.
———. *The Glory of the Lord: A Theological Aesthetics, Volume III: Studies
in Theological Styles: Lay Styles.* Trans. Andrew Louth, et al. San Fran-
cisco: Ignatius Press, 1986.
———. *The Glory of the Lord: A Theological Aesthetics. Volume V: The
Realm of Metaphysics in the Modern Age.* Ed. John Riches; trans. Oliver
Davies et al. San Francisco: Ignatius Press, 1991.
———. *The Glory of the Lord: A Theological Aesthetics, Volume. 7: The
New Covenant.* Trans. Brian McNeil. San Francisco, CA: Ignatius
Press, 1989.
———. *Theo-Drama: Theological Dramatic Theory, Volume V: The Last
Act.* Trans. G. Harrison. San Francisco: Ignatius Press, 1998.
Beauvoir, Simone de. *The Second Sex.* Trans. H.M. Parshley. New York:
Vintage Books, 1989.
Beilin, Elaine V., ed. *The Examinations of Anne Askew.* Oxford: Oxford
University Press, 1996.
Belting, Hans. *The Invisible Masterpiece.* Trans. Helen Atkins. Chicago:
University of Chicago Press, 2001.

Berdyaev, N.V. *The Fate of Man in the Modern World.* Trans. Donald Lowrie. 1935; reprt., Ann Arbor, MI: University of Michigan Press, 1961.
———. *The Russian Idea.* Trans. R.M. French. 1947; reprt. Hudson, NY: Lindisfarne Press, 1992.
———. "Studies Concerning Jacob Boehme, Etude II: The Teaching about Sophia and the Androgyne. J. Boehme and the Russian Sophiological Current." Trans. S. Janos with Michael Knetchen, www.berdyaev.com (2002), section 6, par. 2. Originally published as "Iz etiudov o yak. Beme. Etiud ii. Uchenie o sophii i androgine," *Put'* 21 (Apr 1930): 34–62.
Berkel, Klaas van and Arie Johan Vanderjagt, eds. *The Book of Nature in Early Modern and Modern History.* Leuven: Peeters, 2006.
Blake, William. *The Complete Poetry and Prose of William Blake.* Ed. David V. Erdman, commentary by Harold Bloom, rev. ed. Berkeley and Los Angeles: University of California Press, 1982.
Blok, Alexander. *Poems of Sophia.* Trans. and ed. Boris Jakim. Kettering, OH: Semantron Press, 2014.
[Boehme, Jacob] Jacob Behmen. *Concerning the Election of Grace, or of Gods Will towards Man, commonly called Predestination...* Trans. John Sparrow. London, 1655.
———. *The Fifth Book of the Author, in Three parts. The First; Of the Becoming Man or Incarnation of Jesus Christ the Sonne of God, That is, Concerning the Virgin Mary...* [Trans. John Sparrow]. London, 1659.
———. *Mysterium Magnum, or An Exposition of the First Book of Moses called Genesis...* [Trans. John Ellistone and John Sparrow]. London, 1655.
———. *The Second Booke concerning The Three Principles of the Divine Essence of the Eternal Dark, Light, and Temporary World...* [Trans. John Sparrow]. London, 1648.
———. *The Third Booke of the Author, being the High and Deepe Searching out of The Threefold Life of Man through* [*or according to*] *the Three Principles.* Trans. John Sparrow. London, 1650.
———. *Several Treatises of Jacob Behme not printed in English before...*Trans. John Sparrow. London, 1661.
———. *Signatura Rerum: Or the Signature of all Things...* Trans. J. Ellistone. London, 1651.
———. *The Way to Christ Discovered.* Trans. attributed to John Sparrow. London, 1648 [1647].
Bonio, Serge-Thomas, ed. *Surnaturel: A Controversy at the Heart of Twentieth-Century Thomistic Thought.* Trans. Robert Williams, rev. Matthew Levering. Naples, FL: Sapientia Press, 2009.
Bouyer, Louis. *The Seat of Wisdom: An Essay on the Place of the Virgin Mary in Christian Theology.* Trans. A.V. Littledale. New York: Pantheon Books, 1962.
Brann, Noel L. *Trithemius and Magical Theology: A Chapter in the Controversy over Occult Studies in Early Modern Europe.* SUNY Series in Western Esoteric Traditions. Albany, NY: State University of New York Press, 1999.
Brinton, Howard. *Mystic Will: Based upon a Study of the Philosophy of Jacob Boehme.* New York: Macmillan, 1930.

Bibliography

Brogan, Walter A. *Heidegger and Aristotle: The Twofoldness of Being*. Albany, NY: SUNY Press, 2005.

Bulgakov, Sergius. *The Bride of the Lamb*. Trans. Boris Jakim. Grand Rapids, MI and Edinburgh, UK: William B. Eerdmans Publishing Company and T&T Clark, 2002.

———. *A Bulgakov Anthology: Sergius Bulgakov 1871–1944*. Trans. Natalie Duddington and James Pain; ed. James Pain and Nicolas Zernov. London: SPCK, 1976.

———. "From Marxism to Sophiology." *Religion in Life* 1, no. 4 (1937): 361–8.

———. *The Holy Grail and the Eucharist*. Trans. Boris Jakim. Hudson, NY: Lindisfarne Books, 1997.

———. *Philosophy of Economy: The World as Household*. Trans. and ed. Catherine Evtuhov. New Haven, CT: Yale University Press, 2000.

———. *Sophia, the Wisdom of God: An Outline of Sophiology*. Trans. Patrick Thompson, O. Fielding Clarke, and Xenia Braikevitc, revised. Hudson, NY: Lindisfarne Press, 1993.

———. *Unfading Light: Contemplations and Speculations*. Trans. and ed. Thomas Allan Smith. Grand Rapids, MI: William B. Eerdmans Publishing Company, 2012.

Cady, Susan, Marian Ronan, and Hal Taussig. *Sophia: The Future of Feminist Spirituality*. San Francisco: Harper and Row, 1986.

Caldecott, Stratford. *The Radiance of Being: Dimensions of Cosmic Christianity*. Tacoma, WA: Angelico Press, 2013.

Cassirer, Ernst. *The Myth of the State*. New Haven: Yale Univ. Press, 1946.

The Catechism of the Council of Trent. Trans. Rev. J. Donavan. Baltimore: Fielding Lewis, n.d.

Chantraine, Georges. "The Supernatural: Discernment of Catholic Thought according to Henri de Lubac." In *Surnaturel: A Controversy at the Heart of Twentieth-Century Thomistic Thought*. Ed. Serge-Thomas Bonino; trans. Robert Whalen; rev. by Matthew Levering. 21–40. Naples, FL: Sapientia Press of Ave Maria University, 2009.

Copleston, Frederick C. *Medieval Philosophy*. New York: Harper Torchbooks/The Cathedral Library, 1961.

Craven, J.B. *Dr. Robert Fludd (Robertus de Fluctibus), The English Rosicrucian: Life and Writings*. Kirkwall, UK: William Peace & Son, 1902.

Cyre, Susan. "Fallout Escalates Over 'Goddess' Sophia Worship." *Christianity Today* (April 4, 1994): 74.

David, Zdenek V. "The Influence of Jacob Boehme on Russian Religious Thought." *Slavic Review* 21, no. 1 (March 1962): 43–64.

Davies, Oliver. "Von Balthasar and the Problem of Being." *New Blackfriars* 79, no. 923 (Jan 1998): 11–17.

Deane-Drummond, Celia E. *Creation through Wisdom: Theology and the New Biology*. Edinburgh: T&T Clark, 2000.

Desmond, William. *The Intimate Strangeness of Being: Metaphysics after Dialectic*. Studies in Philosophy and the History of Philosophy 56. Washington, D.C: The Catholic University of America Press, 2012.

———. *Is There a Sabbath for Thought?: Between Religion and Philosophy*. Perspectives in Continental Philosophy 45. New York: Fordham University Press, 2005.

Dickson, Donald R. *The Tessera of Antilia: Utopian Brotherhoods and Secret Societies in the Early Seventeenth Century.* Leiden: Brill, 1998.

Donne, John. *Essayes in Divinity, being Several Disquisitions Interwoven with Meditations and Prayers.* Ed. Anthony Raspa. Montreal: McGill-Queen's University Press, 2001.

———. *The Sermons of John Donne,* vol. 6. Ed. Evelyn M. Simpson and George R. Potter. Berkeley, CA: University of California Press, 1953.

Dupré, Louis. *Passage to Modernity: An Essay in the Hermeneutics of Nature and Culture.* New Haven: Yale University Press, 1993.

———. *The Quest of the Absolute: Birth and Decline of European Romanticism.* Notre Dame, IN: University of Notre Dame Press, 2013.

Eichner, Hans. "The Eternal Feminine: An Aspect of Goethe's Ethics." *Transactions of the Royal Society of Canada,* series 4, vol. 9 (1971): 235–44.

Estrade, J.B. *My Witness, Bernadette: The Authentic Source-Book of the Apparitions at Lourdes by an Eyewitness.* Trans. J.H. le Breton Girdlestone. 1946; reprt., Springfield, IL: Templegate, 1951.

Evdokimov, Paul. *Woman and the Salvation of the World: A Christian Anthropology on the Charisms of Women.* Trans. Anthony P. Gythiel. Crestwood, NY: St. Vladimir's Seminary Press, 1994.

Feingold, Lawrence. *The Natural Desire to See God According to St. Thomas Aquinas and His Interpreters.* Naples, FL: Sapientia Press, 2010.

Fiorenza, Elisabeth Schüssler. *Jesus: Miriam's Child, Sophia's Prophet: Critical Issues in Feminist Christology.* New York: Continuum, 1994.

Florensky, Pavel. *The Pillar and Ground of Truth: An Essay in Orthodox Theodicy in Twelve Letters.* Princeton: Princeton University Press, 1997.

Foltz, Bruce V. *The Noetics of Nature: Environmental Philosophy and the Holy Beauty of the Visible.* Groundworks: Ecological Issues in Philosophy and Theology. New York: Fordham University Press, 2014.

Fludd, Robert. *Apologia Compendaria, Fraternitatem de Rosea Cruce.* Leydae, 1616.

———. *Clavis Philosophiae et Alchymiae Fluddanae.* Francofurti, 1633.

———. *Integrum Morborum Mysterium, sive Medicinae Catholicae, Tomi Primi...* Francofurti, 1633.

———. *Medicina Catholica, seu Mysticum Artis Medicandi Sacrarium...* Francofurti, 1629.

———. *Mosaicall Philosophy, Grounded upon the Essentiall Truth or Eternall Sapience.* London, 1659.

———. *Philosophia sacra et vere Christiana seu meterologia cosmica.* Francofurti, 1626.

———. *Sophiae cum Moria Certamen...* Frankfurt, 1629.

———. *Tractatus Apologeticus Integritatem Societatis de Rosea Cruce defendens.* Lugduni Batavorum, 1617.

———. *Tractatus Theologo-Philosophicus...* Oppenheim, [1617].

Foster, Michael. "Greek and Christian Ideas of Nature." *Free University Quarterly* 6 (1959): 122–27.

Fox, Matthew. *The Coming of the Cosmic Christ.* San Francisco, CA: HarperOne, 1988.

Freeman, Veronica G. *The Poeticization of Metaphors in the Work of Nova-*

lis. Studies on Themes and Motifs in Literature 78. New York: Peter Lang, 2006.

Freud, Sigmund. *Civilization and Its Discontents*. Trans. James Strachey. New York: W.W. Norton and Company, 1961.

Frick, Peter. *Divine Providence in Philo of Alexandria*. Texts and Studies in Ancient Judaism 77. Tübingen: Morh Siebeck, 1999.

Gallaher, Brandon. "The Christological Focus of Vladimir Solov'ev's Sophiology." *Modern Theology* 25, no. 4 (2009): 617–46.

Gassendi, Petri. *Theologi Epistolica Excercitatio...* Parisiis, 1630.

Gauchet, Marcel. *The Disenchantment of the World: A Political History of Religion*. Trans. Oscar Burge. New French Thought. Princeton: Princeton University Press, 1997.

Gibbons, B.J. *Gender in Mystical and Occult Thought: Behmenism and its Development in England*. Cambridge: Cambridge University Press, 1996.

Gillespie, Gerald. "Classic Vision in the Romantic Age: Goethe's Reconstitution of European Drama in *Faust II*." In *Romantic Drama*. Ed. Gerald Gillespie. 379–98. Amsterdam: John Benjamins Publishing Company, 1994.

Goethe, Johann Wolfgang von. *Autobiography: Truth and Poetry, from My Own Life*, vol. 1. Trans. John Oxenford, revised. London: George Bell and Sons, 1897.

———. *The Collected Works: Scientific Studies*, vol. 12. Princeton: Princeton University Press, 1988.

———. *Maxims and Reflections*. Trans. Elisabeth Stopp; ed. Peter Hutchinson. London: Penguin, 1998.

———. *Faust, Parts One and Two*. Trans. George Madison Priest. New York: Alfred A. Knopf, 1950.

———. *Theory of Colours*. Trans. Charles Lock Eastlake. London: John Murray, 1840.

———. *Wilhelm Meister's Travels*. Trans. and ed. Edward Bell. London: George Bell and Sons, 1885.

Graham, Loren and Jean-Michel Kantor. *Naming Infinity: A True Story of Religious Mysticism and Mathematical Creativity*. Cambridge: Harvard University Press, 2009.

Gray, Madeleine. *The Protestant Reformation: Beliefs and Practices*. Brighton, UK: Sussex Academic Press, 2003.

Gray, Ronald. *Goethe: A Critical Introduction*. Cambridge: Cambridge University Press, 1967.

Grayling, A.C. *Descartes: The Life and Times of a Genius*. New York: Weller & Company, 2005.

Gregory, Brad S. *The Unintended Reformation: How a Religious Revolution Secularized Society*. Cambridge: Harvard University Press/Belknap Press, 2012.

Groberg, Kristi A. "The Feminine Occult Sophia in the Russian Religious Renaissance: A Bibliographic Essay." *Canadian-American Slavic Studies*, 26: 1–3 (1992): 197–240.

Gschwandtner, Christina M. *Postmodern Apologetics?: Arguments for God in Contemporary Philosophy*. Perspectives in Continental Philosophy. New York: Fordham University Press, 2013.

Heidegger, Martin. *On the Way to Language*. Trans. Peter D. Hertz. New York: HarperOne, 1982.
———. *Poetry, Language, Thought*. Trans. Albert Hofstadter. New York: Harper & Row, 1971.
———. *The Question Concerning Technology and Other Essays*. Trans. William Lovitt. New York: Garland Publishing, 1977.
Henderson, Fergus. "Novalis, Ritter and 'Experiment': A Tradition of 'Active Empiricism.'" In *The Third Culture: Literature and Science*. Ed. Elinor S. Shaffer. 153–69. Berlin: Walter de Gruyter, 1998.
Henry, Michel. *I Am the Truth: Toward a Philosophy of Christianity*. Trans. Susan Emanuel. Cultural Memory in the Present. Stanford, CA: Stanford University Press, 2003.
Herrick, Robert. *The Complete Poetry of Robert Herrick*. Ed. J. Max Patrick. New York: W.W. Norton & Company, 1968.
Hessayon, Ariel and Sarah Apetrei, eds. *An Introduction to Jacob Boehme: Four Centuries of Thought and Reception*. New York and London: Routledge, 2014.
Hildegard of Bingen. *Letters of Hildegard of Bingen, Volume I*. Trans. and ed. Joseph L. Baird and Radd K. Ehrman. Oxford: Oxford University Press, 1994.
———. *Symphonia: A Critical Edition of the* Symphonia Armonie Celestium Revelationum. Ed and trans. Barbara Newman. 2nd ed. Ithaca, NY: Cornell University Press, 1998.
Hölderlin, Friedrich. *Hyperion and Selected Poems*. Ed. Eric L. Santer. The German Library 22. New York: Continuum, 1994.
Hooker, Richard. *Of the Lawes of Ecclesiastical Politie. Eyght Bookes*. London, [1593].
Hopkins, Gerard Manley. *Poems*. Ed. Robert Bridges and W.H. Gardner, 3rd ed. New York and London: Oxford University Press, 1948.
[Hotham, Durant]. *The Life of one Jacob Boehmen, Who Although He Were a Very Meane man, yet wrote the most wonderfull deepe knowledge in Natural and Divine things...* London, 1644.
Huffman, William H. *Robert Fludd and the End of the Renaissance*. London: Routledge, 1988.
Hughes, J. Donald. "Francis of Assisi and the Diversity of Creation." *Environmental Ethics* 18 (Fall 1996): 31–20.
Huizinga, J. *The Waning of the Middle Ages: A Study of the Forms of Life, Thought and Art in France and the Netherlands in the XIV*th *and XV*th *Centuries*. 1924; reprt. New York: St. Martin's Press, n.d.
Hutton, Ronald. *The Rise and Fall of Merry England*. Oxford: Oxford University Press, 1996.
———. *The Stations of the Sun: A History of the Ritual Year in Britain*. Oxford: Oxford University Press, 1996.
Ingram, Mrill. "Biology and Beyond: The Science of 'Back to Nature' Farming in the United States." *Annals of the Association of American Geographers* 97, no. 2 (Jun 2007): 298–312.
John Paul II. *Fides et Ratio*.
Johnson, Elizabeth. "The Maleness of Christ." In *The Special Nature of Women?* Ed. Anne Carr and Elisabeth Schüssler Fiorenza. 108–16.

Philadelphia, PA: Trinity, 1991.

Josten, C.H., ed. "*Truth's Golden Harrow*: An Unpublished Alchemical Treatise of Robert Fludd in the Bodleian Library." *Ambix* 3 (1949): 91–150.

Julian of Norwich. *The Shewings of Julian of Norwich.* Ed. Georgia Ronan Crampton. Kalamazoo, MI: TEAMS-Medieval Institute Publications, 1994.

Keating, Thomas. *Open Mind, Open Heart: The Contemplative Dimension of the Gospel.* Lexington, NY: Continuum Publishing, 2002.

Keefe, Alice A. "Visions of Interconnectedness in Engaged Buddhism and Feminist Theology." *Buddhist-Christian Studies* 17 (1997): 61–76.

Kerényi, Carl. *Dionysos: Archetypal Image of Indestructible Life.* Trans. Ralph Manheim. Bollingen Series LXV, 2. Princeton: Princeton University Press, 1976.

Kleingeld, Pauline. "Romantic Cosmopolitanism: Novalis's 'Christianity or Europe.'" *Journal of the History of Philosophy* 46, no. 2 (2008): 269–84.

Knuuttila, Simo. "Philosophy and Theology in Twelfth-Century Trinitarian Discussions." In *Medieval Analyses in Language and Cognition: Acts of the Symposium, The Copenhagen School of Medieval Philosophy.* Ed. Sten Ebbesen and Russell L. Friedman, Historisk-filosofiske Meddelelser 77. 237–50. Copenhagen: The Royal Danish Academy of Sciences and Letters, 1999.

Krenglinger, Gisela H. *Storied Revelations: Parables, Imagination, and George MacDonald's Christian Fiction.* Distinguished Dissertations in Christian Theology. Eugene, OR: Wipf and Stock, 2013.

Krimmer, Elisabeth. "'Then Say What Your Religion Is': Goethe, Religion, and *Faust*." In *Religion, Reason, and Culture in the Age of Goethe.* Ed. Elisabeth Krimmer and Patricia Ann Simpson. Studies in German Literature, Linguistics, and Culture. 99–119. Rochester, NY: Camden House, 2013.

Küng, Hans. *Does God Exist?: An Answer for Today.* Trans. Edward Quinn. New York: Doubleday, 1980.

Lead, Jane. *A Fountain of Gardens,* vol. 1. London, 1696.

Lemna, Keith. "Louis Bouyer's Sophiology: A Balthasarian Retrieval." *The Heythrop Journal* 52, no. 4 (June 2011): 628–42.

Lewis, C.S. *Mere Christianity.* London: Collins, 1967.

Libavius, A. *Examen philosophiae novae, quae veteri abrogandae opponitur.* Frankfurt, 1615.

Lissau, Rudi. *Rudolf Steiner: Life, Work, Inner Path and Social Initiatives.* Wallbridge, UK: Hawthorn Press, 1987.

Long, Steven A. *Natura Pura: On the Recovery of Nature in the Doctrine of Grace.* Moral Philosophy and Moral Theology. New York: Fordham University Press, 2010.

Lossky, Vladimir. *The Mystical Theology of the Eastern Church.* Trans. Fellowship of St. Alban and St. Sergius. 1957; reprt., Crestwood, NY: St. Vladimir's Seminary Press, 2002.

Louth, Andrew. "French *Ressourcement* Theology and Orthodoxy: A Living Mutual Relationship?" In *Ressourcement: A Movement for Renewal in Twentieth-Century Catholic Theology.* Ed. Gabriel Flynn and Paul

D. Murray with Patricia Kelly. 495–507. Oxford: Oxford University Press, 2012.

Lubac, Henri de. *At the Service of the Church: Henri de Lubac Reflects on the Circumstances that Occasioned His Writings.* Trans. Anne Elizabeth Englund. San Francisco: Communio Books/Ignatius Press, 1993.

———. *The Eternal Feminine: A Study on the Poem by Teilhard de Chardin followed by Teilhard and the Problems of Today.* Trans. René Hague. New York: Harper & Row, Publishers, 1970.

———. *The Mystery of the Supernatural.* Trans. Rosemary Sheed. New York: Herder and Herder, 1967.

———. *Surnaturel: Études historiques.* 1946; reprt., nouvelle edition, ed. Michel Sales. Paris: Desclée de Brouwer, 1991.

McGrath, Alister. *Christian Theology: An Introduction,* 5th ed. Oxford: Wiley-Blackwell, 2011.

———. *In the Beginning: The Story of the King James Bible and How It Changed a Nation, a Language, and a Culture.* New York: Doubleday, 2001.

———. *A Scientific Theology, Volume I: Nature.* Grand Rapids, MI: William B. Eerdmans Publishing Company, 2001.

McInerny, Ralph. *Praeambula Fidei: Thomism and the God of the Philosophers.* Washington, DC: The Catholic University of America Press, 2006.

Maier, Michael. *Atalanta Fugiens, hoc est Emblemata Nova de Secretis Naturae Chymica...* Oppenheimii, 1618.

Manoussakis, John P. "The Phenomenon of God: From Husserl to Marion." *American Catholic Philosophical Quarterly* 78 no. 1 (2004): 53–68.

Marion, Jean-Luc. *Cartesian Questions: Method and Metaphysics.* Chicago: University of Chicago Press, 1999.

———. *God Without Being: Hors-Texte.* Religion and Postmodernism. Trans. Thomas A. Carlson. Chicago: University of Chicago Press, 1991.

Martin, Michael. *Literature and the Encounter with God in Post-Reformation England.* Farnham, UK: Ashgate Publishing, 2014.

Mascall, Eric. *Corpus Christi: Essays on the Church and the Eucharist.* London: Longmans Green and Co., 1958.

Merchant, Carolyn. *The Death of Nature: Women, Ecology, and the Scientific Revolution.* 1980; reprt., New York: Harper One, 1990.

Merton, Thomas. *Conjectures of a Guilty Bystander.* Garden City, NY: Doubleday & Company, 1966.

———. *A Search for Solitude: Pursuing the Monk's Life.* Ed. Lawrence S. Cunningham. San Francisco, CA: Harper, 1997.

Meyendorff, John. *Living Tradition.* Crestwood, NY: St. Vladimir's Seminary Press, 1978.

———. "Wisdom-Sophia: Contrasting Approaches to a Complex Theme." *Dumbarton Oaks Papers* 41. Studies on Art and Archaeology in Honor of Ernst Kitzinger on His Seventy-Fifth Birthday (1987): 391–401.

Midgley, Mary. *Science as Salvation: A Modern Myth and Its Meaning.* London: Routledge, 1992.

Milbank, John. "Beauty and the Soul." In *Theological Perspectives on God and Beauty.* Ed. John Milbank, Graham Ward, and Edith Wyscho-grod. 1–34. Harrisburg, PA: Trinity Press International, 2003.

———. "Sophiology and Theurgy: The New Theological Horizon." In *Encounter between Eastern Orthodoxy and Radical Orthodoxy.* Ed. Adrian Pabst and Christoph Schneider. 45–85. Farnham, UK: Ashgate, 2009.

———. *The Suspended Middle: Henri de Lubac and the Debate concerning the Supernatural.* Grand Rapids, MI/Cambridge, UK: William B. Eerdmans Publishing Company, 2005.

Miller, Geoffrey. *The Mating Mind: How Sexual Choice Shaped the Evolution of Human Nature.* New York: Anchor Books, 2001.

Mitchell, Nathan. *Cult and Controversy: The Worship of the Eucharist outside Mass.* New York: Pueblo Publishing Company, 1990.

Mongrain, Kevin. "Rule-Governed Christian Gnosis: Hans Urs von Balthasar on Valentin Tomberg's *Meditations on the Tarot.*" *Modern Theology* 25: 2 (April 2009), 285–314.

Montgomery, John Warwick. *Cross and Crucible: Johann Valentin Andreae (1586–1654), Phoenix of the Theologians,* 2 vols. The Hague: Martinus Nijhoff, 1973.

Mowbray, Malcom de. "Philosophy as Handmaid of Theology: Biblical Exegesis in the Service of Scholarship." *Traditio* 59 (2004): 1–37.

Naumann, Walter. "Goethe's Religion." *Journal of the History of Ideas* 13, no. 2 (April 1952): 188–99.

Nesteruk, Alexei V. *Light from the East: Theology, Science, and the Eastern Orthodox Tradition.* Minneapolis, MN: Augsburg Fortress, 2003.

Nieto, José C. *Mystic, Rebel, Saint: A Study of St. John of the Cross.* Travaux d'humanisme et Renaissance, no. 168. Geneva: Droz, 1979.

Novalis [Georg Philipp Friedrich Freiherr von Hardenberg]. *The Birth of Novalis: Friedrich von Hardenberg's Journal of 1797, with Selected Letters and Documents.* Trans. and ed. Bruce Donehower. Albany, NY: State University of New York Press, 2007.

———. *Christianity or Europe: A Fragment.* In *The Early Political Writings of the German Romantics.* Ed. and trans. Frederick C. Beiser. Cambridge Texts in the History of Political Thought. Cambridge: Cambridge University Press, 1996.

———. *The Disciples at Sais and Other Fragments.* Trans. F.V.M.T. and U[na] C.B[irch]. London: Methuen & Co., 1903.

———. *Hymns to the Night.* Trans. Dick Higgins. Rev. ed. New Paltz, NY: McPherson & Company, 1984.

———. *Hymns to the Night and Spiritual Songs.* Trans. George MacDonald. London: Temple Lodge Publishing, 1992.

———. *Werke,* vol. 4. Ed. Gerhard Schulz. München: Verlag C.H. Beck, 1981.

Oakes, Edward T. "The *Surnaturel* Controversy: A Survey and a Response." *Nova et Vetera,* 9, no. 3 (2011): 625–56.

O'Connor, Flannery. *The Habit of Being: Letters.* Ed. Sally Fitzgerald. New York: Vintage Books, 1980.

O'Meara, John. *The Way of Novalis: An Exposition on the Process of His Achievement.* Ottawa, ON: Heart's Core Publications, 2014.

O'Neil, Dennis. *Passionate Holiness: Marginalized Christian Devotions for*

Distinctive People. Victoria, BC: Trafford Publishers, 2009.

O'Regan, Cyril. *The Anatomy of Mis-Remembering: Von Balthasar's Response to Philosophical Modernity, Volume 1: Hegel.* New York: Herder & Herder, 2014.

———. *Gnostic Apocalypse: Jacob Boehme's Haunted Narrative.* Albany, NY: State University of New York Press, 2002.

Pearson, Irene. "Raphael as Seen by Russian Writers from Zhukovsky to Turgenev." *Slavonic and East European Review* 39, no. 3 (July 1981): 346–69.

Pfefferkorn, Kristin. *Novalis: A Romantic's Theory of Language and Poetry.* New Haven: Yale University Press, 1988.

Portier, William L. "Twentieth-Century Catholic Theology and the Triumph of Maurice Blondel." *Communio* 38 (Spring 2011): 103–37.

Pramuk, Christopher. *Sophia: The Hidden Christ of Thomas Merton.* Collegeville, MN: A Michael Glazier Book/Liturgical Press, 2009.

Prokofieff, Sergei O. *The Case of Valentin Tomberg: Anthroposophy or Jesuitism?* Forest Row, UK: Temple Lodge Press, 1998.

———. *Valentin Tomberg and Anthroposophy: A Problematic Relationship.* Forest Row, UK: Temple Lodge Press, 2005.

Pyman, Avril. *Pavel Florensky: A Quiet Genius: The Tragic and Extraordinary Life of Russia's Unknown Da Vinci.* New York: Continuum, 2010.

Ratzinger, Joseph Cardinal [Pope Benedict XVI]. *The Spirit of the Liturgy.* San Francisco, CA: Ignatius Press, 2000.

Rice, Jr., Eugene F. *The Renaissance Idea of Wisdom.* Cambridge: Harvard University Press, 1958.

Richards, Robert J. *The Romantic Conception of Life: Science and Philosophy in the Age of Goethe.* Science and Its Conceptual Foundations. Chicago: The University of Chicago Press, 2002.

Rigby, Kate. *Topographies of the Sacred: The Poetics of Place in European Romanticism.* Charlottesville, VA: University of Virginia Press, 2004.

Rilke, Rainer Maria. *The Selected Poetry.* Ed. and trans. Stephen Mitchell. New York: Random House, 1982.

Robbins, Brent Dean. "New Organs of Perception: Goethean Science as a Cultural Therapeutics." *Janus Head* 8, no. 1 (2005): 113–26.

Rommel, Gabriele. "Romanticism and Natural Science." In *The Literature of German Romanticism.* Ed. Dennis F. Mahoney. The Camden House History of German Literature, Volume 8. 209–27. Rochester, NY: Camden House, 2004.

Roten, Johann. "The Two Halves of the Moon: Marian Anthropological Dimensions of the Common Mission of Adrienne von Speyr and Hans Urs von Balthasar." In *Hans Urs von Balthasar: His Life and Work.* Ed. David L. Schindler. San Francisco: Communio Books and Ignatius Press, 1991.

Ruether, Rosemary Radford. *Goddesses and the Divine Feminine: A Western Religious History.* Berkeley: University of California Press, 2005.

Schaberg, Jane. *The Illegitimacy of Jesus: A Feminist Theological Interpretation of the Infancy Narratives.* San Francisco: Harper and Row, 1987.

Schafer, Lothar. *In Search of Divine Reality: Science as a Source of Inspiration.* Fayetteville, AR: University of Arkansas Press, 1997.

Schickler, Jonael. *Metaphysics as Christology: An Odyssey of the Self from*

Kant and Hegel to Steiner. Aldershot, UK: Ashgate, 2005.

Schillebeeckx, E. *The Eucharist.* Trans. N.D. Smith. New York: Sheed and Ward, 1968.

Schipflinger, Thomas. *Sophia-Maria: A Holistic Vision of Creation.* Trans. James Morgante. York Beach, Maine: Samuel Weiser, 1998.

Schleiermacher, Friedrich. *On Religion: Speeches to Its Cultured Despisers.* Trans. John Oman. New York: Harper & Brothers, 1958.

Schmemann, Alexander. *The Eucharist: Sacrament of the Kingdom.* Trans. Paul Kachur. Crestwood, NY: St. Vladimir's Seminary Press, 1987.

———. "Trois Images." *Le Messager Orthodoxe: Centenaire du P. Serge Boulgakov (1871–1971): Etudes et Textes* 27, no. 1 (1972): 2–20.

———. *Ultimate Questions: An Anthology of Modern Russian Religious Thought.* New York: Holt, Rinehart & Winston, 1965.

Schneider, Helmut J. "Saint Mary's Two Bodies: Religion and Enlighten-ment in Kleist." In *Religion, Reason, and Culture in the Age of Goethe.* Ed. Elisabeth Krimmer and Patricia Ann Simpson. Studies in German Literature, Linguistics, and Culture. 141–65. Rochester, NY: Camden House, 2013.

Schreiner, Susan E. *Are You Alone Wise?: The Search for Certainty in the Early Modern Era.* Oxford: Oxford University Press, 2011.

Schulz, Gerhard. "From 'Romantick' to 'Romantic': The Genesis of Ger-man Romanticism in Late Eighteenth-Century Europe." In *The Liter-ature of German Romanticism.* Ed. Dennis F. Mahoney. The Camden House History of German Literature, Volume 8. 25–34. Rochester, NY: Camden House, 2004.

Sepper, Dennis L. *Goethe contra Newton: Polemics and the Project for a New Science of Color.* Cambridge: Cambridge University Press, 1988.

Sharpe, Lesley, ed. *The Cambridge Companion to Goethe.* Cambridge: Cambridge University Press, 2002.

Sherrard, Philip. *The Eclipse of Man and Nature: An Enquiry into the Ori-gins and Consequences of Modern Science.* West Stockbridge, MA: Lind-isfarne Press, 1987.

Shlapentokh, Dmitry. *The French Revolution and the Russian Anti-Demo-cratic Tradition: A Case of False Consciousness.* New Brunswick, NJ: Transaction Publishers, 1997.

Shumaker, Wayne. *The Occult Sciences in the Renaissance: A Study in Intel-lectual Patterns.* Berkeley: University of California Press, 1972.

Skelton, Stephen. *Viticulture: An Introduction to Commercial Grape Grow-ing for Wine Production.* London: SP Skelton, 2007.

Slesinksi, Robert. *Pavel Florensky: A Metaphysics of Love.* Crestwood, NY: St. Vladimir's Seminary Press, 1984.

Smith, John H. "Living Religion as Vanishing Mediator: Schleiermacher, Early Romanticism, and Idealism." *The German Quarterly* 84, no. 2 (Spring 2011): 137–58.

Soloviev, Vladimir. *The Heart of Reality: Essays on Beauty, Love, and Ethics.* Ed. and trans. Vladimir Wozniuk. Notre Dame, IN: University of Notre Dame Press, 2003.

Solovyov, Sergey M. *Vladimir Solovyov: His Life and Creative Evolution.* Trans. Aleksey Gibson. Fairfax, VA: Eastern Christian Publications, 2000.

Solovyov, Vladimir. *Lectures on Divine Humanity.* Trans. Peter Zouboff (1948); rev. and ed. Boris Jakim. Hudson, NY: Lindisfarne Press, 1995.
———. *The Religious Poetry of Vladimir Solovyov.* Trans. Boris Jakim and Laury Magnus; ed. Boris Jakim. 2008; rept. Kettering, OH: Semantron Press, 2014.
———. *Russia and the Universal Church.* Trans. Herbert Rees. London: Geoffrey Bles, 1948.
———. *A Solovyov Anthology.* Ed. S.L. Frank; trans. Nathalie Duddington. 1950; repr., Westport, CT: Greenwood Press, 1974.
Sorrell, Roger D. *St. Francis of Assisi and Nature: Tradition and Innovation in Western Christian Attitudes toward the Environment.* New York and Oxford: Oxford University Press, 1988.
Spasskij, T. "L'Office liturgique slave de la 'Sagasse de Deiu.'" *Irénikon* 30 (1957): 164–88.
Stein, Edith (Sister Teresa Benedicta of the Cross, Discalced Carmelite). *Knowledge and Faith.* Trans. Walter Redmond. Washington, D.C.: ICS Publications, 2000.
Steiner, Rudolf. *Agriculture: A Course of Eight Lectures.* Trans. George Adams. 1958; reprt., London: Rudolf Steiner House, 1974.
———. *An Autobiography.* Trans. Rita Stebbing. Blauvelt, NY: Rudolf Steiner Publications, 1977.
———. *Bees.* Trans. Thomas Braatz. Great Barrington, MA: Anthroposophic Press, 1998.
———. *Cosmic and Human Metamorphoses.* 1926; reprt., Blauvelt, NY: Spiritual Research Editions, 1989.
———. *Faculty Meetings with Rudolf Steiner, 1919–1922, Volume I.* Trans. Robert Lathe and Nancy Parsons Whittaker. Hudson, NY: Anthroposophic Press, 1998.
———. *Isis Mary Sophia: Her Mission and Ours: Selected Lectures and Writings.* Ed. Christopher Bamford. Herndon, VA: Steiner Books, 2003.
———. *Karmic Relationships, Volume VI: Esoteric Studies.* Trans. E.H. Goddard, D.S. Osmond and M. Kirkcaldy. 1971; reprt. Forest Row, UK: Rudolf Steiner Press, 1989.
———. *The Redemption of Thinking: A Study in the Philosophy of Thomas Aquinas.* Trans. and ed. A.P. Shepherd and Mildred Robertson Nicoll. London: Hodder and Stoughton, 1956.
Taylor, Charles. *A Secular Age.* Cambridge: Harvard University Press/Belknap Press, 2007.
Teilhard de Chardin, Pierre. *Writings in Time of War.* Trans. René Hague. New York: Harper & Row, Publishers, 1965.
Thompson, E.P. *The Making of the English Working Class.* 1963; reprt. Harmondsworth: Penguin, 1986.
Tilton, Hereward. *The Quest for the Phoenix: Spiritual Alchemy and Rosicrucianism in the Work of Count Michael Maier (1569–1622).* Arbeiten zur Kirchengeschichte, Band 88. Berlin: Walter de Gruyter, 2003.
Tomberg, Valentin. *Anthroposophical Studies of the Old Testament,* 2nd ed. Spring Valley, NY: Candeur Manuscripts, 1985.
———. *Covenant of the Heart: Meditations of a Christian Hermeticist on the Mysteries of Tradition.* Trans. Robert Powell and James Morgante. Rockport, MA: Element Books, 1992.

Bibliography

[Tomberg, Valentin]. *Meditations on the Tarot: A Journey into Christian Hermeticism.* Trans. Robert Powell. Warwick, NY: Amity House, 1985.

Tracey, James D. *Erasmus: The Growth of a Mind.* Avaux d'Humanisme et Renaissance CXXVI. Geneva: Librairie Droz, 1972.

Traherne, Thomas. *Centuries.* Wilton, CT: Morehouse-Barlow, 1985.

———. *The Poetical Works of Thomas Traherne, 1636?–1674.* Ed. Bertram Dobell, 2nd ed. London: Published by the Editor, 1906.

Ullrich, Heiner. *Rudolf Steiner.* Trans. Janet Duke and Daniel Balestrini. Continuum Library of Educational Thought 11. London: Continuum, 2008.

Vattimo, Gianni. *After Christianity.* Trans. Luca D'Isanto. New York: Columbia University Press, 2002.

Vaughan, Henry. *The Complete Poetry of Henry Vaughan.* Ed. French Fogle. New York: New York University Press, 1965.

Vaughan, Thomas, ed. *The Fame and Confession of the Fraternity R.C., commonly of the Rosie Cross.* 1652.

Vaughan, Thomas. *The Works of Thomas Vaughan.* Ed. A. Rudrum with the assistance of Jennifer Drake-Brockman. Oxford: Clarendon Press, 1984.

Wahl, Jean. *Poésie, Pensée, Perception.* Paris: Calmann-Lévy, 1948.

Walker, Adrian J. "Love Alone: Hans Urs von Balthasar as a Master of Theological Renewal." *Communio* 32 (Fall 2005): 1–24.

Wallace, Dewey D. *Shapers of English Calvinism, 1660–1714: Variety, Persistence, and Transformation.* Oxford Studies in Historical Theology. Oxford: Oxford University Press, 2011.

Wallace, William A. "Appendix 8. Hexaemeron: Medieval Background." In Thomas Aquinas, *Summa Theologiae, Volume 10: Cosmogony.* 1a 65–74. 1967; reprt. Cambridge: Cambridge University Press, 2006.

Ward, Graham. *True Religion.* Blackwell Manifestos. Malden, MA: Blackwell Publishing, 2003.

Webb, Timothy. "Catholic Contagion: Southey, Coleridge and English Romantic Anxieties." In *Romanticism and Religion from Cowper to Wallace Stevens.* Ed. Gavin Hopps and Jane Stabler. 75–92. Aldershot, UK: Ashgate, 2006.

Weil, Simone. *An Anthology.* Ed. Siân Miles. New York: Weidenfeld & Nicolson, 1986.

———. *First and Last Notebooks.* Trans. Richard Rees. London: Oxford University Press, 1970.

Welburn, Andrew. *Rudolf Steiner's Philosophy and the Crisis of Contemporary Thought.* Edinburgh, UK: Floris Books, 2004.

Westfall, Richard S. "The Scientific Revolution of the Seventeenth Century: The Construction of a New World View." In *The Concept of Nature: The Herbert Spencer Lectures.* Ed. John Torrance. 63–93. Oxford: Clarendon Press, 1992.

Whalen, Teresa. *The Authentic Doctrine of the Eucharist.* Kansas City, MO: Sheed and Ward, 1993.

Wolters, Gereon. "The Catholic Church and Evolutionary Theory: A Conflict Model." *Scientific Insights into the Evolution of the Universe and of Life: Pontifical Academy of Sciences, Acta* 20 (2009): 450–70.

Wordsworth, William. *The Poetical Works* [vol. 4]. Ed. E. de Selincourt and Helen Darbshire. Oxford: The Clarendon Press, 1947.

Yates, Frances A. *Rosicrucian Enlightenment.* 1972; reprt., Boulder, CO: Shambhala, 1978.

Young, George M. *The Russian Cosmists: The Esoteric Futurism of Nikolai Federov and His Followers.* Oxford: Oxford University Press, 2012.

Zohar: Book of Enlightenment. Trans. and introduced by Daniel Chanan Matt with a preface by Arthur Green. New York: Paulist Press, 1983.

Zordan, Davide. "De la Sagesse en théologie: Essai de confrontation entre Serge Boulgakov et Louis Bouyer." *Irénikon* 79, no. 2–3 (2006): 265–86.

Index

Desmond, William 11, 41–42, 95, 147
Digby, Kenelm 7–8, 30, 87
Dionysius the Areopagite 187
Donne, John 18, 73–74
doxa 184
dualism 22, 27, 128
Dupré, Louis 21–22, 37, 118, 122–23, 161

ecology 96, 131, 159, 164–65, 174
economy 34, 158–59
education 64, 101, 115, 130, 131–34
Ehrman, Radd 176
Enlightenment 29, 70, 98–99, 100–01, 115–16, 121, 134, 137, 171–72, 175, 177, 195, 203
epoche 151, 206
Erasmus, Desiderius 170–71
eschatology 8, 37, 167, 188
Eucharist 16–19, 87, 128, 165, 180

Fatima 8n19, 143, 155
Fedorov, Nikolai 8
feminism, feminist theology 1, 3–5, 175, 207–08
Ficino, Marsilio 100
Fiorenza, Elisabeth Schüssler 5
Florensky, Pavel 10, 140, 143, 146n19, 147, 149ff, 156, 159, 167–68, 189
Fludd, Robert 2, 62ff, 97, 100, 128, 137, 139, 150, 156, 161, 176, 179, 186, 194–95, 205
folk religion 170–72
Foltz, Bruce V. 96, 99
Fox, Matthew 4
Francis of Assisi, St. 13, 174–75
Frank, Simon 147
French Revolution 98
Freud, Sigmund 104, 125

Gallaher, Brandon 155
Gassendi, Pierre 70, 72, 75, 80, 95
Gauchet, Marcel 32, 35
gender 32, 35, 37, 43, 45, 91, 93–94, 105, 201, 203, 207–08
glory (of God) 10, 28, 48, 67, 72, 82, 105, 120, 130, 154–55, 157, 164–67, 169, 179, 184–87, 204
GMO (genetically modified

organism) 34–35
gnostic, gnosticism 2–3, 35, 53, 131, 136, 142, 144–45, 148, 162, 196
secular gnosticism 27ff
Goethe, Johann Wolfgang von 100–02ff, 111–12, 120, 122, 125, 131, 137, 150, 195

Hagia Sophia 141, 158, 182
Harrison, Peter 68, 76
Hart, David Bentley 148
Heidegger, Martin 33, 35–36, 41–42, 60, 86, 110, 156, 200
Hermeticism 14
Herrick, Robert 172
Hildebrand, Dietrich von 203
hláfmæsse 171
Hobbes, Thomas 12, 29, 138
Hölderlin, Friedrich 97, 101, 119
Holy Grail 164–66
Hooker, Richard 73
Hopkins, Gerard Manley 169, 177
Hughes, J. Donald 175
Huizinga, Jan 113
Husserl, Edmund 125, 177
hypostasis 148, 152–53, 159, 168, 180, 200

icon, iconography 60, 140–41, 142, 154, 189
Ivanov, Vyacheslav 168

Jerome, St. 81–82
Joan of Arc, St. 155
John of the Cross, St. 22
John Paul II, St. 13, 34–35, 60–61, 174
Julian of Norwich 39

kabbalah 43, 144
Kant, Immanuel 28–29, 97
Kepler, Johannes 70, 75
Keyserlingk, Carl von 134
Kuhlman, Quirinus 141
Kühn, Sophie von 117, 122
Küng, Hans 28

Lady of All Nations 195–97
Law William 63, 139
Lead, Jane 1–2, 5, 63n4, 107, 188, 207

Index

Leadbeater, C.W. 125
Levshin, Platon 142
Libavius, Andreas 66, 70–71, 95
Louth, Andrew 26n43, 181
Lubac, Henri de 20, 24–27, 85, 156, 167, 178, 179–80, 183, 189
Luther, Martin 15, 17, 21, 64

McGrath, Alister 29–30, 68, 73
Maier, Michael 62, 65, 139
Manoussakis, John Panteleimon 60, 111
Marion, Jean-Luc 3–4, 28, 203
marriage 32, 35, 37, 55, 116, 191, 201
Marxism, Marxist 5, 145, 157–58
materialism 32, 35, 38, 66, 69, 99, 119, 125, 128–29, 139, 148
Mebes, Gregory Ottonovitch 190
Merton, Thomas 181–83
Mersenne, Marin 28, 70, 75, 95
metaphor 40, 58, 85, 91, 94, 128, 185, 200, 207
metaphysics 3, 5, 10, 14–15, 35–36, 44, 58, 71, 84, 92, 97, 105, 111, 118, 122, 138, 158, 161, 184, 207–08
metaxu, metaxological 11, 41, 140, 148, 151, 168, 208
Midgley, Mary 30–31
Milbank, John 24, 32, 84, 94, 156, 168, 201
Mongrain, Kevin 194n69
More, Henry 23, 63
More, St. Thomas 170
Murphy, Francesca Aran 29

Nag Hammadi 3
natura pura (see "pure nature")
Neo-Pagans 171
Newton, Isaac 30, 40, 108
nominalism 5, 14, 17–18, 21–3, 27, 29, 30, 32–33, 35, 36–38, 59, 97, 137, 175
Norderman, Konrad 141
Nouvelle Théologie 177
Novalis (Georg Philipp Friedrich Freiherr von Hardenberg) 41, 101, 111ff, 125, 128, 131, 137, 179, 209

Office of Sophia, Wisdom of God 140–41

Olcott, H.S. 125
ontology 54, 127, 186
Opus Dei 202
Organon 11, 15
O'Regan, Cyril 42, 53, 188
ousia 152, 159

panentheism 80
pantheism 80, 146n19, 150, 161
Paracelsus 177
Parousia 33, 86, 100, 119, 163
Pasqually, Martinez de 139
Péladan, Joséphin 139
Peerdeman, Ida 196
phenomenology 6, 45, 86, 108, 110, 122, 125, 140, 151, 202–03, 206
Philadelphian Society 63, 141
physis 184
Pico della Mirandola, Giovanni 100
Pietism 63, 107, 188
Pius XII 24
poetic perception, poetic intuition 1, 11, 22, 41–42, 47, 54, 58–59, 99, 103–05, 110–12, 115, 118, 122, 138, 144–45, 156, 165–66, 168–69, 177–78, 183–85, 200, 205, 208
Plato, Neoplatonism 14, 56, 87, 161
Pramuk, Christopher 183
pure nature (*natura pura*) 19–29, 31–32, 37, 48, 64, 66–67, 69, 75, 78, 85, 97, 111, 128, 131, 167, 175, 178
Pythagoras 161

Quaker 63

rationality, reason 13, 18, 20, 23, 28–29, 31–32, 36, 38, 41, 44, 56, 58–59, 64, 97–100, 112, 137, 151–52, 155, 168, 170–72, 205–06
reading holographically 54–55
realism 14, 17, 18
Reformation 15–17, 19, 27, 30, 32, 64, 114, 116, 170, 172, 198
ressourcement 24, 26, 177–78, 181–82
Rigby, Kate 98–99, 119, 123
Rilke, Rainer Maria 12
Robert Grosseteste 175
Roscelin 14

226

www.ingramcontent.com/pod-product-compliance
Lightning Source LLC
Chambersburg PA
CBHW032043090426
42733CB00030B/493